24.75 4/82

GIFFORD LECTURES

THE INTERPRETATION OF
RELIGIOUS EXPERIENCE

AMS PRESS
NEW YORK

#5195643
9-7-82

THE INTERPRETATION
OF
RELIGIOUS EXPERIENCE

THE GIFFORD LECTURES

DELIVERED IN THE UNIVERSITY OF GLASGOW
IN THE YEARS 1910-12

BY

JOHN WATSON, LL.D.

PROFESSOR OF MORAL PHILOSOPHY IN QUEEN'S UNIVERSITY
KINGSTON, CANADA

PART FIRST. HISTORICAL

GLASGOW
JAMES MACLEHOSE AND SONS
PUBLISHERS TO THE UNIVERSITY
1912

Library of Congress Cataloging in Publication Data

Watson, John, 1847-1939.
  The interpretation of religious experience.

  Reprint of the 1912 ed. published by J. Maclehose, Glasgow; which was issued as the Gifford lectures, 1910-1912.
  Includes index.
  1. Religion—Philosophy. 2. Experience (Religion)
I. Title. II. Series.
BL51.W35 1979   200'.1   77-27216
ISBN 0-404-60510-9

First AMS edition published in 1979.

Reprinted from the edition of 1912, Glasgow. Text area and trim size have been altered in this edition. [Original text area: 9 × 15.2 cm; original trim size 13.5 × 20.8 cm.]

International Standard Book Number:
Complete Set: 0-404-60510-9
    Volume 1: 0-404-60511-7

MANUFACTURED
IN THE UNITED STATES OF AMERICA

PREFACE

ANYONE who attempts to construct a philosophy of religion at the present time is met by two difficulties: he finds, on the one hand, that popular theology contains many ideas that have not been subjected to criticism, and, on the other hand, that there is no recognized philosophy which he can apply in criticism of them. These difficulties seem less formidable, however, when we reflect that our ideas have come to us as the result of a long process of development, and that, if we have faith in the essential rationality of man, we must conclude that neither in his ordinary religious consciousness nor in his reflective formulation of its contents can he have fallen into absolute error. It would thus seem that any attempt to interpret our religious experience must be based upon a critical estimate of the results of experience, both in its direct and in its reflective forms. To ignore the process by which ideas have come to be what they are, must result in an abstract and one-sided theory. No doubt one may have made an historical study of the development of experience, and, having in this way reached conclusions satisfactory to himself, he may not think it necessary to trouble the reader with an account of the process through which he has himself passed; but this method, while it may be satisfactory to oneself, can hardly be convincing to others. In any case a neglect of the historical method seems to me to explain to some extent the inadequate results reached by some recent thinkers. Instead of adopting and consistently following out an evolutionist point of view, a number of discordant facts of the religious consciousness are gathered together, without any attempt being made to consider them in the light of the stage of historical evolution in which they appear. It is therefore not surprising that anything like a system of theology is held to be beyond our reach. The same method is also applied to the study of philosophy itself. The speculations of Plato and Aristotle, of Descartes, Spinoza and Leibnitz, of Locke, Berkeley and Hume, of Kant and Hegel, are ignored, and an attempt is made to begin from immediate experience—as if there were any element of our experience that is not saturated with the thought of the past. Convinced that no fruitful results can in this way be secured, I have endeavoured to follow with a critical eye the main current of reflection upon religion, and especially upon Christianity, with the idea that in this way some assured result might be obtained. It will of course be evident to anyone familiar with the subject that in the constructive part of the undertaking I have found in Hegel, and in his English exponents, the most suggestive ideas for my purpose; but I think it well to add that I do not accept the doctrine presented as Hegelian in the works of some English and German exponents and critics. If the philosophy of Hegel, as Lotze holds, is simply a pan-logism; or if its fundamental principle is an abstract and indeterminate Absolute; or if it denies all freedom to man, and regards him as but the passive organ of an underlying Something-not-ourselves; then anyone who reads the following pages will see that it is widely different from the view I have tried to express. But this is not my reading of Hegel, as I have explained in various parts of this book, and more particularly in the ninth and tenth lectures; on the contrary, what seems to me most valuable in him is his insistence upon the essentially concrete character of the Absolute, as summing up and manifesting, but never abolishing, all that we mean by self-conscious reason. No doubt Hegel denies such one-sided doctrines as that of Lotze and his followers; but he does so, I conceive, because the separation of the world, man and God from one another must result in the logical annihilation of all three. Hegel was perhaps too ready to claim for his philosophy the support of popular theology; but I think he was right in maintaining that the doctrine of the Holy Spirit constitutes the essence of Christian theology; and that doctrine recognizes that without the response of the human soul to the spirit of God, as actually operative in it, and not beyond it, there can be no religion. Not to recognize the importance of this principle seems to me the main defect in much recent theological speculation. Nor does the claim to superior originality, advanced by the exponents of Radical Empiricism, the New Realism and Personal Idealism, seem to me justified. Radical Empiricism is still infected with the vice of the older Empiricism, the vice of denying the real identity of the mind and therefore logically resolving it into fragments; while I am unable to see that the New Realism has added anything essential to the principles of Locke, or Personal Idealism to those of Berkeley and Leibnitz. The form of Idealism for which I contend may be untenable, but it is not fairly open to the objection that it has been superseded by systems which in principle belong to an earlier stage of thought. With the Absolutism of Dr. Bradley, as I need hardly say, I have the greatest sympathy; but I do not think that it successfully avoids in all cases the vice of Spinozism —though, in insisting upon the idea of " degrees of reality," it seems to me to come very near to an abandonment of the abstract Absolutism elsewhere apparently contended for.

I am unable to say how far my discussion of theological and philosophical writers in the first course of lectures has been coloured by the various books read by me in the course of their preparation. I may, however, make special reference to Edward Caird's *Evolution of Theology in the Greek Philosophers*, Dr. Karl Marti's *Geschichte der Israelitischen Religion*, Loofs' *Leitfaden der Dogmengeschichte*, Harnack's *Lehrbuch der Dogmengeschichte*, Mr. T. R. Glover's *Conflict of Religions in the Roman Empire*, Dr. Bigg's *The Christian Platonists of Alexandria*, Dean Inge's *Christian Mysticism*, and Leslie Stephen's *English Thought in the Eighteenth Century*. In preparing the second course of lectures I have received much assistance from the late Principal Caird's *Fundamental Ideas of Christianity*, Professor J. B. Baillie's *Idealistic Construction of Experience*, Dr. R. Otto's *Naturalism and Religion*, Signor Varisco's *I Massimi Problemi*, M. Henri Bergson's *Essai sur les données immédiates de la conscience* and *L'Évolution créatrice*, Dr. W. McDougall's *Body and Mind*, the late Professor W. Wallace's *Life of Schopenhauer*, Professor J. Ward's *Naturalism and Agnosticism*, and his Gifford Lectures on *The Realm of Ends*. I am also indebted to Mr. H. H. Joachim's *The Nature of Truth* and Dr. Hastings Rashdall's *Philosophy and Religion*, and to articles by Professor J. Arthur Thomson, Dr. F. H. Bradley, Mr. H. W. B. Josephs, and Professors J. S. Mackenzie, Sir Henry Jones and J. H. Muirhead, which appeared in *Mind*, *The Philosophical Review*, *The International Journal of Ethics* and *The Hibbert Journal*. Dr. Bosanquet's *Essays and Reviews* I also found suggestive, but I have not been able to profit sufficiently by his recent very important work on

PREFACE

The Principle of Individuality, having only received it after my lectures were in shape for the press. I ought to add, however, that to his various other works, as well as to those of Dr. Bradley and the late Dr. Edward Caird, I owe more than I can well estimate.

With the numerous books on biblical or historical criticism published within the last fifty years, I cannot pretend to have the detailed acquaintance of an expert. In such matters I am only too glad to avail myself of the invaluable labours of a long line of scholars from Spinoza in the sixteenth century to such accomplished writers of our own days as my colleagues, the Rev. W. G. Jordan, M.A. (Lond.), D.D. (Queen's Univ. Can.), and Dr. Ernest Scott, M.A. (Glasg.), LL.D. (St. Andrews), whose names are familiar to students of theology and philosophy on both sides of the Atlantic. Intercourse with men of this type for some forty years has made it possible for me to speak with some authority, even on the problems with which it is their business to deal. The same remark applies to the discussions on scientific subjects, including the principles of physics, chemistry, biology, and medicine.

To my nephew, Mr. W. W. Henderson, M.A., I am much indebted for the extreme care he has exercised in reading the proofs.

JOHN WATSON.

QUEEN'S UNIVERSITY,
  KINGSTON, CANADA,
    2nd September, 1912.

CONTENTS

PART FIRST. HISTORICAL

LECTURE FIRST

DEVELOPMENT OF GREEK RELIGION AND THEOLOGY

Object of first course of lectures to trace the influence of philosophy upon the evolution of Christianity. The supreme principle and the three aspects of religion. The problem of theology. Development of Greek religion and philosophy. The theology of Plato. Critical estimate of Plato's theology. The philosophy of Aristotle. Critical estimate of Aristotle's theology. The theology of the Stoics. Opposite tendencies in Greek philosophy - - - - - - - - - - - 1

LECTURE SECOND

PRIMITIVE CHRISTIANITY AND ITS EXPONENTS

Development of the Hebrew religion. The religion of Jesus. Early Christian theology. Conflict of Christianity with Judaism. Conflict with paganism. Gnosticism. The theology of Marcion. The early Apologists. The epistle of Diognetus and Justin Martyr. Critical account of the theology of Clement of Alexandria - - - - - - 25

LECTURE THIRD

FROM ORIGEN TO THOMAS AQUINAS

Theology of Origen. Arius, Athanasius and the Nicene Creed. The theology of Augustine. Critical estimate of Augustine's theology. History

xii CONTENTS

of the Roman Church. Theology of Anselm. The Rationalism of Abelard. The Mysticism of Bernard of Clairvaulx. Theology of Thomas Aquinas - - - - - - - - - - - 57

LECTURE FOURTH

DANTE'S THEOLOGY AND POLITICS

General character of the Middle Ages. Dante's relation to his time. His opposition of faith and reason. Conception of God in his relation to the world. Differentia of Man. Original sin, freedom, responsibility and redemption. The Virgin Mary. Natural and theological virtues. The Politics of Dante based on the idea of one Emperor, one Pope, one God. His arguments in support of this idea inconclusive. His reasons for holding that the Empire must be Roman equally inconclusive. State and Church held to be of co-equal authority. A universal Empire and a universal Church an unrealizable and undesirable ideal - - - 99

LECTURE FIFTH

ECKHART, DESCARTES AND SPINOZA

The Mysticism of Eckhart and his successors. The Renaissance and the Reformation. The philosophy of Descartes not completely "critical." Method of philosophy. Meaning of the *Cogito ergo sum*. Proofs of the being of God. Reality of the external world. The three kinds of Substance. Criticism of the Cartesian philosophy. Greater consistency of the philosophy of Spinoza. God and his Attributes. Spinoza's criticism of the Cartesians. The infinite modes. Body and soul. The three phases of the intellectual life. The three phases of the moral life. Spinoza's conception of immortality. Critical remarks on the philosophy of Spinoza - - - - - - - - - - - 148

LECTURE SIXTH

LEIBNITZ, LOCKE AND THE ENGLISH DEISTS

Leibnitz' criticism of Cartesianism. The Monads and the Pre-established Harmony. The theory of knowledge. Will and freedom. God and the world. Metaphysical, physical and moral evil. Contrast of Spinoza and

CONTENTS   xiii

Leibnitz. The nature of religion. Critical estimate of Leibnitz. Locke's denial of innate ideas. Truth and falsehood. Meaning of "substance." The nature of knowledge. Certainty of the idea of God. General estimate of Locke's theological ideas. The English deists   -   -   190

LECTURE SEVENTH

BERKELEY AND HUME

Various senses of the term "mind." Locke's confusion of the feeling of touch with solidity. Berkeley's denial of an independent "matter." His reference of ideas of sensation to God as their cause. His doctrine leads to Nominalism. Distinction between Berkeley's Idealism and Objective Idealism. Criticism of his theory of knowledge. His conception of the self and of God untenable. Hume reduces consciousness to impressions and ideas. Rejects all arguments for the existence of God. His reply to Butler's arguments in favour of providence and a future state. His *Natural History of Religion*. Transition to Kant -   -   -   -   233

LECTURE EIGHTH

THE CRITICAL PHILOSOPHY

Kant's relation to Leibnitz and Hume. How the *a priori* synthetic judgments of mathematics and physics are possible. No independent self an object of knowledge. A self-complete world equally unknowable. No valid theoretical proofs of the existence of God. Freedom, immortality and God based upon the moral consciousness. The regulative idea of purpose as connecting link of the sensible and the supersensible. This idea essential in the explanation of living beings and involved in the aesthetic ideas of beauty and sublimity. Moral teleology the basis of theology. The doctrines of sin, salvation, the incarnation, justification by faith and the Church as interpreted by Kant -   -   -   -   -   260

LECTURE NINTH

HEGEL'S RELATION TO KANT

Hegel's denial of the opposition of phenomena and noumena. His criticism of Kant's view of the categories. Importance of the doctrine of the "transcendental unity of self-consciousness." The "transcendental

xiv CONTENTS

judgment" suggestive of a truth deeper than Kant has formulated. Contrast of understanding and reason in Kant and Hegel. The critical problems of the soul, the world and God not insoluble. Solution of the Paralogisms. Solution of the Antinomies. Defence of proofs of God's existence. Criticism of Kant's ethical doctrine. The postulates of God, freedom and immortality really demonstrable Principles. The idea of purpose not merely "regulative" - - - - - - - 286

LECTURE TENTH

HEGEL'S PHILOSOPHY OF RELIGION

General character of the Hegelian philosophy. Religion the self-consciousness of God. Christianity as the "revealed" religion. Hegel's reinterpretation of the idea of creation. The permanent and the transitory in Historical Christianity. Kingdom of the Father: the speculative idea of God as expressed in the doctrine of the Trinity. Kingdom of the Son: God as manifested in the spiritual nature of Man: Evil and its Atonement. Kingdom of the Spirit: the invisible Church. The Sacraments. Relations of Church and State. The philosophy of Religion - - - 330

INDEX - - - - - - - - - - 362

PART FIRST. HISTORICAL.

LECTURE FIRST.

DEVELOPMENT OF GREEK RELIGION AND THEOLOGY.

THE main object of the following lectures is to determine whether, and how far, a reconstruction of religious ideas may be necessary in view of the long process of development through which the human spirit has passed. An enquiry into the origin and development of Christianity will first be made; but, in the course of that enquiry, particular attention will be devoted to the systematic formulation of religious experience in theology, and especially to the influence of philosophy in determining the form that theology has successively assumed. This will cover the ground dealt with in the first course of lectures; while the second course will endeavour to give such an interpretation of religious ideas as may seem to be required by the greater complexity and comprehensiveness of modern thought.

So far as he is religious, man is raised above the divisions and distractions of his ordinary consciousness, and attains to peacefulness and serenity. No doubt religion means much or little according to the stage of development that has been reached, but, in its earliest as in its latest form, the whole being of the religious man is filled with the divine as it appears to him, and therefore in religion he feels that he is in perfect unity with himself and with the deeper nature of the universe. The possibility of religion is bound up with the essential nature of man as a rational and spiritual being, and rationality or spirituality presupposes as its primary condition the consciousness of a unity which embraces all distinctions, and more particularly the fundamental distinction of the world and the self. So far as he has merely immediate presentations or feelings, man is but potentially rational; it is only as these are lifted out of the flux of immediacy, and grasped in their relation to the world as a rational system, that he realizes his birthright as a self-conscious intelligence. It is in virtue of this inalienable capacity that he creates arts, sciences and political institutions, all of which imply the elevation of what immediately presents itself to the rank of an intelligible object. That object is possible at all only because of the self-activity which is implied in the power of turning immediate things into the means of expressing the will. Now, when man, as a rational subject, finds, or believes that he finds, the world to be a cosmos and human life intelligible, and refers both object and subject to a supreme principle, he adopts the attitude of religion. Thus religion is not one sphere alongside of others, but the single all-embracing sphere in which all distinctions are but elements that have no reality or meaning when they are severed from the single principle upon which they depend. Religion cannot be subordinated to any higher form of consciousness; it is not a means to something else, but all else is a means to it. No doubt there are various forms of religion, but in all of them man has the consciousness of having grasped the inner truth of things and attained to the completion of his being. Whether the divine is believed to be immediately present or to be far off, there is never any doubt of its absolute reality

Religion, then, in all its forms implies a belief in some power higher than man, the source of all that is best and noblest in his life, and the object of his reverence and worship. Variously as this power may be conceived, it is always regarded as distinct both from man himself and from any particular object in the world around him. But, though this belief in what may be called "divine" is involved in religion, and indeed is its indispensable condition, it does not of itself constitute religion. Animism, for example, is a very early form of belief, but it is a mistake to say that the belief in spirits is a form of religion. For there is a belief in spirits that does not call forth any religious emotion, but is rather the source of fear and repulsion; and such a belief is manifestly independent of religion. The belief in a higher power, in fact, is simply a very early form of theology—if we may apply so august a title to so undeveloped a form of consciousness—and may therefore be held independently of religion. But, though it is thus capable of separation from religion, animism at the stage when it arises is the *sine qua non* of religion. What is required to transform this belief into a religion is that the spirits believed to exist should bear a special relation to those who have faith in them. Nor is it true that any relation whatever to the individual which affects his life is entitled to be called religion. No less a thinker than Goethe has said that the "ethnic" religions are adequate to fear, but not to reverence, and this view has been frequently repeated, and indeed is held by some contemporary writers. Unless I am mistaken, religion never has its source in fear, but always in a lower or higher degree of reverence. No doubt primitive man fears certain spirits; but his dread of these is not religious; on the contrary, it excludes religion. For the spirits that he dreads are those which are beyond the circle of humanity, whereas the spirits that he reverences are those with which he enters into sympathetic and friendly relations. It is true that a more developed form of religion may contain an element of fear as well as of reverence, but this is due to the inclusion within the objects of worship of spirits that had formerly been regarded as unfriendly " demons," and had not yet been entirely transformed into " gods."

As the first element in religion is belief, so the second element is worship. For religion implies not only a belief in powers that are able and willing to help man, but some form of worship through which his reverence is expressed. And there is a third element, which is found in the lowest as well as in the highest religion. Not only is there a belief in some power higher than man, not only is this power an object of worship, but religion involves a conformation of the life to what is believed to be the will of the divine being. Thus religion is a life, as well as a creed and a ritual. I am aware that the connection of religion and morality has been questioned, and indeed is expressly denied by some modern thinkers, but the facts seem to show that religion in all its forms inevitably carries with it an influence upon the whole conduct of those who believe in it.

What has been said may help us to avoid certain fallacies. Thus it is sometimes held that religion is entirely independent of theology, and, in fact, is the enemy of theology; and we are asked to abandon all efforts to imprison it within the iron framework of theological abstractions. Such a view seems to rest upon a false idea both of religion and of theology. It is true enough that a religion may contain elements that are not formulated in the theology which claims to represent it; but, when this is the case, a discrepancy arises, which can only be overcome by a reconstitution of the theology. Over and over again in the history of religion theology has failed to embody the higher truth to which religion had attained. But the true inference surely is that, as religion develops, theology must also develop. Moreover, it is just as true that theology may be in advance of religion, as that religion may be in advance of theology. When Plato had developed a monotheistic theology of a pure and lofty kind, the religion of Greece as it existed in the popular consciousness was still steeped in the inconsistencies and superstitions of an earlier faith. What should be shown therefore is not that there is a discrepancy between the religion and the theology of a particular age, but that a religion can exist without any theological ideas whatever. But this proposition is obviously absurd, unless we identify theological ideas with the systematic exposition of religious belief. To remove from religion all beliefs, and thus to identify it with pure feeling, is to destroy its fundamental character as rational. Without the belief in friendly spirits, for example, there can be no religion corresponding to the stage of animism, and such a belief constitutes the theology of this primitive stage of intelligence. Nor does it introduce any fundamental difference that the beliefs lying at the basis of religion are taken hold of by the reflective intellect, and formed into a more or less consistent system; for this system merely formulates what is already present in the unreflective consciousness, with no other change than is implied in placing those beliefs upon a rational basis and bringing them into harmony with one another. And if religion cannot exist without belief, neither can it be identified with the forms in which reverence for the divine expresses itself. Whatever may be said of the necessity of ceremonial and ritual, it will not be denied that religion does not consist in ceremonial and ritual, since a man who has no belief in the divine, and therefore no reverence for it, may perform the so-called religious act of worship, and yet be essentially irreligious. Religion, in fact, is incompatible with the elimination of any of the elements that have been mentioned. A religion without belief in the divine is a superstition; a religion that has no influence upon conduct is a contradiction in terms; a religion that substitutes external ceremonial acts for the higher life is an empty formalism.

Of the three elements involved in religion—belief, ritual and reverence—the first presents a double aspect, failure to perceive which has been the source of some confusion. No man can be religious who has not a belief in the divine; but it does not follow that he is able to throw his belief into a systematic form, much less that he is able to assign the rational grounds on which it rests. Thus, although religion presupposes belief in the divine, it does not necessarily presuppose an explicit theology. The latter only arises when the belief is subjected to examination, and expressed in the form of a connected system of ideas. But, when belief in the divine is identified with a system of theology, it may be argued that, as it can exist without theology, religion does not necessarily imply any belief whatever in the divine. Thus arises the fallacy that religion does not in any way depend upon what a man believes, but is purely a matter of feeling or religious experience; a proposition which is true only if by feeling or religious experience is meant the total concrete religious consciousness, including thought as well as emotion and will. While, therefore, it may be admitted that a systematic theology is not the indispensable condition of religion, it by no means follows that there can be a religion which excludes all definite ideas. It is certainly true that, unless religion already exists, theology can have no material to organize, but its special task is to show that nothing short of union with the divine can give satisfaction to a rational being. This will involve a demonstration of the dependent or limited character of all other interests. The problem of theology is, therefore, to demonstrate the truth of that which the religious consciousness already believes. The necessity of giving this proof is bound up with the very nature of man as a being who not only feels but thinks, and not only thinks but reflects. In our day, at least, the more reflective minds cannot be satisfied with anything short of a scientific theology or philosophy of religion, and this demand at once raises all the difficulties that surround the attempt to determine the ultimate nature of things.

Bearing these general considerations in mind, we may go on to consider very shortly the development of the religious consciousness in Greece. The pre-Hellenic idea of the divine was that of spirits not yet definitely characterized, but believed to dwell in unwrought stones. Gradually, from contact with the East and South, and, above all, by the influx of the Northern tribes, the undifferentiated gods obtained personality. The Homeric poems, while they contain distinct traces of earlier beliefs, indicate a marked advance both in religious ideas and in the conception of human life and conduct. Nevertheless, the mysticism associated with the names of Dionysus and Orpheus preserved and developed the deeper aspect of the popular religion. Especially in Orphism, with its doctrine of immortality and its belief in the union of the worshipper with the divine, a phase of religion was reached, which acted powerfully on the later poets and the philosophers of Greece. In the beginning Greek philosophy made no clear distinction between the external object and the human spirit. In a sense it repeated on a higher level the same process as had been undergone by religion, attempting at first to solve its problem by referring the sensible world to a principle affirmed to be itself sensible.

The object of the early philosophers was to find some primary substance which remained at unity with itself in all the changes of things. In the world, it was said, there was a continual process of coming to be and ceasing to be, and hence no stable reality could be found in particular objects. Yet there must be something which is eternal and imperishable. This is the unconscious logic involved in a pantheistic conception of the universe. In this first phase Greek philosophy was rather indifferent than hostile to the popular religion, but it was inevitable that the latent antagonism of the two should become explicit, and only then could an advance be made to the reconstruction of the idea of the divine on a rational basis. This antagonism came to expression in the sceptical attitude of the Sophists. In the religion of Greece there was implied, however, a higher principle than Greek philosophy in its earlier form explicitly grasped—the principle that in man there is something akin to the divine—and this principle was divined by Socrates, and brought to clear and systematic statement in the philosophies of Plato, Aristotle, the Stoics and the Neo-Platonists.

A thorough-going Idealism would seem to demand that the world properly understood must be regarded as a perfect manifestation of the Divine Intelligence, though at even the most advanced stage of knowledge reached by us we cannot show this in detail. Plato, however, is not prepared to go so far ; all that he will admit is that the world is as perfect as the nature of the sensible and finite will allow it to be. If the world were perfect, he thinks, it would be above genesis and decay, for the perfect admits of no change. It is true that the finite world is not a scene of mere disorder and lawlessness ; it has in it an ordering principle which keeps it within bounds, thus setting a limit to the " unlimited " (τὸ ἄπειρον) ; but as the unlimited is perpetually chafing against this limit, it ultimately prevails and the thing is dissolved, giving place to another finite thing, which is subject to the same remorseless process. True reality, then, is eternal and unchangeable, whereas the phenomenal world is transient and changeable. The former is self-active, self-caused or self-determined; the latter is subject to a cause beyond itself or is passive. Nevertheless, the phenomenal is an image or adumbration of the real or intelligible, as is proved by the fact that it contains beautiful objects, which express the ideal in sensible form. On the other hand, the fact that objects are ugly as well as beautiful shows that the good is not perfectly realized in them. The cosmos, then, is the product of the Divine Intelligence, but of the Divine Intelligence operating under the conditions of the sensible. For the Divine Intelligence is good, and therefore it seeks to produce a world as like itself as possible. The relation between the intelligible and the phenomenal is not accidental, though there is in the latter an accidental element due to the inevitable limitations inseparable from the finite. The rationality of the phenomenal, upon which Plato still insists, implies that the world is not a dead mechanism but a living or self-active being, as completely rational as reason acting under the conditions of the sensible can be. For soul is self-identical and yet cannot completely realize its self-identity in a world where all things are conditioned by space and time. There is an approximation to the perfection of the Divine Intelligence in the ever-recurring movements of the heavenly bodies, and in the perpetuity of animal species; but, after all, these are only approximations to the perfection of the Divine Intelligence, which is eternally complete and unchanging. As the phenomenal is ever changing, we come to figure it as a series of changes which take place in an unchanging substrate. This substrate is that which imposes spatial and temporal conditions. It cannot be defined, because it has no determinate form of its own, and indeed we are led to maintain it by a kind of "spurious reasoning," because space is always present as a condition of the sensible, and so we think of it as a substance. Thus the unity of the *idea* is never completely realized, but is broken up into fragments, associated only in an external way. The phenomenal world is therefore subject to necessity, though necessity is in a certain degree subject to reason. To this Plato adds that the phenomenal is not merely that which lies side by side in space or follows in time, but it is reduced to a certain order by number and measure. Lastly, Plato conceives of the universe as a "Second God"; *i.e.* though derivative, it is relatively self-complete and self-sufficient, and is the source of the being and well-being of all other creatures.

From what has been said it seems evident that there is a certain vacillation in Plato's conception of reality. On the one hand, he seems to hold that the real is a synthesis of the one and the many, that the principle which explains the living movement of the phenomenal world is self-active intelligence, and that the Divine Intelligence communicates its own nature to finite things. If this line of thought were followed out consistently, it would lead to the conclusion that, properly understood, the world of our experience must be an absolutely rational system, conformable to the nature of the Divine Intelligence. On the other hand, Plato does not admit this to be the result of his own statements. For he maintains that the phenomenal world is subject to a necessity which is not the necessity of reason, but something to which even reason must submit; he draws a strong contrast between that which is self-moved and that which is moved by another, viewing the latter as falling beyond the domain of the intelligible; and he opposes the ever-changing sensible, with its spatial self-externality and its temporal evanescence, to the self-centred activity and unity of the intelligible world. One reason for this vacillation seems to be the confusion between the phenomenal as a special sphere of being contrasted with the intelligible, and the phenomenal as the intelligible when it is only imperfectly comprehended by us. It is one thing to say that the sensible world is opposed in its own nature to the intelligible world, and another thing to say that in man, as a being whose " knowledge grows from more to more," the sensible world seems to be imperfectly intelligible. If we take the former view, it is hard to see how we are to escape from dualism and pessimism; for a world which, by its very nature, contains an irrational element can never completely realize the good; so that evil is not a disappearing phase of it, but is inseparable from its very existence. On this theory it seems obvious that the intelligible world—or, what is the same thing, the Divine Intelligence—cannot be the sole principle of reality. Opposed to it is a world which, at the most, it can only modify, but of which it is not the cause. Hence, we seem forced to conclude that the Divine Intelligence is limited and incomplete; a conclusion which Plato himself regards as untenable. Why, then, did Plato take the view that the phenomenal world is only partially rational and intelligible? To some extent, no doubt, because of the elementary state of the physical sciences. So much seemed to be beyond the possibility of solution, so complicated appeared the interplay of mechanical causes, that Plato may be excused for thinking that the manifestations of cause and effect lay for ever beyond the reach of our knowledge. But no doubt the main reason for his hesitancy arose from a belief in the limitations of human faculty. " Each of us," he says, "seems to know everything as in a dream, and, again, in waking reality to know nothing at all."[1] There is indeed a real difficulty in the apparent contradiction between the claim to a knowledge of reality and the obviously limited extent of our knowledge, a contradiction which can only be solved, when we see that there are certain presuppositions which alone make any knowledge whatever, and even any appearance of knowledge, conceivable. The main presuppositions are, that the universe is intelligible and that all intelligences are in their essential nature identical. On this rational faith we must build, otherwise the world and our own life cease to have any meaning. Nothing less seems to be demanded by the idea of religion, and if Plato was not able to reach, or at least to keep at this level, he has presented the problem so clearly that we need not despair of its solution.

Aristotle agrees with Plato in seeking the ultimate principle of knowledge and existence in reason, and in denying that the objects of experience are a perfect realization of reason, though they do realize it as far as their finite nature will allow. Plato, while he holds that the world is on the whole a rational system, finds in it an element of non-being or finitude that prevents it from being completely rational. This element is described by him in much the same terms as those employed by Aristotle to characterize that to which he gives the name of "matter" (ὕλη). Prior to the determinate form which it assumes, a thing cannot be said to be "this thing"; yet it is not nothing, but that which "will be" this thing, when it receives a determinate "form"; or, otherwise stated, that which this thing is "potentially." "Matter" may therefore be called either the "substrate" or the "potentiality" of a determinate thing. By "form," on the other hand,

[1] *Politicus*, 277 D.

is meant the determination which is given to the " matter," and which constitutes it " this thing." As we have no experience of anything but things so formed or individualized, nothing exists that is not a combination of " matter " and " form." As that which " becomes " is " sensible," it follows that whatever is " sensible " contains " matter," and that whatever contains " matter " is " sensible." Hence that which does not imply " matter," that which is immaterial, is not subject to change, but must eternally persist. Moreover, sensible things are by their nature contingent, since they may either be or not be ; and this contingency arises from their possession of a " matter " which is capable of opposite determinations ; it is, therefore, the " form " which determines whether a thing should be this or that.

Beginning with the idea of " matter " as the ultimate basis of all things, Aristotle goes on to describe the world as displaying an ever-increasing complexity, and indeed he has fixed the bold lineaments of the world for all time. The first and simplest forms imposed upon primitive matter are displayed in the four elements. More complex bodies are formed by a mixture of those elements, which must not be conceived as a mere mechanical combination, but as the product of the reciprocal action of the opposite qualities of the elements combined. In this way arises the distinction of organic and inorganic things. Plants and animals, again, are composed of different kinds of homogeneous parts combined into a whole. A body is essential as an organ of the soul, the latter not being a separate entity, but the sum of functions in which the life of the being consists. Aristotle's conception of " soul " as the principle which differentiates living from non-living beings is a new and original contribution to philosophy. " Soul " is defined by him as the " first actuality of a natural organized body which possesses life potentially." In this definition he indicates the fact that soul or the principle of life is found only in organized beings, not in products of art or even in natural inorganic things, and that it is the form which actualizes or brings into activity the capacities of the organized body. Soul and body are therefore correlative. The body is not, as with Plato, an independent substance, having a nature of its own which bears no necessary relation to the soul temporarily inhabiting it, but it is essentially relative to the body. Hence Aristotle rejects the whole principle of the transmigration of souls, maintaining that the soul of the plant is relative to the plant-body, the soul of the animal to the animal-body, the soul of the man to the human-body. "Body" is not "body" apart from "soul," for "soul" is the principle through which the latent capacities of "body" are realized; and therefore body and soul are not separable, but are properly only distinctions within the one concrete living being. In this conception of soul Aristotle makes a distinct advance upon Plato; for Plato saw nothing inconsistent with reality in the conception of soul as an independent substance, which is capable of existing apart from body, and therefore has only external relations to it. Such a conception obviously divides up the world into two independent halves, either of which may exist apart from the other. Aristotle's conception of soul, as the form in which the capacities of the organized body are realized, is therefore inconsistent with the dualism of Plato. Further, as soul is essentially the correlate of body, the specific form of the soul implies the specific character of the body. Hence, in proportion as the body possesses more complex capacities, the soul displays higher functions, and thus there are different stages in the ascent towards a perfect unity. Such a unity, it is true, is never realized in any

THE THEOLOGY OF ARISTOTLE

finite being; for the life of such a being is a perpetual struggle to maintain its individuality, a struggle in which it is finally worsted, though it passes on the task to its offspring.

Aristotle, however, does not carry out the idea of correlativity with perfect consistency. Reason or intelligence, he holds, in its own nature is entirely independent of the bodily organs. From reason proper Aristotle therefore excludes feeling, memory, imagination and discursive thought. In this opposition of pure reason to the passions and interests of the individual life, the correlativity of matter and form, which on the whole he maintains in its application to the lower functions of the soul, is expressly abandoned, and we are presented with an absolute dualism of nature and mind, one of the results of which is seen in the abstract opposition of the theoretical and the practical sides of human nature. A true theory would seem to demand that man should be regarded in the whole of his life as implicitly or explicitly rational. The most elementary form of knowledge must, therefore, be supposed to contain the same elements, though in an undeveloped or inchoate state, as are found in the most developed form of knowledge; and, similarly, the simplest form of action must be regarded as governed by the same principle as that which comes to clear consciousness in the highest form; while knowledge and action, thought and will, must be viewed as but distinguishable aspects of the same rational subject. Aristotle, however, does not so conceive of the matter. Man, he admits, is always potentially rational, *i.e.* he is perpetually striving to live the life of reason, but in the sphere of practice he can never realize this end. In knowledge he is self-determined and deals with purely intelligible objects; but in action, where he has to work with a material that is beyond his control, the utmost that reason can do is to attain to the relative subordination of a foreign and recalcitrant matter to its own ends. In its theoretical use reason is dealing with universal principles and their logical consequences; and as these can be grasped by thought, it can attain its end irrespective of any limitations implied in the character of the particulars; but, in its practical use, where it has to deal with the world and the actual nature of man, it is compelled to ask what can be realized by the agent under particular circumstances and in consistency with his whole nature, animal and rational. Hence no absolute laws can be laid down in regard to action; all that can be done is to prescribe what must be done under given conditions, external and internal. Hampered by the character of the material with which it has to work, reason does not in the sphere of action reach its own proper form. That form is pure contemplation, as is evident from the fact that we conceive of the divine being as enjoying the absolute felicity of uninterrupted self-contemplation.[1] No doubt in the case of man the State is the necessary condition of the theoretical life; for, without the organization of the State no one would be free to devote himself to purely intellectual pursuits; but pure contemplation is in its own nature independent of all external aid, and if man cannot through it realize perfect happiness, that is only because he is unable to maintain for any length of time the activity of pure thought.[2] For Aristotle, then, it is only as theoretical that reason reveals its true nature, for only theoretical reason is capable of grasping the universal and eternal. In contemplating the principles involved in things—the end toward which they are striving, or the form which constitutes their essential nature—the mind attains to that freedom and self-satisfaction which is the result of its

[1] *Eth.* 1178 b, 7-11.   [2] *Eth.* 1177 b, 27.

THE THEOLOGY OF ARISTOTLE 17

apprehension of that which is akin to itself. Aristotle is led to exalt theoretical above practical reason by his assumption that things as presented to us in immediate experience contain an element which cannot be shown to be essential to the constitution of an organic whole.

The world is a cosmos, or rather is ever tending towards a cosmos, in which all things exhibit an effort after self-completeness; an effort, however, which is never completely realized. The perpetual change and mutation of the phenomenal world is an indication at once of the actual imperfection of things and of their effort to "make themselves eternal." In a certain sense, indeed, man is able to rise above his finitude. So far as he participates in pure reason, he can contemplate reality as in its ideal completeness it is. Hampered as he is by his animal nature, he can never actually realize in himself this ideal completeness; but, in rare moments, he is able to transcend the limits of his finitude, and to contemplate the world as it would be were the striving after perfection of each being actually realized. Now, this ideal is actually realized in God; and it is by reference to the idea of God that we must explain that divine unrest which will not allow a finite being to be satisfied with anything short of absolute completeness.

The outer sphere of the universe, that in which the fixed stars are set, as a substance in unceasing circular motion, is eternal, and therefore a cause of this motion is required, which must also be an eternal substance. This substance, however, as the ultimate cause, must itself be unmoved. Now, there is in each being a desire for an end, which is not changeable but is involved in the very nature of the being in which the desire is operative. In rational beings this is the object towards which the whole of the rational life is directed. Here we have a fixed or unchangeable principle, which yet is the moving principle in the whole life of the beings in whom it is operative. There is, therefore, perfect agreement between the primary object of desire and the primary object of thought. It is not possible to account for the persistent tendency towards this object by saying that it seems to us to be "good" because we "desire" it; the only possible explanation is that we "desire" it because we judge it to be "good," *i.e.* because the mind grasps the principle which will give satisfaction to the effort after the rational, and which is therefore fitted to satisfy desire. Thus desire is dependent upon thought, not thought upon desire. Now, the highest object of thought, and therefore the highest object of desire, is the Substance which is first and simple or self-complete. This Substance, as the object of rational desire, acts upon finite beings by being loved. In itself it is absolutely unchangeable, but it produces the primary motion of the heavens, and secondarily all the other forms of motion or change. As the only absolute, the first mover is good. This, then, is the principle of the heavens and the world of nature. "The life of God," says Aristotle, "is like the highest kind of activity in us; but while we can maintain it but for a short time, with him it is eternal; for it is an activity which is at the same time the joy of attainment."[1]

Thus Aristotle seeks to explain the nature of God by a reference to the activity of contemplation in us, which he regards as the highest form of activity of which we are capable. For, in contemplation, he holds, the mind is not thwarted in its activity, but comes directly into the presence of an object, the apprehension of which is accompanied by the joy of attainment. If man could live entirely in contemplation, there would no longer be a contrast between the end after which he strives and the process in which it

[1] *Met.* 1072 a, 75; b, 15.

is sought. But, as the limitations of our human life compel us to live mainly in the lower sphere of action, it is only at rare moments that we are able to attain to the blessedness of complete self-realization. In God, on the other hand, there is no opposition between process and realization; in other words, it is the nature of God to experience eternally that absolute identity of thought with its object which in us is experienced only in rare moments. We are not to think of God as devoid of all activity or joy, but, on the contrary, as exercising an infinite activity, and therefore experiencing an infinite satisfaction. His activity is that of pure intelligence, which is the only activity that admits of complete realization. God, in Green's words, is an "eternally complete self-consciousness." There is thus a marked contrast between the nature of God and all forms of finite being; for each of these begins and ends in time, and only partially realizes its end or nature. It is true that the world as a whole never began to be, and can never cease to be, but every single substance in it is produced by another substance, which again produces a new substance of the same species; and this perpetual process, in which new beings are perpetually arising and perishing, stands in marked contrast to the completely realized activity characteristic of the divine nature.

Now, if the world is a scene of ever-renewed change, in which nothing persists beyond a limited time, while the life of God is an unchanging and eternally complete activity, how are we to conceive of the relation between the world and God? If God is by his very nature complete in himself, can it be said that he is the cause of the changes which take place in the world? The life of God, Aristotle seems to maintain, consists solely in the activity of self-consciousness, and it is hard to understand how a being thus self-complete apart from the world should in any way act upon it. Aristotle argues that we must go beyond the world in order to explain it, for there cannot be an endless series of changes unless there is something which does not itself change. Thus we seem compelled to hold that the totality of changes in the world must be referred to an " unmoved mover," or an unchangeable principle of change. But how are we to make such a principle intelligible to ourselves ? Aristotle answers that there is in every finite being a desire for its own completeness, a desire which in rational beings takes the form of a will or love of the good. Thus the influence of God upon the world must be conceived as due to the inherent tendency of every being to complete itself or to attain to the perfection eternally realized in God.

The difficulty we feel in accepting this solution is that it does not seem to account for any influence of God upon the world, but at the most only for the process in the world itself. In the case of finite beings, there is an opposition between the actual and the ideal, an opposition which is displayed in the effort after a perfection not yet possessed ; but, since God is already perfect, it does not seem that there can be anything in his nature corresponding to desire, and therefore he must apparently remain in eternal isolation and self-completeness. The method of extrication afterwards followed by Christian thinkers, who adopt the idea of creation, was not open to Aristotle, for in his view the world is eternal. It thus seems to be a contradiction in terms to speak of God as in any way related to the world. What is called the action of God upon the world can only be the tendency of finite things to strive after completeness, a completeness which is no doubt held to be realized in God, but realized in entire independence of the process which goes on in the world. When Aristotle says that there is " something divine " in all creatures, this can only properly mean that there is in all creatures something of the same kind of nature as exists in God, since they cannot be satisfied with anything short of the divine perfection: it cannot in strictness mean that God communicates his nature to the finite being, but only that the finite being bears a certain resemblance to God. It must also be observed that the only finite being that can properly be said to seek for perfection is man, for other beings move blindly towards an end of which they are not themselves conscious. Aristotle no doubt speaks of "nature" as "aiming at the best," but this is merely a figure of speech, for "nature" is but a name for the way in which things occur, and even animals, not to speak of inorganic things, do not in any strict sense consciously seek their own good. Granting, then, that the world, as a finite existence in space and time, is not self-explanatory but must be referred to some principle other than itself, it does not follow that this principle can be identified with a Being who is conceived to be absolutely perfect apart from the world, and therefore apparently incapable of entering into any relation whatever with it.

Aristotle is not prepared to admit that the imperfection of the world is only apparent; for him the world in itself is imperfect, while only in God is there realized that which the world would be if its effort after perfection were actually realized. In this view there are two main difficulties. In the first place, if God sees what the world would be, were its tendency towards completeness realized, he must also apprehend it in its imperfect form. But this is in contradiction to Aristotle's own statement, that God can apprehend nothing lower than himself. In the second place, if God only contemplates the world as it is in idea, he can have no influence upon the world as it actually is. Thus we come back to the old difficulty: that the changes in the world, granting that they must be referred to a principle beyond the world, yet cannot be connected with God, who is complete in himself independently of the world. Or, as we may also express the difficulty, a world which from an ultimate point of view is imperfect, cannot be the product of a perfect being. Aristotle's conception of " matter," as the persistent element which prevents the perfect realization of the " form," is thus seen to lead logically to the severance of any real connection between God and the world ; and it thus prepared the way for those mystical systems in which all knowledge of God was denied, and the mind in despair fell back upon a supra-rational ecstasy.

The problem of the nature of God and his relation to the world was therefore left unsolved by Aristotle. The only satisfactory solution of it would seem to consist in conceiving God, not as entirely transcending the world, but as manifested in it. The first step towards this mode of solution was taken by the Stoics. Their main problem was to combine the freedom of man with his absolute self-surrender to God. The energy with which each being seeks to realize itself is in man capable of being expended in the realization of the divine principle, and indeed, struggle as he may to escape from it, he must " obey it all the same," as Cleanthes says. The main value of Stoicism lay in its tendency to free morality and religion from national or racial limits. Its conception of God was no doubt abstract, but it served as the nucleus from which a positive philosophy of religion might be developed. By removing the barriers which prevented man from coming into direct contact with the divine, the way was prepared for the religious philosophy of the Neo-Platonists. Just because they fixed upon self-consciousness or personality as constituting the essential nature of man, the Stoics maintained that the world is a rational unity. This monistic doctrine is the main source of their strength. A pluralistic universe is a contradiction in terms; for, unless there is a principle which unites all parts of the world, however diverse they may seem to be, we can say absolutely nothing that is intelligible. The weakness of Stoicism is that it tends to regard all differences as merely accidental and superficial. It did much to make the idea of humanity as a whole familiar to men's minds, but the secret of a spiritual life, which shall preserve the ideal of morality and yet be capable of actual realization, could only be discovered by a philosophy which neither opposed God and man as abstract opposites nor obliterated the distinction between them.

Looking back over the path traversed by Greek philosophy, we can see that it is harassed by a conflict between two opposite tendencies which it is unable to reconcile. On the one hand, in Socrates, Plato and Aristotle the divine is on the whole conceived of as absolutely complete in separation from the world, and morality is identified with the form of the Greek municipal state; on the other hand, in Stoicism the divine is believed to be immanent in and inseparable from the universe, while morality is identified with the good of humanity as a whole. Thus we have a conflict between an abstract theism and an equally abstract pantheism, and between a limited conception of social morality and a comprehensive but empty cosmopolitanism. It was therefore only natural that Neo-Platonism should attempt to heal these divisions by setting up a principle that was beyond the opposition altogether. Such a method of solution, indeed, was foredoomed to failure, but in the continuous experiment which constitutes the history of man, it was a great and perhaps an indispensable step. At any rate it is certain that but for Neo-Platonism Christianity would have had a much less sure grasp of its own principle—the principle that the divine is neither beyond the world nor identical with it, but is manifested in the world while remaining identical with itself—and therefore it would have failed to discern that the only true morality is that in which the utmost satisfaction is given to the spiritual nature of every man, while yet all men are seen to be members of the one organism of humanity.

LECTURE SECOND.

PRIMITIVE CHRISTIANITY AND ITS EXPONENTS.

THE genius of the Hebrew religion was shown in the living energy by which it transformed the crude material supplied to it in the Babylonian myths. At each stage of its history there emerged a new element, which effected a transformation of the old. It is a disputed point whether it was, or was not, originally totemistic, but there can be no doubt that in the Old Testament itself there are traces of a stage when animistic beliefs prevailed. The spirits worshipped were believed to reside in a tree, a stone, or some other inanimate thing. At this stage "holy" merely meant "dedicated." Then the rough blocks of stone were shaped into pillars, and poles were substituted for sacred trees. The transition to the next stage was very gradual, and it is not impossible that it was through the influence of Moses that Jehovah came to be worshipped by all the Hebrew tribes, though it was only after the conquest of Canaan that he was definitely acknowledged as the national God, and incorporated certain of the nobler attributes of Baal along with his own. His worship was carried on at a number of holy places, "on the tops of mountains, under oaks and poplars and terebinths" (Hos. iv. 13). With the advent of the great prophets a new phase ·began. Holiness was now conceived in an ethical instead of a ceremonial sense, and God as a spiritual being, whose glory fills the heavens and the earth, and whose purposes are realized in the creation and preservation of the world and in the history of nations. In the second half of the seventh century Jehovah was held to be not only the greatest of all gods but the only God, though he was still conceived to stand in an unique relation to Israel. The bond, however, was no longer that of nationality; only so long as Israel obeyed the holy will of Jehovah could she escape the uttermost punishment: "You only have I known of all the families of the earth; therefore I will visit upon you all your iniquities" (Amos iii. 1). Even before the prophetic religion had reached its highest point in Jeremiah and Deutero-Isaiah a new phase had arisen from the amalgamation of the popular with the prophetic religion. Its central principle was the Law, which was at first conceived to register the commands of Jehovah as revealed through the prophets, but gradually came to be viewed as of absolute and independent value. The power of the Deuteronomic Law was strengthened and consolidated by the exile. Its prophet was Ezekiel, who emphasized the importance of ritual. From his circle proceeded the Law of Holiness (Lev. xvii.-xxvi.), which attached great importance to sacred actions, persons, gifts and times. The fear of God became almost the same thing as the fear of divine punishment. Yet genuine piety was not destroyed, and in the Psalms powerful expression was given to the longing for purity of heart and communion with God. The Book of Job was a passionate revolt against the dogmatic creed based upon Legalism, while Palestinian Judaism was its inevitable development. When it is assumed that the will of God is completely expressed in a written document, from it must be extracted, by the method of casuistry, rules for guidance in all possible circumstances, and this can only be plausibly effected by an irrational method of interpretation, in which passages and even words are torn from their context. And as God was too sublime even to be named, the doctrine of angels was more and more elaborated. The legal regulation of worship and conduct was expected to usher in the happy Messianic period foretold by the prophets, and with this Messianic hope was closely connected the belief in a resurrection. The blending of Jewish and Greek ideas was most marked among the Jews scattered over Asia Minor, Cyrene and the new Greek cities, and especially among the Jewish population of Alexandria. The influence of Plato and the Stoics is manifest in the *Wisdom of Solomon*, though its fundamental ideas are derived from the Old Testament. Especially in his doctrine of the pre-existence of the soul and its incarnation in the body the author departs entirely from the traditions of his countrymen. Philo is, however, the most important representative of Hellenistic Judaism. God he affirms to be one, eternal, unchangeable, free and self-sufficient; but, as these attributes are conceived in a purely negative way, the inner nature of God is indefinable and unknowable. As the first begotten Son of God the Logos is neither unbegotten like God nor begotten like man, its function being to reduce the world to order and system. As man is made after the image of God, Philo holds that he may at times have a direct intuition of God even here, though only when his spirit is freed from its imprisonment in the body can he attain to the full fruition of the ecstatic vision, and experience that perfect peace ($\dot{\alpha}\tau\alpha\rho\alpha\xi\acute{\iota}\alpha$), which in common with the Stoics Philo regarded as the supreme end of life. Thus by divergent paths the Greek and the Hebrew religions finally reached a stage at which God was conceived to be raised so far above the world that no positive definition of his nature could be given. When this point had been reached, no further development was possible without an entire transformation of the whole idea of the divine in its relation to the world and to human life. The fulness of the time was come for the advent of a new form of religion and a new theology.

By a long and toilsome path the Hebrew religion had at last reached the definite consciousness that there is but one just and holy God, and with this belief was connected the hope of a resurrection from the dead. On the other hand, as the counterpart of the abstract idea of God, it was held that man only knew God in the revelation which God had given of himself in the Law ; and therefore the pious man, it was said, will keep himself undefiled by all that is " unclean," he will lay up merit for himself and even for others, and he will hold himself aloof from a wicked and sinful world. Jesus attacked this whole conception of religion. God, he declared, is not incomprehensible and unknowable : he is our Father, and his love is so inexhaustible that it can be chilled by no sin of his children. The theology and religion of his day he therefore read with the eyes of the prophets, and like them he spoke with the authority of his own direct vision. All externalism and legalism he swept away by insisting on the simple yet profound principle, that the whole of morality proceeds from a spontaneous love to God, which is inseparable from the equally spontaneous love of man. The early Church was unanimous in holding that Jesus was, and believed himself to be, the Messiah ; but that idea in his own consciousness loses its earthly and limited character. In complete surrender to the divine influence lay the secret of the " free and friendly eyes " with which he looked out upon the world. With the clearest comprehension of the forces that make for evil, he combined the faith that nothing can ultimately withstand the power of goodness.

The immediate followers of Jesus, though they conceived of the advent of the Messianic Kingdom as bringing in the reign of righteousness, were unable to free themselves from the external and miraculous features embedded in the popular belief. Upon the conviction that Jesus was the Messiah the earliest form of Christian theology was based. In defending this thesis the eternal validity of the Jewish religion was assumed. To the objection that the death of Jesus effectually disposed of his claim to be the Messiah of prophecy, the Christian apologist answered, that his death was a voluntary sacrifice for the sins of the world; that God had raised him from the dead, thus reversing the condemnation passed upon him by his countrymen ; that by miracles and signs he had shown himself to be more than man ; and that he would give a final demonstration of his Messiahship by his speedy return in glory. Agreeing on these points, there was considerable divergence among Christians in other respects, ranging from those who followed Jesus in maintaining the eternal obligation of the Law to the free Christianity of St. Paul, who was the first to see with absolute clearness that a Judaized Christianity was incompatible with the spiritual religion of its Founder and with its claim to universal dominion. Christ, the " man from heaven," the apostle argued, was sent into the world for the express purpose of freeing men from the belief that they can become righteous by a slavish obedience to the Law.

The splendid idealism of St. Paul freed Christianity from bondage to the customs and ideas peculiar to the Jewish people. The first conflict of Christianity in the sub-apostolic age was with Judaism. The ostensible subject of dispute was whether or not Jesus was the Messiah, a problem which also involved the question whether he was the Son of God from heaven. The dialogue of Justin Martyr with Trypho may be taken as substantially identical with older disputations on these points. In this dialogue Trypho argues that Jesus did not possess the characteristics assigned by the prophets to the Messiah; to which Justin replies by a lavish use of the allegorical method of interpretation. Yet, false as this method was, it enabled the early Christian to retain the Old Testament as a Christian book.

The next problem was to come to terms with the heathen State and religion. From 90 A.D. the State was openly hostile to Christians, and thus there grew up a longing for the end of the world, when the kingdom of God should be established. Three views of heathen religion were held: its gods were regarded either as literally animals, trees or stones, or with Euhemerus they were held to be deified heroes, or finally they were believed to be demons or evil spirits. The Fourth Gospel, however, expresses the claim of the Church to the exclusive possession of the truth, though it is also unconsciously influenced by Greek ideas. All that is reasonable and spiritual in the world, it is held, has proceeded from the Logos, and Christianity is but a clearer revelation of God in the person of Jesus. Justin, again, maintains that Greek Philosophy, not less than the Jewish Law, has been a " schoolmaster to bring men to Christ." The first complete view of Christianity advanced by a Gentile Christian is, however, contained in the Ignatian Epistles. The writer starts with the idea that mankind made in Christ an absolutely new beginning. Prior to his advent men lived under the power of Satan, though it is conceded that the prophets were raised above ordinary humanity, and therefore escaped from the general doom. Before the creation of the world God planned the salvation of man, and with the earthly life of Jesus this purpose began to be realized. His life, death and resurrection ensure the immortality of believers, because in him is revealed the essential nature of the divine life. Jesus was " truly born and ate and drank, was truly persecuted under Pontius Pilate, was truly crucified, and died in the sight of those in heaven and those on earth, and He was truly raised from the dead by his Father."

In these assertions Ignatius was consciously opposing the doctrines of the Gnostics, who held that the sacred writings must not be taken literally; that the God of the Jews was not the true God; that the chief end of man is to escape from this world and return to God; that Christ was in reality a spiritual being who was neither born nor died; that redemption consists in the acquirement of the higher wisdom; and that the true Church is composed of the sons of light, who alone after death enter the heavenly kingdom. Starting from the conception of the unity of God, and assuming his absolute transcendence, a commonplace of Jewish-Alexandrian speculation, their problem was to determine the nature of God and to give some explanation of his relation to the world and to human life. So convinced were the Gnostics of the absoluteness of God that they refused to allow that he can be defined by any predicate applicable to the finite, while claiming that this was not due to any defect in him, but on the contrary to the inexhaustible riches of his nature. The ultimate logical result of this negative method was to deny that even " being " can be predicated of God. This is the conclusion expressed by Basilides, undoubtedly the greatest of the Gnostics, who tells us that " the God that was not (ὁ οὐκ ὢν θεός) made the world that was not out of that which was not." This is as consistent an expression of the unknowability of the Absolute as could well be given. The difficulty of predicating anything of that of which nothing can be predicated has never been exhibited in a stronger way, and indeed this is the necessary result of all doctrines which consistently maintain the absolute transcendence of God. It has been strangely held that in this doctrine of the Gnostics we have an anticipation of the Hegelian Absolute. As we shall see, when we come to treat of Hegel, the principle of Basilides is the exact opposite of that of Hegel, who is almost unique in insisting upon the possibility and indeed the necessity of conceiving the Absolute, not as indeterminate, but as infinitely determinate, and in affirming the futility of all attempts to separate the Absolute from the Relative. No doubt Hegel declares, in his paradoxical way, that " pure being is pure nothing " ; but what he means, and indeed says, is that " pure being " is neither thinkable nor imaginable nor perceivable, but is in fact nothing " in heaven above or the earth beneath or the waters under the earth." Basilides was therefore right in denying that " being," on the premises from which he started, can be predicated of God ; but the conclusion he ought to have drawn was that an indefinable God is nothing whatever but the *caput mortuum* of a false philosophy.[1]

Another distortion of the central ideas of Christianity is associated with the name of Marcion, who, although he was partly influenced by Gnosticism, was not a Gnostic, since his interest did not lie in cosmological speculations, but in the method of salvation. Marcion's main characteristic is a hard logical common sense, which excluded all speculative subtlety or flexibility of imagination. Oriental mysticism, Hellenic philosophy and the allegorical interpretation of Scripture are in his eyes equally preposterous. His main thesis is that the Church had not shown itself able to comprehend the plain and simple Christianity taught by St. Paul, but, on the contrary, had never freed itself from the beggarly elements of Judaism. Nor indeed is this liberation possible, until it is recognized that the whole of

[1] For a more detailed treatment of Gnosticism the writer may refer to his *Philosophical Basis of Religion*, pp. 249-298.

THEOLOGY OF MARCION

the Old Testament gives a false conception of the divine nature. God is love, and from men what is required is a correspondent love, while the God of the Old Testament is a stern, jealous, wrathful and variable God, who demands from his servants blind obedience, fear and outward righteousness. Such a finite and imperfect God, who cares only for his own people, is not the true God, and indeed is not even aware of the existence of the true God. Marcion rejects with contempt the effort to save the Old Testament for Christianity by the false and pernicious method of allegorical interpretation, nor would he have anything to do with speculations on the Logos, which to him seemed to be nothing but a perverse obscuration of the simple truth of the Gospel.

In this controversy between Marcion and the orthodox Christianity of his day, the truth was by no means altogether on the side of the latter. Marcion was of course right in maintaining that in the Old Testament, as literally interpreted, there is contained a very inadequate presentation of the divine nature; and as the exponents of orthodoxy agreed with him in holding that history was all on one plane, they were unable to escape from the consequences of their initial false assumption. On the other hand, Marcion, with his coarse common sense, did not see that the allegorical method of interpretation had in it this amount of truth, that the higher idea of God, brought to light by Jesus and taught by St. Paul, was implicit in the Old Testament. Thus, while his opponents were able to profit by the rich treasures of religious experience preserved in it, Marcion, by his abrupt denial of all truth to the Old Testament, was deprived of this priceless possession. What was required to reconcile the opposite points of view was an idea which lay beyond the horizon of the age: the idea of the evolution of religion. It is characteristic of

Marcion's aggressive and uncompromising attitude, that he was blind to that suggestive conception of history which was St. Paul's substitute for the modern idea of development. Finding in the Old Testament a conception of God that was in contradiction to that of Jesus and St. Paul, he came to the conclusion that the Old Testament was speaking of a different God altogether. There really existed, he thought, a God such as was there portrayed, but he was not the Supreme God, and indeed was ignorant even of the existence of the Supreme God. Marcion therefore honestly believed that he was expressing the true mind of St. Paul, when he maintained that the stern God of the Old Testament, who was also the Creator of our world, was a different being from the loving God of Christianity, the Father of the Lord Jesus and the Creator of the higher world.

The main representatives of Christian thought rejected both Gnosticism and the one-sided doctrine of Marcion, though they were not entirely unaffected by them. Apologists like Justin attempt to show that Christianity is the only absolutely true philosophy, because it contains truths that have been divinely revealed, and is therefore free from the errors and inconsistencies found in the systems of pagan philosophers. The object of the Apologists is, by stating and defending this Christian philosophy, to strengthen the faith of believers. The main topics dealt with are the nature of God, the moral law, and the belief in immortality. In dealing with the first of these subjects the Apologists borrow the language of Hellenistic philosophy, applying to God such predicates as inexpressible, ungenerated, unchangeable, eternal, reason and spirit. On the other hand, when they speak of God as almighty, and assert the creation of the world out of nothing, they are on Christian ground. Thus, though the idea of God is not entirely cleansed of its

THE CHRISTIAN APOLOGISTS 35

Hellenistic colouring, it is, we may say, Christian theology speaking in terms of an alien philosophy. This, in fact, is a phenomenon which accompanies the whole course of Christian theology for centuries. What was essentially a non-dualistic conception struggled to express itself by means of dualistic categories, with the result that the fitting terms were never found. We therefore find that the Apologists attempt to get rid of the opposition of God and the world by conceiving the Logos as a self-conscious personality; for the Logos, though not identical with God the Father, yet proceeds from the Father as light goes forth from the sun; indeed, the Logos is the manifested God. Here we see the essentially Christian idea of a self-manifesting and self-conscious God expressed in inappropriate terminology. God the Father, who in his own nature is inexpressible, expresses himself in the Logos and in this expression reveals himself as Spirit. In their ethics the Apologists start from the idea that man, as essentially rational and free, is capable of acting morally. The moral ideal is declared to be in accordance with reason, but as actually conceived it tends to asceticism. It is true that by Justin and others all real knowledge and all good action are said to proceed from the Logos; but this does not really modify the rationalism of their doctrine, for what is meant is that the germ of reason ($\sigma\pi\acute{\epsilon}\rho\mu\alpha$ $\tau o\hat{v}$ $\lambda\acute{o}\gamma ov$) is implanted in all men; which is merely one of the popular renderings of the familiar Stoical idea that certain common ideas ($\kappa o\iota v\alpha\grave{\iota}$ $\acute{\epsilon}vvo\iota\alpha\iota$) are found in the minds of all men. This thought, however, is rare among the Apologists; for, while it is admitted that real knowledge and a right life are possible for all men, the value of the admission is virtually destroyed by the doctrine that this possibility is seldom realized, so great is the influence of the " demons " in seducing men into a belief in polytheism and the practice of immorality. It was, in fact, to counteract this evil influence that the Logos assumed the nature of man. The need of truth was proclaimed by the prophets, and from their inspired writings the philosophers borrowed their ideas; but, so misled have men been by the demons, that at last the Logos appeared as man, in order to teach the true morality. Thus Christianity does not reveal truth for the first time; on the contrary, the teaching of Jesus is identical with that eternal truth which was proclaimed by the prophets, and can be elicited by a proper interpretation of their writings. Besides this rational theology the Apologists accept as true many traditional ideas which they do not attempt to justify philosophically. They hold the resurrection of the body, as well as the whole of the primitive Christian eschatology, including the belief in the millennium, they maintain the inspiration of the Old Testament, and they assume such ideas as that of the Holy Ghost, expressed in the formula customary at baptism.

At the end of the second century the main problem of the Church was to effect a reconciliation between Greek culture and Christianity. The appropriation of the Old Testament scriptures had already been effected, partly by St. Paul and other writers of the New Testament, and partly by the formal defence of such thinkers as Justin Martyr, who, as we have seen, employed the allegorical method in proof of the prophetic and inspired character of the Hebrew writings, maintaining that they gave an intimation, patent to those who were possessed of the Spirit, of the advent and history of Jesus the Messiah. This problem no longer burdened the Christian mind, and was only argued, if at all, as one of the stock defences of the faith against assailants. The writer of the epistle to Diognetus betrays the distinct impress of Hellenic culture. For him " Christians are in the world what the soul is in the body ": the spiritual Christ is firmly established by God in the heart of man, and Christianity is the explicit recognition of this truth. Justin Martyr again was steeped in the culture and philosophy of his day, having successively passed through the phases of Stoicism, Aristotelianism, Pythagoreanism and Platonism, until he found in Christianity complete satisfaction for the needs of his intellectual and moral nature. It cannot be said that Justin was possessed of speculative genius; like other thinkers of his day he had no comprehension of the free spontaneous movement of thought by which the great masters of philosophy were dominated, but valued different systems according as they appealed to his common sense and his conscience. For him Christianity was the true philosophy; by which he meant that it was not contradictory of pagan philosophy, but the highest expression of that divine reason which is everywhere diffused throughout the world. Justin is the first writer to maintain that God had not confined the revelation of himself to the Jewish people, but had revealed himself to the heathen world, not only in the world of creation, but through his Son, who is the divine reason in every man.

That Greek philosophy, as well as the Law of the Hebrews, has been a " schoolmaster to bring men to Christ," is an idea which is strongly insisted upon by Clement of Alexandria. Had not Christianity come to terms with Greek culture, and with philosophy as its highest expression, it would have remained as the exclusive possession of the common people; while, on the other hand, had it not preserved its independence and originality, it would have been engulfed in such crude metaphysical speculations as that of the Gnostics, or swamped by a flood of oriental superstition. Clement clearly saw these opposite dangers, and therefore he endeavoured to preserve the heritage of thought bequeathed by the ancient world, while maintaining the distinctive ideas of Christianity. Whatever defects may be found in his theology, it is difficult to overestimate the service he rendered to Christianity. His large and reasonable reading of it commended itself to the minds of the wealthy and educated classes. The days of the uncultured Christian were past, and it was important that the fantastic speculations of the Gnostics should be avoided, while due allowance was made for the inextinguishable desire of the human mind to construct an organized system. As in our own day there were not wanting people who rejected all speculation as an unjustifiable concession to the arrogant claims of the human intellect, and fell back upon " the old faith of the fathers." Clement refused to take this narrow view. Loving the poetry of Greece and familiar with its great philosophers, he sought to secure and employ the dialectic of philosophy as a weapon of the Christian armoury. It is true, he admits, that men who call themselves Christians have employed philosophy to destroy the central idea of Christianity, the love of God, and therefore not unnaturally simple souls have been led to condemn all philosophy. " I know quite well," says Clement, " what is said over and over again by some ignorantly nervous people, who insist that we should confine ourselves to the inevitable minimum, to what contains the faith, and pass over what is outside and superfluous, as it wears us out to no purpose and occupies us with what contributes nothing to our end. Others say philosophy comes of evil and was introduced into life for the ruin of men by an evil inventor."[1] But, how can anyone condemn philosophy without philosophizing ? To refute philosophical opinion it is necessary to examine it. " You cannot condemn the Greeks on the basis of mere statements about

[1] Strom. i. 18, 2.

CLEMENT OF ALEXANDRIA

their opinions, without going into it with them, till point by point you discover what they mean. It is the refutation based upon experience that is reliable."[1]

Greek philosophy, then, must not be simply set aside; it is essential in the process of the higher education of the individual; as the foe of superstition, it prepares the way for Christianity, which is the final philosophy. Clement, however, does not regard all philosophy as admirable. For the idea of philosophy as a free and independent discipline, which, even in its greatest aberrations, is contributing some element to the edifice of truth, he was not prepared. The test that he applies to a philosophy is, whether it confirms the fundamental truths of religion and morality; and where it seems to him in opposition to those truths, he rejects it altogether. He will not admit, for example, that Epicureanism is a genuine philosophy, because it denies the Providence of God and regards pleasure as the end of life. From Stoicism, again, he derives his main ethical ideas; yet there are passages in which he condemns its theology unreservedly, as when he tells us that "the Stoics, in saying that God, being corporeal, pervades all matter, even the most dishonourable, shame philosophy."[2] The philosophers whom he prefers are Pythagoras and Plato. The Pythagoras whom he admires is not the historical Pythagoras, but the saint of the Pythagoreans constructed out of legend. His greatest reverence is reserved for Plato, whom he never ventures to criticize. "Plato," he says, "is the friend of truth, he is inspired by God himself." It is thus obvious that Clement does not come to philosophy with an open mind. He approves or condemns a philosophy according as it does or does not harmonize with his ideas of God, man and the world. Whether a system has consistently derived its

[1] Strom. vi. 80, 5; 162, 5; i. 19, 2. [2] Protr. 66, 3.

theological or ethical conclusions from its premises, he does not trouble to ask; enough for him that it contains elements which he regards as true. " I call philosophy," he says, " the sum of doctrines which teach justice and piety, of which each school furnishes a part."[1] Clement, in short, exhibits the eclectic spirit characteristic of the philosophy of the second and the two preceding centuries. His object is not to enquire into the foundation of truth itself, but to construct a philosophy which will enable men to find true satisfaction in life. We can therefore readily understand his antipathy, not only to Epicureanism, but to the Sophists of his time, who " make the worse appear the better reason " by their fatal gift of rhetoric. For the same reason he is not interested in logical, metaphysical or physical enquiries; like Seneca, Epictetus and Plutarch, his thoughts are almost entirely confined to theology and morality. Philosophy he therefore conceives as " the science of divine things," and by a " philosopher " he means one who lives in the practice of religion and virtue. To be a philosopher for him means to be a Christian. The great philosophers of Greece were to their nation what the prophets were to the Hebrews; they supplied the indispensable training in the conception and practice of morality. Philosophy therefore comes from God. This thesis he seeks to establish, partly from Scripture by the usual ingenious but perverse use of allegory, partly by the argument that philosophy like all good things must proceed from God. To the Greeks God in his providence gave the gift of Philosophy, just as the Law was revealed to the Hebrews. No doubt God is not the immediate source of philosophy; but he works through the philosophers, just as health and vigour are directly due to the physician and the teacher of gymnastic, and wealth to commerce.

[1] Strom. i. 37.

CLEMENT OF ALEXANDRIA

With a certain reluctance Clement distinguishes between Greek philosophy and Holy Scripture, maintaining that the former does not directly proceed from God, while the latter does; and there is little doubt that he had a strong inclination to regard philosophy as a direct revelation of truth to the Greeks before the final revelation of Christ. "Before the advent of the Saviour," he says, "philosophy was necessary to the Greeks, in order to teach them justice; now it is useful for the development of piety, being, for those who come to believe by reason, a kind of preparatory and preliminary discipline. For, as Scripture says, 'thy foot will not slide,' if you refer to Providence that which is excellent, whether it is Greek or not Greek. For God is the cause of all good things; some in the first degree and directly, such as the Old and the New Testaments, others consequentially or indirectly, as is the case with philosophy. Perhaps indeed philosophy may have been given directly to the Greeks at the time when the Saviour had not yet called the Greeks to repentance. For philosophy also served to the Greeks as a schoolmaster to bring them to Christ, as did the Law to the Hebrews. Thus it is a preparation for the perfect revelation of Christ."[1]

Clement further seeks to prove that philosophy proceeds from God by employing the argument, first advanced by Philo, that the Greek thinkers derived their main ideas from Moses; a proposition which he seeks to establish by a comparison of the words of Scripture with a crowd of passages more or less analogous from the poets and philosophers of Greece. Fallacious as the whole argument was, it served to silence those who regarded philosophy as the work of the devil; for obviously that which came indirectly from the oracles of God must ultimately be of divine

[1] Strom. i. 28.

origin. Clement, however, is not always consistent with himself. Sometimes he suggests that philosophy was the product of the independent effort of Greek thinkers and harmonized with divine wisdom by a sort of divine accident; while, on the other hand, his deepest thought is that there is diffused everywhere, but more especially in the human breast, a universal reason, which assumes the forms of intuition, knowledge, faith, or art, according as it deals with first principles, with demonstrative truth, with religious ideas or with production. It is from participation in this divine reason that Greek thinkers have been able to attain to a measure of truth. Philosophy, however, has no knowledge of absolute truth: it " knows only in part, for all that it has clearly proclaimed are the doctrines of providence and of reward and punishment after death."

Having argued that Greek philosophy is a preparation for the fuller truth of Christianity, and that it must be studied if the Christian is to obtain a clear grasp of the whole truth, Clement could hardly avoid the question as to the relations of faith and knowledge. His repugnance to the aristocratic severance of Christians into two diverse classes, as maintained by the Gnostics, is sufficiently clear and emphatic. Faith, as it exists in the soul of the simple Christian, is the necessary basis of knowledge. It is therefore an entire perversion of " the common Faith " to say that the truth is hidden from the " babes " and revealed only to the " wise." God gives no imperfect gifts, and therefore the simple Christian who has faith in God is in possession of the whole truth; his eyes have been opened, so that he has the power to see God. No doubt this faculty is still in a sense potential, and indeed it will never be completely developed until after the resurrection; nevertheless Christians are not divided into " gnostics "

CLEMENT OF ALEXANDRIA 43

and "psychics," but all are at one in the renunciation of sin and in faith in him who alone is perfect. Thus in the common faith of all Christians the highest knowledge is implicit. The true gnostic is therefore merely the simple believer who realizes all that is involved in his faith. To make the transition from faith to knowledge no doubt a process of ratiocination is needed, but without faith that process would be but beating the air. True gnosis always remains in perfect harmony with the divine Word. It consists in the personal assent of the whole being to the idea of God. Faith believes that the Son is the Son, that he has come to earth, that he has appeared under a certain form, for a certain purpose, and has suffered for man's redemption; while knowledge interprets the facts so accepted. Thus Clement does not agree with Tertullian that faith excludes all enquiry; on the contrary, he holds that the very nature of faith as an immediate or intuitive apprehension of the truth naturally leads to its expansion into knowledge. At the same time Clement does not really differ fundamentally from Tertullian; for he justifies knowledge purely on the ground that it must remain within the limits of faith. The content of Christian truth is in no sense doubtful; and it is because of this conviction that for Clement there can be no conflict between faith and knowledge. This attitude must obviously lead later to the Scholastic doctrine of authority. No doubt Clement regards the truths of Christianity as an expression of the universal reason, and therefore as having the certification of reason; but, in so far as he identifies these truths with the special doctrines accepted in his day, he obviously lies open to the objection, that he does not allow reason to do its perfect work. Even when it is admitted, for example, that there is a providential government of the world, it does not follow, as Clement maintains it does, that no proof of the fact can be demanded, and that even the raising of the question is impious.

Apart from this inconsistency, however, Clement regards faith as the foundation of knowledge, because it contains that which can be demonstrated by reason. Indeed, faith is for him the foundation of all knowledge. There are four ways by which we obtain truth: sensible perception, opinion, science and reason. In the order of nature reason is primary, but in the order of our apprehension we begin with sensible perception. Even when reason has done its perfect work, we have not attained to the ultimate principle of things; and therefore the Greeks, because they were wanting in faith, did not know the true God. There can be no doubt, I think, that Clement has not succeeded in adjusting two entirely different conceptions of the relation of faith to knowledge. According to the one, faith is the foundation of knowledge, but it differs from knowledge in being an implicit comprehension of that which in knowledge becomes explicit. In this sense knowledge is evidently the highest stage of faith: it is in fact faith which is distinctly conscious of its own content. The other view of the relations of faith and knowledge is different. By faith is now meant that comprehension of truth as a whole which is given in Christianity, and by knowledge that inadequate grasp of truth which falls short of the highest, and which is attained only in Greek philosophy. Thus faith is higher than knowledge because its *content* is higher. Faith, in fact, consists in the comprehension of the true nature of things, knowledge in that measure of truth which at the best is only a preparation for the truth as revealed in Christianity. Here, in fact, there comes to light that contradiction in Clement's thought which is due to his endeavour to regard Greek philosophy as at once a preparation for Christianity and as differing from it in kind. If we follow out the former view, we shall be led to hold that Greek philosophy was only a less adequate comprehension of the truth than Christianity, and Christianity but a further stage in the comprehension of the truth. Clement undoubtedly had a strong inclination to endorse this view, but he was withheld from adopting it by his preconception that in some sense Christianity, or rather the form of Christianity prevalent in his day, differed *toto coelo* from all other forms of truth, being the final revelation of the Absolute directly communicated by God himself. Nothing but a compromise could result from such a doctrine, and therefore Clement holds both that Greek philosophy was a partial comprehension of the truth and that it entirely failed to comprehend the truth. The former view he adopts when he is defending philosophy from the attacks of the traditionalists; the latter, when he is seeking to prove the absolute truth of current Christian theology. Thus he exposed himself to attack from representatives of both parties. To the traditionalist he seemed to be sacrificing religion to philosophy; to the exponent of philosophy, to be sacrificing philosophy to religion. Nothing short of a thorough reconstruction of his whole doctrine could have met the attacks of both parties. It would have been necessary to admit that faith and knowledge, religion and philosophy, are not two diverse kinds of truth, but can only be contrasted as lower and higher. Within Greek religion the contrast of faith and knowledge obtains as well as within the sphere of Christianity. Faith in both cases is the intuitive apprehension of the truth explicitly set forth in knowledge; and therefore knowledge is in both higher in a sense than faith. On the other hand, faith is the assent of the whole man to the truth, and as such it is, as Clement said, the foundation of knowledge. When, therefore, we are contrasting Greek wisdom with

Christianity, it is a confusion of ideas to argue that " reason " is lower than " faith," because its content is not the " truth " ; for, in this way, we are employing the term " faith " as equivalent to the comprehension of truth, and " reason " as identical with a false conception of truth. Obviously, what we should say is, that " reason " includes and goes beyond Christian " faith " ; just as " reason " includes and goes beyond Greek " faith." When, therefore, we compare the one with the other, our conclusion must be, that Greek reason is Christian reason in a less developed form, or, what is the same thing, that Greek faith is Christian faith at a lower or less developed stage ; what we are not entitled to do, is to oppose Greek reason to Christian faith, interpreting the latter as the comprehension of the truth, and the former as the comprehension of a lower kind of truth, *i.e.* of that which strictly speaking has no title to the name of truth at all.

In Clement's conception of God there is a curious blending of philosophical and traditional ideas, with the result that no real synthesis is reached. In different degrees we can trace the influence, on the one hand, of Platonism and Stoicism, and, on the other hand, of Christian ideas as expressed in the New Testament, and indeed in the Old Testament as interpreted by the allegorical method. Clement is aware that the Christian faith may be distorted and indeed traversed by an illegitimate use of this method, but he does not therefore abandon it, but trusts to the inspiration of Christ in the soul to guard against the false interpretation of Scripture. In attempting to explain the nature of God, he employs the language of Platonism. What especially attracted him in the writings of Plato was not the dialectic method, but the positive ideas in regard to God, providence and immortality that he found in them. But, when he comes to deal with the idea of God, he pushes

CLEMENT OF ALEXANDRIA

certain elements in the Platonic doctrine to a point of abstraction which strongly reminds us of Basilides and Valentinus. All attempts to define the nature of God, he tells us, are futile. For God is not only beyond the whole phenomenal world, but even beyond the intelligible world as well. It is only by a process of abstraction that we are able to approximate to the conception of God. By the elimination of all the concrete properties of things, and by a gradual ascent from less to more general ideas, we ultimately reach the highest and most abstract of all conceptions. Clement has himself given an account of the process. "By analysis we reach the first conception, starting from things that are subordinate to it and stripping off from bodies their physical properties. In this way we abstract from the three dimensions of length, breadth and depth. The residuum is a point, or, as we may say, a unit occupying a certain position. Eliminate position, and what is left is simply the conception of unity. Now if, removing from bodies the properties that are inherent in them, and from incorporeal things the properties by which they are characterized, we throw ourselves into the greatness of Christ and by the energy of holiness advance to his immensity, we shall in a sense reach to the comprehension of the Almighty, understanding not so much what he is as what he is not. For we must not suppose that the terms used in Scripture, such as *figure, motion, state, throne, place, right hand, left hand*, are literally applicable to the Father of the universe. The First Cause is not in space, but beyond space, beyond time, beyond language and thought." [1] Now, a Being who is of this abstract character is obviously not an object of science, nor can his nature be expressed in human language. We have indeed a vague and indefinable intuition of God, but what knowledge we

[1] Strom. v. 11.

have of him is purely a gift of his grace. " It is difficult," says Clement, " to apprehend the principles of things, and *a fortiori* much more difficult to apprehend the First Cause, the Cause which is the principle of all other things. For, how can we define that which is neither genus nor species, nor difference, nor individual, nor number, nor accident, nor that to which accident belongs ? We cannot properly call him the All, for the All implies magnitude. Nor can we speak of his parts, for the One is indivisible and infinite, not as incomprehensible, but as being without dimensions or limits. Nor can we say that God has shape or name. If we speak of the One, the Good, Reason, Being in itself, or even of Father, God, Creator, Saviour, we employ terms that are not strictly appropriate. Such high names we employ because of our impotence to find the veritable name, in order that the mind may have something to rest upon and steady it. None of these names taken separately expresses God ; combined, they but indicate his omnipotence. We designate things by their qualities, or by the relations they bear to one another ; but we cannot do so in the case of God. Nor can he be apprehended by demonstrative knowledge ; for such knowledge presupposes better known principles, and there is nothing prior to the Uncreated. It follows that our idea of the Unknown is solely the effect of divine grace." [1] We must eliminate from the idea of God all that savours of anthropomorphism. God has no passions or desires ; nor has he need of senses, but directly perceives all things by pure thought ; and when we find Scripture attributing sensation and emotion to God we must regard the language as symbolical.

Clement is here under the influence of that false method of abstraction, of which there are traces in Plato and Aristotle, but which only displayed its full influence in the

[1] Strom. v. 81, 82.

CLEMENT OF ALEXANDRIA

Gnostics, Philo and the Neo-Platonists. The logical basis of the doctrine is a false conception of the process of thought. It is assumed that universals are obtained purely by the method of abstraction or elimination. As Clement himself explains the process, we start from particular things with their properties, and, by abstracting from these, we obtain the conception of a unity; and if we apply the same process to incorporeal things, we finally reach the conception of Being as that which is the *prius* of all particular things. Clement tells us that the idea of God which is thus obtained is negative rather than positive; but he does not see that he has really emptied the idea of all meaning; so that, strictly speaking, it is neither positive nor negative, but is simply the empty abstraction of the unintelligible. The great defect in this conception of the process of thought is that it isolates the universal side of thought, and the universal, grasped in its abstraction, is nothing that can be said either to exist or to be thinkable. There is no such reality as " humanity," when " humanity " is conceived as the object of abstract thought; the true humanity is that which is realized in individual men. Similarly, a God who is regarded as the ultimate result of a process of abstraction, continued until all the attributes by which knowable objects are characterized have been eliminated, is simply the empty idea of that which is the principle of all that is, but which is itself devoid of all being. To comprehend God it is necessary that he should be conceived, on the one hand, as the Supreme principle of all things—that which gives them reality—and, on the other hand, as the principle which is expressed in all things. God, in other words, must be at once the absolutely universal and the absolutely individual. He must be conceived, not as an abstract unity, but as a unity that is infinitely differentiated. Clement sees only the one side.

God is for him the ultimate principle of all things; but, as incapable of being identified with anything less comprehensive than the All, this principle seems to him to be beyond and above the All; what he does not see, is that a principle which is not self-differentiating is not a living principle, but a bare abstraction.

Clement undoubtedly means something very different from the empty Being or Nothing that he declares God to be. Like all Absolutists he assumes that the categories, by which, as a matter of fact, we characterize God, are in some way analogous to the essence of God, as he would appear to us could we transcend the limitations of human thought and speech. In this view we have an implicit affirmation that the true universal is not absolutely indeterminate, but on the contrary is infinitely determinate. Thus there are in Clement's mind two opposite conceptions of thought, which are not, and cannot legitimately be, harmonized: on the one hand, the conception of thought as operating with the abstract universal, and, on the other hand, the conception of it as working with the concrete universal, *i.e.* with a universal that is realized in the particular, and so is individual.

If Clement were perfectly self-consistent, having defined God as the indefinable, he would deny that of God either mental or moral qualities can be predicated. But to do so would do violence to the whole Christian idea of God; and therefore we find him, by a noble inconsistency, not only declaring that God is absolutely good, but that he is absolutely good because goodness is the expression of his self-conscious personality. This doctrine he derives, not from Greek philosophy, but from Christianity; for it is characteristic of Christianity to conceive of the attributes of God, not after the analogy of properties inherent in and constituting the nature of a thing, but as involving a rational self-conscious will. Similarly, Clement's idea of Providence as extending to the minutest detail of life is distinctively Christian; for providence, in his thought, is the process by which the believer is gradually perfected. Thus he regards the whole history of man as a manifestation of the divine purpose. " Our Father," he says, " full of tenderness, does not cease to exhort us, to warn us, to discipline us, for He does not cease to save us." This is the other side of Clement's thought; for obviously a God whose love is infinite and eternal is very different from the abstract Being of whom we can strictly speaking predicate nothing.

It is, however, in his doctrine of Christ as the Logos that Clement to a great extent escapes from the abstractions of his conception of God, though here too there is an imperfect fusion of the metaphysical idea of the Logos, which is borrowed from Philo, and the religious view of the Logos as the author of redemption. In Philo the Logos is the mediator between the Absolute One and the world. The problem that he sought to solve was how God, who in his inner nature is absolutely self-complete, can be brought into relation with the world. This was a problem that had engaged the mind of thinkers ever since the days of Plato. Strictly speaking, no solution was possible on Philo's premises, since a Being who is absolutely self-complete apart from the world cannot possibly manifest himself in the world; but Philo found in the conception of the Logos, as at once thought and its expression, a means of plausibly explaining how the inexpressible may be expressed. God is not himself manifested in the world, but remains secluded within himself, but the Logos, filled with the divine nature, creates and organizes the world, manifesting himself as the divine power from which the unity of the world proceeds. Thus God is conceived to be at once self-involved and self-manifested. In all the metaphors by which Philo seeks to characterize the Logos —the "Idea of Ideas," the "Power of Powers," the "Ambassador of God," the "Interpreter," etc.—the fundamental notion is that of mediation between God and the world. Now, Clement agrees with Philo in the conception of the Logos as the mediator; but there is this fundamental difference, that whereas Philo is seeking to account for the creation of the world and its natural order, Clement's main conception is of the Logos as the mediator between God and man, his interests being almost entirely religious and moral. Just because of this predominance of interest in the redemption of man his conception of the Logos as such is somewhat vague and indefinite. Like that of Philo, the Logos of Clement has two sides: on the one hand, as a pre-existent Being, it exists not only beyond the visible world, but even beyond the intelligible world; and, on the other hand, it is the primary source of all motion and change. Not God, but the Logos, pervades all things, from the highest to the lowest; and, in this aspect of it, it is regarded as immanent in the world and in the innermost depths of the human soul. Clement agrees with Philo in holding that the Logos is the Master of the world, who introduces order and harmony into that which otherwise would be a mere chaos of irreconcilable elements, above all creating man in its own image.

While Philo personified the Logos, it is doubtful whether he conceived it as a person. Clement, on the other hand, leaves no doubt that in the person of Jesus Christ we have the Logos in human form. Whether the Logos was a person prior to the incarnation Clement is by no means clear, but as the Saviour of men, it is undoubtedly to be conceived as a person. Even before he took upon him the nature of man the Logos was a Saviour. Clement sees

CLEMENT OF ALEXANDRIA

him working everywhere in the past for the redemption of man. It was he that spake to Moses from the burning bush; he it was who delivered Israel from the bondage of Egypt; and it is he who speaks through the mouth of the prophets. Nor is his work confined to Israel; for, in accordance with the general view that Greek philosophy was a preparation for Christianity, Clement maintains that it was the Logos who instructed the Greeks in wisdom.

In accordance with the popular Christianity of his day, Clement insists upon the necessity of knowledge as the converse of pagan error and superstition. Hence he speaks of the Logos as a teacher, who communicates that knowledge which is essential, not to the full development of the Christian, but to salvation. Moreover, it is the Logos who has freed man from the depths of moral degradation into which paganism had sunk. And Clement adopts the current doctrine of his day, that deliverance from past sin, involving illumination, purification and a new birth, takes place at the moment of baptism through the influence of divine grace; for it is characteristic of the Christianity of the second century that, in speaking of the deliverance from sin, he should dwell rather upon the virtue of baptism than upon the death of Christ on the Cross. Lastly, the Logos is the conqueror of death, and has secured immortality for man.

From what has been said it is evident that Clement has not been able to free himself entirely from the initial dualism with which he started under the influence of Philo. His conception of God as absolutely self-involved is not consistent with the assertion that God is manifested in the Logos, and therefore we find him fluctuating between the conception of the Logos as expressive of the attributes of God, and as a distinct person. There is a similar defect in his conception of the Logos, as, on the one hand, the

Creator of the world and the Saviour of men, and, on the other hand, as the incarnation of God in Jesus Christ. From the former point of view the Logos is really a term for divine Providence, as manifested in the whole process of history; from the latter point of view the Logos is concentrated in the man Christ Jesus, who lives an individual life, and can only be said to be identical with the divine Redeemer who always was, in the sense that in him there is manifested in a higher degree than previously the redemptive spirit of God. The implicit contradiction between these two conceptions of the Logos reveals itself in the tendency of Clement to docetism, notwithstanding his protests against it. For, when the Logos is identified with the divine principle manifested in creation and in the process of the world's history, the only escape from contradiction seems to be in some such doctrine as that of docetism, which seeks to avoid the contradiction of identifying the universal divine spirit with the person of a single individual by virtually denying that this person was a man in the ordinary sense of the term. It was therefore almost inevitable that Clement, with his imperfect notion of the Logos, should exhibit a tendency to explain away the purely human side of Christ's nature.

The same defective fusion of Greek philosophy and Christian ideas is also exhibited in Clement's conception of the Christian gnostic, as contrasted with the ordinary Christian. The description of the morality of the simple believer, as set forth in the *Pedagogue*, is substantially that of the Church, while the higher morality of the gnostic expresses the ideal of the Christian life. This distinction contains in germ that fatal opposition between the clergy and the laity, which was afterwards hardened into a dogma, and prevailed all through the Middle Ages. Clement's idea of the gnostic is the natural result of his familiarity

CLEMENT OF ALEXANDRIA

with Plato and the Stoics ; for in Plato's ideal state, the higher citizens, and especially the statesmen, are conceived to combine all wisdom in themselves, while the ideal wise man was one of the commonplaces of the Stoic philosophy. Clement's view is that in Christianity, which is the ultimate philosophy, the man who, by a long process of discipline, has attained to the contemplation and love of Good is the true Christian philosopher or wise man, surpassing others both intellectually and morally. The distinction between the ordinary Christian and the Christian gnostic Clement has no difficulty in extracting from Scripture by the usual method of allegory, a method which had the unfortunate effect in this case of allowing him to traverse the essential spirit of Christianity, which is incompatible with any sharp division of cultured and uncultured, any more than of class or nationality. Clement, however, is so far true to the spirit of Christianity, as to deny that the distinction between the less and the more advanced Christian is due to any fundamental difference of nature : it is purely a question of discipline and education ; and, therefore, no Christian is in principle excluded from the highest life.

The aim of the Christian gnostic is, in a word, to become like to God. When we ask wherein this likeness consists, we do not get from Clement any very definite answer. It is clear, however, that likeness to God, for one who conceives of God as indefinite, must consist in likeness to Christ, the Logos of God ; and indeed Clement, as we have seen, conceives of Christ as the divine schoolmaster who leads the gnostic into all truth. The result is that the gnostic has a higher knowledge than others, a knowledge of the world of ideas or the real world, as distinguished from the world of appearance. This " truly perfect knowledge," Clement tells us, " is related to that which is beyond the cosmos, consisting of things perceived solely by the intelligence, and even things more spiritual still." This higher knowledge enables the Christian to ascend to the first cause from which all things proceed; but it also embraces a true knowledge of man, of morality and of the sovereign good. The gnostic is, therefore, not merely one who knows the highest, but one who attains to the highest virtue. In his conception of the moral life, Clement is largely influenced by Stoicism. To be moral is to love the life of reason. The result is that the gnostic attains to a state of perfect apathy or serenity, in which all the passions are, not so much suppressed, as spiritualized. In this mode of conception, indeed, Clement virtually transforms the negations of Stoicism into affirmations; for, apathy, as he describes it, is not due to a mere abstraction from all that is personal, but rather to the transformation of the purely personal into the spiritual. Hence Clement also speaks of the motive of all action as love. In the end, therefore, his Christianity is too strong for his inadequate philosophy, though there is an unreconciled antagonism between the two. When Clement tells us that the Christian should not merely avoid evil, but should love all that is good, he shows that, though he has borrowed certain details from the Stoics, his ethics is fundamentally Christian. The moral ideal he therefore sums up in the one word "piety," which includes the highest knowledge together with unselfish love and tranquillity of soul.

LECTURE THIRD.

FROM ORIGEN TO THOMAS AQUINAS.

THE philosophical theology of Clement was accepted and developed by his pupil Origen. Adopting the "rule of faith" and Scripture as a basis, he seeks to build up a system of theology on rational grounds. The allegorical interpretation of Scripture he accepts in its integrity, maintaining that in Scripture we find three different senses: the literal, the moral and the spiritual; and in this way he is able to show that the creed and the Bible are in entire accordance with the conclusions that he reaches independently. It is by this method of exegesis that he disposes of the contention of the Gnostics, that because of its moral anomalies the Old Testament did not proceed from the Supreme God, and by the same method he replies to Greek critics like Celsus, who declared that it contained philosophical, vulgar and often unintelligible statements. The six days of Creation, for example, are no doubt indefensible, argues Origen, when understood in a literal sense; and it is contrary to morality to say that the child is punished for the sin of the parent; but, interpreted in the spiritual sense, as they ought to be interpreted, they have a profound meaning. By an application of the same method Origen seeks to show the harmony of the Old and the New Testament, and so to defend the verbal inspiration of Scripture. And finally, the same method is employed in the interpretation of the external world, for Origen contends that all natural objects are symbols of higher things. It is hardly necessary to make any elaborate criticism of a method so long outworn: what rather needs to be emphasized in our day is the fact that it is the expression of a violent but blind effort not to let go what is essential, no matter how imperfect may be the method by which the truth is sought to be preserved. Surely there is a process from higher to lower, whether we consider the relations of the Hebrew religion and Christianity, or the connection of the natural and the spiritual worlds.

In his theology Origen begins with a consideration of the nature of God and of his relation to the supersensible world. Clement had conceived of God as the Absolute Being, who is entirely incomprehensible by the intelligence of man; Origen defines him as the pure spirit, who is eternal, immutable and immaterial. God is, therefore, beyond time and space. Instead of saying that he is in heaven, we should rather say that heaven is in him; in other words "heaven" is not a place in which God dwells, but a characterization of his spiritual condition. We cannot properly say that God is in the world, but rather that the world is in God. The former view leads to pantheism, while the latter makes provision for the infinite heights and depths of the divine nature. Nor can we speak of God as "infinite"; for the "infinite" is that which has in it nothing determinate, and therefore nothing that can be made an object of thought. God again is not almighty in the sense that he can dispose of the world and man as he pleases, but only in the sense that, as the Universe has been created by him on a definite and intelligible plan, there can be nothing in it contradictory of his rational will. Hence Origen prefers to say that God is perfect rather than infinite. And when God is said to be perfect, it must not be supposed that he is devoid of all emotion. He

THEOLOGY OF ORIGEN

feels, but his feeling is always rational. " The Father of all," says Origen, " is long-suffering, merciful and pitiful. The Father himself is not impassive ; He has the passion of love."

The visible world, according to Origen, has come to be and will cease to be. The spiritual world, on the other hand, the world towards which the whole process of the visible world is tending, is beyond the limits of time, and consists of immaterial, incorporeal, invisible spirits. From all eternity this intelligible world has existed, God being its source and its light. As perfect, and therefore absolutely good, God must communicate himself, and this he does by revealing himself eternally in the Son, and in the whole world of spirits, a world which he eternally creates through the Son. The Son is co-eternal with the Father, and is eternally produced by him ; but, while he is an hypostasis distinct from the Father, he subsists only for the purpose of revealing the Father. The Holy Spirit is directly created by the Son, and must be regarded as, like the Son, lower than God. Origen, in fact, is unable really to reconcile the unity of God with the three persons. The Holy Spirit is said to be a Person. He it is that in the beginning moved on the face of the waters. His special function is to sanctify. The Father gives being to all that exists ; the Son imparts reason to all that are capable of the gift ; the Holy Spirit endows all who believe with eternal life.

God in his justice originally made all the spirits or rational natures lower than the Holy Spirit equal ; but, because they have the gift of freedom, they are capable of diverging infinitely from one another. In the exercise of their freedom they have all departed more or less from God, and God, in order to punish and purify them, has created matter, forming out of it the visible world, and has then incorporated the various spirits in material bodies according to the measure of their sin. Thus there is a hierarchy of spirits: the highest being the angels, the lowest the demons, while men occupy an intermediate position. By the exercise of his allegorical method, Origen extorts from Scripture a history of the souls of men before and after their appearance on earth. Not only did this knowledge seem to him valuable in itself, but it was employed to explain the inequalities in body, in local and social environment, and in mental power. Origen found numerous hints of the pre-existence of the soul in Scripture, but the real source of his belief was no doubt Plato's *Republic* and *Phaedo*. The souls of men are spirits that have been "chilled" ($\psi\acute{u}\chi\epsilon\sigma\theta\alpha\iota$), and have been sent down to earth to be purified through suffering. They are incorporated in a body, which corresponds to the moral constitution that they possessed in their pre-existent state. Thus, though the freedom of man is undoubted, every soul comes into the world defiled, and is still further defiled by contact with the body; so that men are subject to the temptation of the demons.[1]

Christ became man in order to bring salvation to men. In time there was a union of the divine Logos with a soul that, in its pre-existent state, was absolutely pure; and therefore in Christ the divine and human natures were combined. Between these two natures Origen draws a sharp distinction, but he supposes that the Logos by the resurrection and ascension has deified both body and soul.

[1] The idea that $\psi v\chi\acute{\eta}$ is connected with $\psi\acute{v}\chi\epsilon\sigma\theta\alpha\iota$ is of course a conceit due to false etymology and defective philosophy. I may take this opportunity of saying that I have devoted less attention, at least in the lectures as now published, to Origen than to Clement, not because I am ignorant of his importance in the history of theological speculation, but (1) because I have dealt so largely with his master, and (2) from considerations of space, the work as it stands being too long, I fear, for the class of readers contemplated by Lord Gifford in his Bequest.

THEOLOGY OF ORIGEN

This deification of Jesus is followed by the deification of his followers. Sometimes Origen conceives of the death of Jesus as a ransom paid to the devil, sometimes as a victory over the demons, and at other times as a representative sacrifice to God. Complete redemption occurs only at death. Origen was the first to deny explicitly the millenarian eschatology. The saints, he maintains, receive a new spiritual body and enter into paradise, while the wicked descend into Hades. The former pass through various stages on their way to a perfect morality, and the latter, after passing through a purifying fire, are ultimately brought back to God. Then God will be all in all, and the visible material world will pass away, though another Fall may lead to a new period of the world. Origen's doctrine of universal restitution has an obvious similarity to the belief in purgatory, the main difference being that it admits the possibility of repentance after death, and includes the heathen as well as Christians in its scope. Thus in Origen we have a fusion of Hellenic culture and Christian tradition. His theology not only added new features to the creed, but even contradicted it, especially in regard to the final restoration of all men.

From the time of Novatian (250 A.D.) to the Synod of Nicaea (325 A.D.) there was no real movement in the theology of the West. In the East, on the other hand, the speculative theology of Origen was developed into a definite Logos-Christology, and new problems were raised by the character of that theology. When it became a dogma of the Church the Logos-doctrine spread more widely, but, as Origen's doctrine of emanation was rejected, it became impossible to hold at once the identity of the substance of Father and Son. Moreover, the theology of Origen, triumphant as it was so far, in many points flatly contradicted the "rule of faith" and the tradition of early Christianity. It denied Millenarianism: it affirmed the eternity of the world of spirits; it maintained the pre-existence of souls; it had a peculiar theory of the foundation of the world; and it denied the resurrection of the body. This led to the attack of Methodius, who returned to the view of Irenaeus in regard to a physical resurrection. Methodius entirely denied any separation or disembodiment, maintaining that salvation consists in a transfiguration of the corporeal. The pessimistic view of the world held by Origen in common with the Gnostics he rejected. The world is in no sense a prison-house of the soul, but all that has been created by God is permanent and capable of transfiguration. Hence Methodius denies the doctrines of the pre-existence of souls and a pre-mundane Fall. Like Irenaeus he inclines to the view that the incarnation is the necessary completion of creation. Mankind before Christ was in a plastic condition, and readily fell into sin, which had a purely external source: it was first consolidated in Christ. Methodius finally came to hold that the descent from heaven, and the death and resurrection of the Logos, must be repeated mysteriously in the heart of the believer. Here, in fact, we have the origin of Monastic mysticism. Every believer must, through participation in Christ, be born as a Christ. At the same time, the history of the Logos-Christ as held by the Church was not a matter of indifference, for the individual soul can only repeat what had first taken place in the Church. Hence the Church must be revered as the Mother of the individual soul. Methodius also held that celibacy is the condition of Christ-likeness.

From the fourth to the seventh century the creed of the Church was formulated and stereotyped. Underlying all the disputes, theological and ecclesiastical, was a definite conception of Christianity, though it was not always clearly present to the minds even of prominent theologians. During the first part of this period (318-456), while the point of view was mainly that of the Alexandrian theology, this was combined with traditions which belonged to primitive Christianity. At first the theology of Origen was regarded as authoritative; but, when once Alexander and more especially Athanasius had modified it, a movement had begun which finally resulted in its complete overthrow. The controversy was occasioned by the contention of Arius, that only God the Father can be said to be unbegotten, while the pre-existent Christ may be said indifferently to be begotten or made. From this point of view Christ becomes a creature like other creatures, differing only in his spiritual rank, for the view of Tertullian that Christ is an emanation of the Father is repudiated by Arius. Holding this view, Arius cannot accept the doctrine of Origen, that the Son is a hypostasis, along with the Father, and has existed from all eternity: the Logos, as he expressly says, is in all respects unlike in substance to the Father; Christ is, therefore, neither truly God nor the eternal Logos in God, but is only called God, because he is in communion with God. At the Synod of Nicaea (held in June, 325 A.D.) Arianism was condemned, and an Anti-Arian confession of faith constructed for the whole Church. To Athanasius is due its acceptance in the East. He maintained that God is one, and that he is by nature the Father of the Son, so that the Logos existed from all eternity. Hence a sharp distinction is drawn between being "begotten" and "made." It is true that there is still a remnant of subordinationism, for the Father is the source from which the Son proceeds; yet this element is virtually made of no account, when it is maintained, that the Father and the Son are the same in substance, equal in honour and glory. This doctrine is not the result of philosophical speculation, but is based upon Scripture as interpreted by the Church.

The first seven centuries of the Christian era resulted in the formulation of the Trinitarian and Christological doctrines, and in the West laid the foundation of the doctrines of Sin and Grace. At the same time during this period various ideas were accepted which modern thought is forced to regard as distortions of Christianity. At the very time when Christian doctrine was in process of formation a large number of persons entered the Church who were unable really to comprehend the subtle views of theologians. The result was that many heathen forms of worship were introduced, and there gradually emerged a distinction between a higher and a lower morality. Thus arose as early as the fourth century the worship of the saints, and in a much less degree of angels, the reverence for the cross and for relics of all kinds, and the worship of Mary as the Mother of God. The tendency to superstition was fostered by monasticism and by the ceremonious and mysterious character of worship. The excessive importance attached to ritual was an index of the disappearance of creative life in the Eastern Church, which, in fact, with the establishment of the doctrines of the Trinity and the Incarnation, underwent no further intellectual development.

Though Tertullian had given an outline of its main tenets, Augustine must be regarded as the real founder of Latin Christianity. In virtue of the response of his spirit to the various forces operative in his day, his doctrines in a measure effect a synthesis of the different competing ideas that in the fourth century were struggling for the mastery. Believing that he was simply expounding and defending the primitive faith, he really gave to the Christian religious consciousness and to Christian doctrine a new form and content.

A glimpse of something higher than the life of sense came

THEOLOGY OF AUGUSTINE

to Augustine from a perusal of Cicero's defence of philosophy, but he was not satisfied that the treatise, eloquent as it was, had penetrated to the true nature of things, and therefore he turned to scripture in quest of a deeper truth. The immediate result was disappointing, for, taken literally, as he assumed it must be taken, he found it deficient in dignity and eloquence. His next incursion was into Manichaeism, which seemed to him to furnish a real solution of the central riddle of the universe, the otherwise inexplicable existence of evil. The original basis of Manichaeism was Babylonian, but it had been gradually modified by elements furnished by the Persian and Christian religions, and possibly also by Buddhism. In Augustine's day the struggle between Manichaeism and Christianity was not yet over. What attracted the ordinary mind in the former was its pictorial representation of God, its plausible solution of the problem of evil, its ascetic morality, and its promise of immortality. The divine was conceived by its founder as a sort of *tertium quid*, which is beyond the distinction of good and evil, of matter and spirit; but, though no attempt was made to explain the diremption, it was held that in the world there are two opposite forces ever at war with each other, the principle of light and the principle of darkness—the former presided over by God, the latter ruled by Satan and his demons. Man repeats in himself the conflict of these two forces, being created by Satan, but containing in his being some particles of good. To free man from the power of Satan various prophets have been sent into the world by God, the last and greatest being Mani himself, who took up the work of the spiritual Jesus. As good and evil are abstract opposites, Manichaeism was naturally strongly ascetic in its ethics, and a distinction was drawn between the elect and the ordinary man.

What mainly attracted Augustine to Manichaeism was its solution of the problem of evil and of human freedom. By the former, the absolute holiness of God seemed to be preserved; by the latter, it was apparently explained how man was led into evil, in direct contradiction of his reason. This view, however, was for Augustine only a temporary halting-place, and, after a short period of scepticism, when he despaired of ever arriving at truth, though he still believed in God, he finally (387 A.D.) was converted to Christianity. God, as he learned from Ambrose, was a spirit, man is the free creation of God, and he is the author of his own actions. This doctrine he was helped to accept by a study of Neo-Platonism, and indeed the influence of Neo-Platonism is manifest in his ideas of God, matter, the relation of God to the world, freedom and evil, though none of the earlier theologians has done more to distinguish it from Christianity. From Neo-Platonism Augustine learned that the true nature of things is to be found in the forms by which material things are converted into a cosmos. These are grasped by the mind which finds them within itself. Moreover, all forms are the expression of God, the supreme beauty, truth and goodness. But, if God is the author of the cosmos, how are we to account for the fact of evil? The answer of Neo-Platonism was that evil is simply the inevitable limitation of all finite things; and that, as the universe must be infinitely differentiated, the whole is perfectly good because perfectly harmonious, moral evil being simply the absence of that good which is the true nature of the soul.

Augustine, however, though his intellect was satisfied, found that he was still as much as ever the slave of passion. From this thraldom he was freed by a renewed study of the scriptures, especially of the epistles of St. Paul, from which he emerged a firm believer in the infinite love of God as revealed in his Son. Convinced of that love, his whole nature responded to this central revelation of the meaning of the universe, and he found in Christianity the force required to enable him to triumph over his evil passions. Man lives by dying, is only himself when he loses himself in God. As Augustine himself expresses it, " God has created us for himself, and our hearts are never at rest till they find rest in Him." [1]

Augustine was the first theologian to impart a Neo-Platonic colouring to the Christian faith. The centre around which all his thoughts revolve is the idea of God, and it was from Neo-Platonism that he adopted the conclusion that God is in no sense material. But, agreeing so far with Neo-Platonism, Augustine found it essentially defective in this, that, though it spoke of the Logos as a manifestation of God, it yet affirmed that the innermost nature of God is beyond the reach of all definite thought. This doctrine Augustine refused to accept, maintaining that God has completely revealed his true nature in his Son, so that he who identifies himself in faith with the Son attains to a real comprehension and union with God. This truth seemed to him to be expressed in the doctrine of the Trinity, which Augustine interpreted to mean, that Father, Son and Holy Spirit are one substance in three persons. It is the same God who is manifested in three functions, each

[1] Augustine's *Confessions*: *Nos tibi fecisti et inquietum est cor nostrum donec requiescat in te.* The reader should consult the references to Augustine in the late Edward Caird's *Evolution of Theology in the Greek Philosophers*, almost his last and perhaps his most important work. I may be permitted to add that the account of Augustine's life and doctrines given in this work and in my *Philosophical Basis of Religion* is based upon his various writings—always naturally conducted in view of the comments and expositions referred to in the Preface, pp. viii-ix—while the critical estimate of his philosophy of religion is of a more developed character than that contained in my earlier book.

of which involves the others, just as memory, intelligence and will constitute the one single mind of man, while yet each involves the exercise of the whole mind. God the Father expresses the self-existence of God, God the Son his self-knowledge or wisdom, God the Holy Spirit his self-satisfaction or love; and yet the whole nature of God is expressed in each. Thus the divine attributes are inseparably united. While they are distinguished by discursive thought, they are again resumed into unity in the vision or intuition of God. Augustine therefore denies the earlier doctrine of the subordination of the Son and Spirit to the Father, and thus gives a more satisfactory formulation of the Christian idea of God as self-conscious, self-determining and self-revealing. It can hardly be said, however, that he is quite free from the idea that there is a distinction between the inner nature of God and his manifestation in three persons. The absolute "simplicity" of God seems to be rather that of a unity which is beyond distinctions than a unity which by its very nature distinguishes itself.

This defect is more obvious when Augustine seeks to explain the relation of God to the world. In the divine mind are contained the invisible and unchangeable "ideas," which give form to the visible and changeable world; but these ideas constitute the divine nature, and must therefore be distinguished from their effect in the phenomenal world. Thus God's knowledge of himself is absolutely separate from his knowledge of the world; the former consisting of the eternal and unchangeable ideas, the latter of the transient and changeable course of events. Moreover, Augustine holds, on the one hand, that what God knows he must also will, and yet he maintains that God does not will but only permits evil.

Augustine's next question is, how the idea of the world

THEOLOGY OF AUGUSTINE

as it existed in the divine mind came to be realized, and that without destroying the absolute completeness of God apart from the world. The difficulty that the origination of the world must add to the sum of being, he meets by adopting the view of Neo-Platonism that finite things as such have no positive being, but are finite just in so far as they have in them an element of non-being; while in their positive being they are identical with the absolute. The creation of the world, therefore, does not add to the totality of being. It is true that the world absolutely began to be, for Augustine denies the doctrine of a pre-existent matter; but its creation was but an expression of what existed from all eternity in the divine mind. We cannot, however, say that God exists *prior* to the world; for God, as absolutely unchangeable, is not in time. Similarly, God is not in space, for space has no meaning except in relation to corporeal things, and God is absolutely incorporeal or spiritual.

Augustine's main religious interest was in the problem of moral evil. Nothing can be evil in itself, or as it comes from the hand of God. Hence the first man as created by God has nothing evil in his nature. Augustine, however, emphatically rejects the doctrine of Pelagius, that man has an absolute freedom of choice, which is unaffected by the exercise of his will, and that Adam was therefore indifferent to good and evil. His own view is that originally man's intelligence and will were directed to what was good, but he was nevertheless capable of willing evil. The freedom of Adam consisted in his power to accept divine aid, an aid which he perversely refused to accept, and so fell into sin. All true being consists in identification with God, and the sin of Adam lay in the pride or self-assertion which led him to affirm himself, *i.e.* to will the negative or unreal. Sin is, therefore, an inversion of man's true nature. Augustine further maintains, in contrast to the Pelagians, that the willing of evil results, not merely from ignorance of what is truly good, but from perversion of the will. Hence it is not true that man is still free to will the good, and in this loss of freedom consists the punishment of sin. The descendants of Adam are, therefore, impotent to will acceptance of the divine aid. It is not merely that they are exposed to evil example and custom, as the Pelagians held, but that even at their birth both their intelligence and their will are infected. Adam's sin was the act of the whole race, his guilt the guilt of the whole race, his punishment the suffering of the whole race. But through Christ original sin may be removed, and man restored to his original state.

The blindness of the intellect of man is bound up with sin, and therefore Augustine holds the absolute necessity of divine illumination. Faith is a gift of God, by which evil is removed from the mind. And as man is impotent to will the good, divine grace is necessary to renovate his will as well as his intellect. Its result is faith, humility and love. The law awakens the consciousness of guilt, but the essential content of Christian faith is the consciousness of our own sinfulness and impotence for good, as well as of the saving grace which is given only in Christ and his work. Christ frees man from sin, guilt and punishment, and restores him to his original state of purity. While sin is contrary to the will of God, the guilt of sin is not guilt against God, nor is there any change in the nature of God. Christ gave his blood as a ransom to the devil, in order that his just claim over sinners might be paid.

As man is impotent to will the good without the aid of divine grace, while yet all things are in harmony with the divine plan of the world, it follows that only those are good who are predestinated to be good. If all things are fore-ordained, it may seem that it is useless to work for the

THEOLOGY OF AUGUSTINE

spread of the Gospel. Augustine's answer is, that predestination does not exclude the employment of external means, and that prayer is one of the means of Grace subordinate to the will of God.

Augustine's influence, not only on the theology, but on the religious consciousness of his age, can hardly be overestimated. He overcame the divorce between religion and morality, he deepened the consciousness of sin and guilt, not healing the hurt of men slightly, but seeking to transcend the radical evil of human nature by an optimism that did not attempt to explain away evil, but to account for it as the condition of good. He put an end in principle to the perpetual oscillation between hope and fear, which led to the performance of fasts, alms-giving and prayer, crossed by an insecure belief in the inexhaustiblity of the grace of Christ. Augustine was the first to regard the fall of man as the central fact. Sin is self-will and therefore unrest, and from this state man can be freed only by union with God through his Son. If sin has terrible power, grace is omnipotent.

It was Augustine's belief that he was adding nothing to the creed of the Church. For him the Church was the only means by which scepticism could be overcome, and he even goes so far as to say that many things he could not believe except on the authority of the Church. He is thus the father of that doctrine of "implicit faith" which was to play so large a part in the subsequent history of Christendom. The worst effects of this doctrine were prevented in Augustine's own case by his living personal consciousness of God, but it was destined to prove a fatal gift, when the authority of the Church came to be held in a way that tended to suppress that consciousness, and when to the sacraments of the Church an almost magical virtue was attributed.

The theology of Augustine has exercised an influence on Western Christianity which can hardly yet be said to be exhausted. To enter into a thorough examination of its doctrines would be to anticipate what I shall have to say in my second course of lectures; and at present I shall only make a few remarks, which I hope may be suggestive of the line of criticism that the development of modern thought compels us to adopt.

(1) Augustine's doctrine of the Trinity bears obvious marks of the pit from which it was digged. He is unable to accept the fundamental idea of Neo-Platonism, that in his essential nature God is absolutely and for ever inscrutable, rightly seeing that in that case any revelation of the nature of God is impossible. This is by no means a dead issue even at the present day, and indeed it has a plausibility that is hard to withstand. When it has apparently been shown that all the categories by which we seek to characterize existence, including the highest of all, that of self-conscious reason, are inadequate as a determination of the ultimate principle of existence, it seems as if nothing were left for us but to admit that God so far transcends our thought as to be absolutely indefinable. This was the logic of the Neo-Platonist, as it seems to be the logic of the modern Absolutist. Now, it seems to me that Augustine rightly rejected this doctrine, though with a certain natural hesitation, due partly to reverence for his teachers and partly to the inherent difficulty of the problem. The Neo-Platonists were not themselves altogether unconscious of the defect of their doctrine, and sought to give it greater plausibility by speaking of the Son of God, by which they meant God as an object for himself. This concession to relativity was, however, rendered perfunctory by their fundamental principle that in an absolute unity the distinction of subject and object cannot exist; for, with the

THEOLOGY OF AUGUSTINE

elimination of this fundamental distinction, the idea of God is stripped of all content, and, in fact, is little better than a deification of the word "not." What gives plausibility to the Neo-Platonic, as to all forms of abstract Absolutism, is the necessity of ascending to a unity that includes all differences, and the seeming impossibility of finding a category adequate to its characterization. We must ascend to an absolute unity, because anything less throws the whole of our knowledge, morality and religion into chaos. Suppose for a moment that there is no such unity: suppose, to express the same thing in the most recent terminology, that there is a plurality of principles; and what is the logical result? The result is that we cannot even say that there is no unity, or that there is a plurality, or indeed anything whatever. This is the πρῶτον ψεῦδος of Pluralism, the new form of the doctrine of Relativity.[1] If there is no unity, there is no reason why there should not be any number of universes, none of which has any connection with the other. Nor is there any reason why that which applies to one of these universes should not be entirely inapplicable to the others. In one universe—say, that with which we are familiar—no change occurs that does not take place in accordance with the principle of causality, but there is no reason why in any of the other hypothetical universes changes should not take place in a perfectly arbitrary and lawless fashion. Similarly, we may be unable at once to affirm and deny the same thing, but in some other universe affirmation and denial may be utterly meaningless. Thus, we are forced

[1] I mean by this that Pluralism is a revival, under the guise of a "new and virile" philosophy—if I may be allowed to use the language of one of its most prominent supporters—of the old doctrine of Relativity, now advocated with so much superficial fervour and, to my mind, with an almost entire absence of philosophical comprehension.

to the conclusion that there can be no significant speech, since, as Aristotle long ago pointed out, the denial of all distinction between opposite assertions makes significant speech impossible. It thus seems to me that a necessary postulate of all thought and existence is that there is but one universe; in other words, that nothing is absolutely isolated: whatever is or comes to be, must be or come to be in consistency with the principle that the universe is an intelligible system. Now, an intelligible system necessarily implies an intelligence that is capable of grasping the system, and such an intelligence implies the possibility of making itself its own object. But such an intelligence not only knows the universe to be intelligible, but it must be capable of knowing that it knows the universe to be intelligible. Surely this implies a self-conscious intelligence—an intelligence which is capable of making a regress upon itself, and which, when it has grasped the unity of existence, becomes aware that it has so grasped it in virtue of its intelligence. It is really of subordinate importance whether we speak of the universe as intelligible or of the mind that grasps it as an intelligence; for the one is impossible apart from the other. If the universe is not intelligible, no possible intelligence can comprehend it; if there exists any intelligence whatever, the universe must be intelligible. I am therefore unable to see how the doctrine that the Absolute is beyond self-conscious intelligence can possibly be established. That which is beyond self-conscious intelligence cannot be an object of any possible intelligence, and indeed is merely at bottom the idea of that which is unintelligible. It may be said that the Absolute cannot be characterized as a self-conscious intelligence, because such an intelligence involves personality, and therefore limitations. To this I should answer, that self-conscious intelligence is not necessarily

THEOLOGY OF AUGUSTINE

identical with personality in the sense of the definite self-consciousness of a particular and therefore limited being.[1] It is perfectly true that the self-conscious intelligence which constitutes the ultimate principle of unity cannot be limited to the definite self-consciousness of a particular being, since it is the principle that gives meaning to all particular beings; but it by no means follows that it is not intelligence and self-conscious. Certainly *our* self-consciousness is inseparable from personality; but this is because, from one point of view, we are, as Green says, " part of this partial world." When we speak of our self-consciousness, we no doubt think of ourselves as a unity which is presupposed in all our consciousness. But we must remember, that while this unity of self-consciousness is the condition of all our knowledge and activity, it is not of itself an ultimate principle. It is not an ultimate principle, because it presupposes a principle more ultimate than itself, upon which it depends. We can have no experience apart from the unity of self-consciousness; but that unity itself presupposes that our intelligence does not produce pictures, but acts according to unchangeable principles. Our self-consciousness, in other words, presupposes that we as persons belong to an intelligible universe, without which we should have no self-consciousness. For, if we make the unity of our self-consciousness the product of the peculiar nature that we chance to have, it is obvious that we are logically reduced to a sceptical distrust of even the simplest assertion. From this point of view there is no world, no cosmos, no intelligence, and in fact we are launched upon a welter of arbitrary impressions. It thus seems to me that our self-consciousness not only implies our personal consciousness, but it implies a self-conscious

[1] See Part II., Lectures Second and Ninth, where the question is discussed more fully.

intelligence that comprehends within itself all modes of existence, and therefore comprehends all modes of personal consciousness. And this self-conscious intelligence certainly is not " personal," in any of the senses in which we speak of ourselves as persons, since it is the absolute unity presupposed in all things and therefore in all " persons." A unity, which is at once an intelligence and is an object to itself, seems to me the only adequate characterization of the ultimate principle of all things, and therefore this conception is not improperly called the Absolute or God.[1] Such an Absolute must be presupposed as the condition of an intelligible universe, and I do not see how it can be denied without a surrender of the claim to make a single true judgment, whether in the region of knowledge, of morality, of art, or of religion. Nor does the admission that the principle of all things must be a self-conscious intelligence involve the preposterous claim on our part to omniscience; all that it involves is that there can be no reality, knowledge, morality or religion except under presupposition of such an intelligence. The idea that we cannot say anything about the principle of existence unless we have absolutely complete knowledge is its own refuta-

[1] There seems to be a disposition at present to distinguish between the Absolute and God, Dr. M'Taggart going so far as to say bluntly that, as the Absolute is not God, there is no God. But surely this is a very "short and easy" way of dealing with the problem. To me it seems obvious that, if the Absolute can be established at all, it is merely paltering with a great problem first to endorse the conception of God held by "the man in the street," and then to declare that God in His essence is not identical with that conception. Of course not. But why we should descend so low I do not understand. What I find it still more difficult to understand is how Dr. F. H. Bradley, whose speculative power no one can for a moment dispute, should seem to lend the weight of his authority to a piece of what in his earlier days he would certainly have called "clap-trap." See the criticism of Matthew Arnold in his *Ethical Studies*.

THEOLOGY OF AUGUSTINE

tion; for, on that ground, we cannot assert anything whatever, not even that we cannot assert anything whatever.[1]

Augustine, then, was perfectly right in maintaining that God is essentially self-knowing, or that in him intelligence is its own object. In holding tenaciously by this principle he was really following out to its consequences the idea expressed in the simplest Christian consciousness, that God is not a God who hides himself behind an impenetrable veil, but is "not far from any one of us, yea, is in our mouths and in our hearts." The same idea is involved in his contention, that the relation between Father and Son is that of Love. What is defective in his explanation of the Trinity is that he makes each of the "persons" express a special "function" of God, and thus he fails to preserve the absolute unity of God. The attempt to assimilate the three "persons" to the faculties of memory, intelligence and will is not successful, because Augustine does not see that these are different phases of the one self-conscious subject, and therefore that, though we may distinguish in God's nature between his being, his wisdom, and his love, these are but logical distinctions in the one unity. I think there can be no doubt that Augustine thought of the "persons" of the Trinity as having a quasi-independent existence, instead of regarding the Father as a term expressing the infinite perfection of the divine nature, the Son

[1] The reader will therefore perceive that, while I sometimes use the term "Absolute," and at other times the term "God," I refuse to distinguish the one from the other. The *true* definition of the Absolute is also the *true* definition of God: just as the *false* definition of God is the *false* definition of the Absolute. Boldness of assertion, I may perhaps be forgiven for saying, is no proof of speculative power: nor is it clear to me how any one "who knows what he is about," as Green used to say, can imagine that he is saying anything when he declares that we know *only* the Absolute, not God.

as the objectification of that nature, and the Holy Spirit as a name for the self-conscious unity of God. And it may be doubted whether it is not misleading, to say the least, to continue using the term "person" to express inseparable distinctions within an absolute unity. In any case, the essential truth for which Augustine was contending is that which would be better expressed by saying that God is the self-conscious principle involved and manifested in the existence and process of the universe.[1]

(2) And this leads us to consider Augustine's doctrine of the relation of God to the world. His explanation of that relation is that what first exists in the divine mind is afterwards realized in the process of the world. And as the divine mind is conceived to be complete in itself apart from the world, knowledge of the former would seem to render knowledge of the latter unnecessary and indeed impossible. Augustine is unable to see how the reality of God can be preserved unless it is distinguished from the reality of the world, and therefore he distinguishes between God's knowledge of himself and his knowledge of the world. There can be no doubt, I think, that his difficulty arises from assuming, after the manner of Neo-Platonism, that God is in his own nature independent of the world. From this point of view the world and its process first exists in the divine mind, and is then realized. But such a dualism assumes that the world is related to God as a machine to the machinist, or a statue to the sculptor; it is something that is produced, and exists in some sense independently of its producer. No doubt Augustine

---

[1] It seems to me undeniable that many of the fruitless controversies, into which we are all apt to fall, arise from our not asking what we mean when we speak of "persons," "substances," "forces," "powers," "creative activity," "intellect," and numerous other ill-defined terms. How could a satisfactory philosophy of religion be based upon so shifting a foundation?

THEOLOGY OF AUGUSTINE

asserts that the world is not formed out of a pre-existent matter, and that we cannot distinguish absolutely between its creation and its preservation; but this does not prevent him from thinking of it as a separate entity. This indeed is involved in his conception of the pure spirituality of God; for a spirituality that excludes corporeality implies that the latter has no right to exist. What seems wanting in Augustine's conception is a dialectical process by which it may be shown that the world, properly understood, is not separate and distinct from God, but is a manifestation of God. No doubt from the point of view of common sense, which Augustine virtually adopts, body and mind, the world and God, are essentially distinct. This is a dualism that was never got rid of till quite recent times, if it can be said to be got rid of even now; and yet it seems to me to be at bottom unmeaning. If the universe is one, it is impossible to hold that *in addition* there is a God who is also one. Two principles of unity are a contradiction in terms. It is therefore necessary to show that the unity of the world has no ultimate meaning except as the intelligible unity which is God. The proof of this proposition involves a whole philosophy, but it is at once obvious that, if two principles of unity are posited, neither can be absolute. If the world is one only in relation to God, it has no unity apart from God; if God is a unity in himself apart from the world, there can be no world that can be said to be a unity. We can, in fact, preserve the unity of either only by showing that there is but one unity, and surely no better name for this unity can be found than the one that is familiar and dear to us all.

(3) In his account of creation Augustine again displays that imperfect fusion of Neo-Platonic and Christian ideas which we have already seen to be involved in his idea of God and of God's knowledge of himself. The world, he contends,

differs from God only in having in it an element of negation, all that is positive in it being identical with the being of God. This doctrine, when pressed to its logical consequences, must result in converting the world into illusion. The principle on which it proceeds is that afterwards expressed by Spinoza in the formula, *omnis determinatio est negatio*, a principle which logically converts reality into the absolutely indeterminate. In contrast to this view, it must be maintained that *omnis negatio est determinatio*.[1] Absolute negation has no real meaning, since, in the absence of all positive being, nothing is negated. Every negation has reference to some specific mode of being. We can predicate that the soul is not mortal, if we mean to deny its identity with that which is mortal, or, what is the same thing, to affirm its immortality; but it is impossible to frame an intelligible judgment that merely removes from the soul the predicate of mortality, without determining anything in regard to its positive

[1] This was pointed out by Hegel as early as the first edition of his *Wissenschaft der Logik*, but of course it was no discovery of his. It was indicated by Plato more than two thousand years ago in his allegory of the cave, repeated by Aristotle in a more consistent way, suggested even by Spinoza himself, and, I believe, is at bottom what our personal idealists, new realists, and empiricists are struggling to express in their own way.

I may take this opportunity of saying that I do not know what Dr. Rashdall means when in his recent valuable work on *Philosophy and Religion* (p. 106 note) he says that the account I have given of his views in my *Philosophical Basis of Religion* "completely misrepresents his real position." If I have "completely misrepresented" his views—which I take leave to doubt—it was certainly not intentionally. When Dr. Rashdall, on the publication of my *Philosophical Basis*, first made this charge (see *Mind*, N.S., No. 69, Jan. 1909) I gave my reply (I think in the subsequent number of the same journal); but, judging from the note just referred to, I do not appear to have convinced my critic that my original statement was a fair account of his doctrine. Wherein I have offended, except by drawing plain inferences from his words, I have not yet been able to discover.

THEOLOGY OF AUGUSTINE

nature. Such a judgment as " a sound is not mortal " is one that no intelligent being would make, because sound belongs to a universe of thought in which the question of its mortality never arises ; for, obviously, mortality has a meaning only by reference to living or self-conscious beings. To frame any negative judgment whatever therefore presupposes that the object thought of has been so far determined, and that the negative judgment is an expression of the step by which the object is further determined. When the soul is said not to be mortal, what is implied is, that having certain attributes which may seem to include it in the class of mortal things, this inclusion is denied, and at the same time it is implied that the soul is included in the class of immortal things. This is the truth of what some logicians have called the " infinite judgment." Now, if it is true that negation implies determination, it is obvious that the world cannot be determined at all, if it is supposed that in itself it is purely negative. All that a pure negation can imply is that the world in itself is nothing at all, or, what is the same thing, has no reality from the point of view of God. And the same result follows, if we suppose God to contain only positive being ; for purely positive being is just as unthinkable as purely negative being. In truth God is conceivable at all only when contrasted with determinate things, and if these are removed from thought, there is nothing for thought to think about. God is the principle that unifies the world, not by eliminating all modes of being, but by taking them up into itself. It is true that in conceiving of God we negate all lower modes of being, but, as in the case of the soul, this negation is relative to lower modes of determination, which are transformed into the highest mode of determination. When God is said to be " spirit," this does not mean that the world has no reality ; what it means is that, from the point of view of God the world is spiritual. Augustine, then, makes a fatal concession to Neo-Platonism, when he grants that the world has no reality in itself. It is true that it has no reality apart from God; but the reason is that apart from God it does not exist. This, however, does not mean that it is in itself purely negative, but, on the contrary, that in God it is infinitely determinate.

While Augustine has not got rid of the preconception that the world as such contains only negation, he virtually contradicts this assumption when he grants it to have a relatively independent existence. The world is not an emanation from God, as the Platonists held, but may be called a continual creation of God. This modified doctrine does not explain how God can be complete apart from the world. Not to repeat the difficulty that the world has no being in itself, Augustine's doctrine of creation is open to the objection, that the world after its creation must in some way add to the totality of being; which is inconsistent with the ascription of all reality to God. From this difficulty there is no escape except by regarding the world as an expression of the divine nature. To speak of the world as existing apart from God is at bottom the same thing as to speak of God as existing apart from the world.

The conflict of opposite points of view is also shown in Augustine's doctrine, that time and space have a meaning only in regard to created things, not from the divine point of view. If they are merely modes of finite reality—in other words, negations—they must be regarded as from an ultimate point of view mere appearances; and it is significant that those who conceive of the Absolute as abstract, also look upon space and time in that way. If from an absolute point of view there is no time or space, all temporal and spatial determinations must be regarded as due to the necessary limitations of our form of knowledge. Hence things-in-themselves, as Kant contends, are not in space and time, these being merely subjective forms belonging to our human and finite point of view. Now, while it is undoubtedly true that the determination of the world as spatial and temporal is a relatively abstract and imperfect mode of characterization, it by no means follows that this mode of characterization is absolutely false. It may well be maintained that co-existence and succession are subordinate points of view, which must be brought into relation to a unity that subordinates them to itself, without granting that they have no meaning whatever from this higher point of view. It seems to me that to make space and time purely subjective is to fall into the same error as that involved in assuming that "all determination is negation." The differentiation of the world is not less important than its integration, and if we eliminate co-existence and succession, and along with it as a consequence motion and energy, we shall find ourselves left with the *caput mortuum* of a reality that is purely general and abstract. God is certainly beyond time and space, in the sense that he preserves his unity in all the changes that go on in the universe, but there would be no unity to preserve, were there no space and time, and therefore no change.

(4) Augustine's doctrine of Sin is an attempt to avoid the opposite defects of Manichaeism and Pelagianism. In contrast to the former he denies that it is inconsistent with the perfection of God to create man as evil, and yet we cannot admit with Pelagius that man as he came from the hand of God was indifferent both to good and evil. The sin of the first man arose from his perverse rejection of the divine aid, though his whole nature was directed to the good. Thus Augustine holds that man had power to will evil, but had no power to will good without the divine aid.

Now, we cannot possibly admit that man can will evil any more than good, independently of God. This no doubt raises the difficulty that it seems to make God responsible for evil. But, in the first place, Augustine himself holds that the perfection of God is not inconsistent with the existence of evil; and, in the second place, to say that man receives from God the power of willing evil or good is not the same as saying that he wills either the one or the other only under compulsion. Thus we must admit that the Pelagian doctrine contains this amount of truth in it, that man must be regarded as free to choose good or evil. On the other hand, Augustine is certainly right in denying that the commission of evil leaves man in his original condition of freedom, though his doctrine of original sin suffers from the defect incidental to the knowledge of his time, arising from the belief that in the history of the race man was at first perfect, and only lost his original purity from the sin of the first man.

(5) The doctrine of predestination, as stated by Augustine, can hardly be accepted. It suffers from the false contrast of God and the World. When God is conceived to be complete in himself apart from the world, whatever takes place in the world must be conceived as due to the purpose conceived by God prior to its actual realization. Hence, as God is perfect, it is held that the whole process of history is pre-ordained. God of his own free will elects that certain persons should be saved. Now, this whole conception of the providence of God is inadequate. We cannot conceive of the mind of God as having in it an unrealized idea, that is afterwards realized. The analogy of an architect who plans a house, or a sculptor who frames an image, is not appropriate when we are speaking of the Infinite. Nor can we properly assimilate the influence of God upon man to the formative activity of an architect

or sculptor on dead unconscious matter. The divine purpose is no doubt realized in the world, but it is not realized without the free activity of man. No arbitrary decree can determine human destiny, for man as a moral being is necessarily free. Augustine partly sees the logical result of his doctrine, when he admits that if we knew, as God knows, those who are predestined to perdition, our attempts to save them would necessarily be abandoned. On the same ground, we cannot help men to attain salvation, if their destiny is already fixed by an eternal and unalterable decree. In this mechanical and indefensible doctrine, we cannot but see a survival of the Manichaean doctrine, that there is a fundamental distinction between men, which nothing can transcend. Here Augustine has almost lost the essential truth of Christianity, which allows of no insuperable distinctions between men, but regards all men as sons of the one Father. Augustine's conception of evil was so vivid, that it leads him to raise an impassable barrier between the elect and the non-elect. No doubt by his doctrine of grace he partly escapes from the logical consequences of his doctrine of predestination, though even here he minimizes the infinite love of God; but he left an impress on the Church from which it has taken centuries to recover.

The influence of the teaching of Augustine has been enormous, not only on theology but on the idea of the Church. This was partly due to the practical task which it fell to its lot to undertake. The genius of Rome displayed its old vigour in the way in which the Church subdued and disciplined the fierce, turbulent and sensuous barbarians, who had overspread the Western Empire and threatened to overthrow civilization. With Gregory the Great (570-604 A.D.) the claim of the papacy to the primacy of the Church became a reality. The Church was, in fact, the symbol to a rude people of the presence of God on earth. It was the mediator between God and man, and only in communion with it was salvation possible. As the Church increased in power, it brought the laity under control of the clergy, the clergy under the authority of the bishops, and the bishops into subjection to the Head of the Church. In consolidating the empire into one great family, united by a common faith and hope, the state lent its aid. Men were converted to Christianity by force, and laws were passed enforcing obedience to the decrees of the Church. After the fall of the new empire, the only bond of unity among the Christian nations of the West was the Church. From this time the primacy of the pope was virtually established. Burdened with the task of discipline, there was little development of doctrine It is true that Joannes Scotus Erigena († *ca.* 880 A.D.) advanced a mystical system of doctrine, but it was only later that it had any real influence. In the ninth century there was a controversy as to whether the Holy Spirit proceeded from the Father alone, or from the Father and the Son. Rome decided in favour of the second alternative, though a change in the Roman Symbol was only made two centuries later. What seems to have commended the doctrine to the Latin mind was apparently the countenance it gave to the idea that, as the Holy Spirit proceeded from the Son as well as the Father, the Church, which was the representative of Christ, was the necessary medium through which the believer entered into communion and fellowship with the Holy Spirit. It was in the ninth century that the doctrine of transubstantiation was first formally discussed. Augustine had maintained that only the elect received the benefits of the sacraments. The monk Radbertus (831 A.D.) in his treatise, *De corpore et sanguine domini*, held that a miraculous change took place at the consecration of the elements. Nothing could more clearly show how far the spiritual idea of the continuous incarnation of Christ in the heart of the believer had been lost. In the mass it was held that the sacrifice of Christ on Golgotha was repeated anew.

In the eleventh century medieval theology entered upon its second stage. The invasion of the Frankish empire by the Huns, of Italy by the Northmen, and of England by the Danes had resulted in a general sense of insecurity, which was intensified by the belief that in the year 1000 the world would be destroyed and humanity summoned to appear before the judgment seat of Christ. In these circumstances the people, in terror of an angry God, voluntarily flew to the Church for refuge from the impending judgment. When the tenth century closed and hope returned, a grateful people expressed their gratitude to heaven by the erection of great cathedrals, embodying their feelings of awe and mystery, and symbolizing their aspirations towards heaven. In this beginning of the " Ages called of Faith," when the popular belief found satisfaction in the rites and ceremonies of the Church, arose that application of human reason in defence of the Church's teaching which we know as Scholasticism. The first and one of the greatest of the long line of Scholastic theologians is Anselm, who strongly insists upon the necessity of belief in the authority of the Church. " It is not my aim," he says, " to understand in order to believe, but I believe in order to understand." Assuming the truth of the doctrines of the Church, he seeks to show that they are in conformity with reason. His theological writings are, therefore, largely occupied in answering objections. Anselm, however, is something more than a mere defender of the traditional creed: he also contributed to speculative theology, especially in his cosmological and ontological proofs of the existence of God, while his *Cur Deus homo ?* is a real attempt to refer all the dogmas of the Church to a single central idea. In this last treatise, he argues that man by his sin has deprived God of the honour that is due to him. Man owes perfect obedience to the divine law, and, as no one has rendered this obedience, it is necessary that satisfaction or punishment should follow. The only adequate punishment is infinite, since the sin has been committed against an infinite being. The divine goodness, however, cannot permit all men to be lost for ever, and therefore the divine wisdom has devised a plan by which goodness may be manifested while justice is satisfied. Man must pay the debt, for man has sinned. But as no mere man can pay the debt, God must become man. Thus both sides of God's nature—his justice and goodness—are satisfied ; for Christ, as God-man, by his obedience even to suffering and death, atones for the infinite guilt of man, and therefore sinners can be pardoned. This doctrine of Anselm gets rid of the idea countenanced by Augustine that the debt paid by Christ is a ransom to the devil. His special solution of the problem presupposes the doctrine of penance, according to which acts that are not obligatory may give satisfaction for sin, and may therefore be meritorious. Death had no claim on Christ, and, therefore, in dying he did a work that was not obligatory and acquired merit which could be imputed to mankind.

While Anselm's doctrine of the atonement is an attempt to get rid of the dualism involved in the notion of a ransom paid to Satan, the conception of God as a being to whom the obedience of man is due as of a subject to his lord, however consonant with the feudalistic ideas of the time, is obviously one that cannot now be endorsed. The whole conception of Sin as the violation of a law proclaimed by God is a revival in another form of that slavery to the

Law against which St. Paul so strongly protested. Christianity differs from Judaism mainly in converting an external law into the true nature of man, which is also the nature of God. In the free assent of his nature to the higher, and the consequent turning away from the lower, man is reconciled in principle with God, and no artificial atonement is required. In the notion that the death of Christ was more than an equivalent for the endless punishment of man, Anselm prepared the way for the later doctrine of the schoolmen, that Christ had created a vast treasury of merit which was at the disposal of the Church, especially when it was increased by the superfluous merit of the saints. Thus he unwittingly laid the foundation of the later doctrine of indulgences.

The hundred and fifty years between Anselm and Thomas Aquinas did very little for the development of theology, though the twelfth century, partly stimulated by the new influence of Greek philosophy, was a period of great intellectual activity. Of its spirit the most representative man was Abelard, whose motto, *Intelligo ut credam*, expressed a half-unconscious revolt against authority and tradition. No doubt by *intelligo* he did not mean any process of free reconstruction, such as the modern world knows; all that he consciously meant was to protest against a kind of faith that was based upon tradition and authority, and which had never called out any real process of thought. When he attempted to explain the doctrines of the Church, he was not altogether successful, partly because of the inadequacy of the dogmas themselves, and partly because of his speculative limitations.

The teaching of Abelard did not go unchallenged. Bernard of Clairvaulx (1091-1153) was alarmed at the seeming recklessness of Abelard, as well as by the extravagant speculations of Roscellinus in regard to the Trinity, and he succeeded in securing Abelard's condemnation. In contrast to the rationalism of these thinkers, Bernard falls back upon a mysticism, the distinctive mark of which, as of all mysticism, is that it virtually abolishes all other relations except that of the individual soul to God, and therefore tends to separate religion from active life by identifying it with pure contemplation. Plotinus, the father of all mystics, went so far as to say that public calamities are to the wise man but stage tragedies; while the moral results of mysticism are shown in the medieval saint, Angela of Foligno, who congratulates herself on the deaths of her mother, husband and children, " who were great obstacles in the way of God." This transcendence of all differences, intellectual and moral, is held to result in the complete union of the soul with God. The motive for this elimination of all definite categories of thought is the conviction that ultimate reality is not the world but God, and therefore that we can know ultimate reality only by leaving the world with its finiteness and definiteness behind, and contemplating God without the interposition of limited forms of thought. In a theology of this kind there are only two ways in which the Absolute can be characterized: we must either state what it is not, or an attempt must be made to suggest its transcendence of all limited modes of being by heaping up metaphor upon metaphor. The motive for both modes of characterization is the same; for it is because all definite categories are regarded as inadequate that a refuge is sought in metaphors, which do not claim to be literal predicates, but only serve to suggest that which is beyond all predication. Thus Dionysius the Areopagite describes God as " the Unity which unifies every unity," the " super-essential essence," " irrational mind," " unspoken word," " the absolute no-thing which is above all existence." At the same time he speaks of God as a Unity that does not abolish but comprehends all differences within itself. Yet in order to have the vision of this Unity, the mystic " must leave behind all things both in the sensible and in the intelligible world, till he enters into the darkness of nescience that is truly mystical." This " Divine darkness " is " the light unapproachable." Here, by the express union of contradictions, an attempt is made to suggest the infinite fulness of the divine nature, which for us is its absolute emptiness.

The mystics have often been accused of Pantheism, but the charge is really due to a confusion of thought. Mysticism refuses to admit that the world has any reality from an absolute point of view, whereas Pantheism insists on its reality, and only denies its independent existence, maintaining that in it the Infinite is present in all its fulness. When Dionysius tells us that " Being is in God, but God is not in Being," he is purposely seeking to avoid the charge of identifying God with the world. " Being is in God," but not in its finite form ; while " God is not in Being," because he is all in all, and " Being " has therefore no reality in itself.

In Augustine, with his many-sidedness, the highest stage of which man is capable is " the vision and contemplation of truth." The blessedness of this state he celebrates in words that have a distinctly mystical tone. " I entered, and beheld with the mysterious eye of my soul the light that never changes, above the eye of my soul, above my intelligence. It was higher than my intelligence because it made me, and I was lower because made by it." From this side of Augustine's theology the mysticism of Bernard of Clairvaulx was partly derived. Of a sensitive and yet practical type, his mind recoiled from hard and inelastic dogmas, and he was not possessed of sufficient speculative power to dissolve their rigidity and to raise them into the light of a higher dialectic. On the other hand, his theology was a faithful reflection of his experience. Whatever brought man nearer to God seemed to him true. Such a man in such an age naturally accepted the creed of the Church as an absolute revelation, but its truth was really proved to him by his own intuitions. Hence, while he held that the Scriptural writers were directly illumined by God, he also maintained, in common with other mystics, that in a less degree this divine illumination is experienced by all believers. By grace the mind is able tò transcend the finite and to enter into direct communion with God. Only those so illuminated can penetrate to the true sense of Scripture. As usual this fatal method of exegesis opened the door to all sorts of fanciful interpretations only kept in check by Bernard's practical sense and moral sensibility. As strongly as Anselm he insisted upon faith as the condition of knowledge; but knowledge, by which is meant the direct contemplation of invisible things, is the disclosure of what in faith is only implicit. This highest state of the mind is reached by a sudden exaltation, in which the soul, " collecting itself within itself, and receiving divine assistance, abstracts from all human things, and attains to the direct contemplation of God." Bernard was satisfied with nothing less than this exaltation above sense and flesh, above logical thought and ardent sentiment, and to secure this union with the divine no self-denying labour was too great. The Church was for him the mystical body of Christ, and its truth was the higher truth that is inaccessible to mere reason. But he was keenly aware that this ideal church is by no means identical with the actual, and he does not hesitate to contrast the pride and pomp of the Pope with the humility of Peter, whose representative he is. The sacraments were symbols, by which Christ was manifested to those who could only bear the vision of him when he was enshrouded in a lucent cloud.

A mystic like Bernard naturally felt the strongest antagonism to the rationalism of Abelard. The latter, for example, explains the Trinity as a necessary idea of reason, the Father representing the divine power and majesty, the Son the divine wisdom, and the Holy Ghost the divine benignity and love. This whole mode of thought, as well as Abelard's self-confident temper, was hateful to Bernard, with his humility and his profound reverence for the divine mysteries. The conflict of the two men was really a conflict of opposite types of mind, and inevitably led to opposite systems of thought. At the Council held in 1140 Bernard cited passages from Abelard's writings, fourteen of which were condemned, especially those concerning the Trinity, the Divine Nature of Christ, his redemptive work, man's dependence on saving grace, and the nature of sin. Abelard was condemned by Innocent and silence was imposed upon him. The battle between mystic piety and rational Christianity was however only begun, and could only be brought to anything like a successful issue, when in the modern world it was carried on without the traditional preconceptions of Bernard, and with a deeper philosophical grasp than that of Abelard. These two men, like the systems they represent, are really complementary of each other ; for, if it is true that the highest reach of the mind must consist in the contemplation of the Absolute, it is not less true that this contemplation must contain within itself the specific distinctions of reason. This indeed was partly recognized by Thomas Aquinas, who sought to combine reason and faith, philosophy and religion, rationalism and a mystical intuition, and perhaps more fully by Dante, the poet, who sums up the thought, the art and the religion of the middle ages.

In the first centuries of the Middle Ages the only treatises of Aristotle that were known were the *De Categoriis* and the *De Interpretatione* ; but from the beginning of the thirteenth century his complete works were available in Latin translations. Scholastic theologians, accepting the " Book of Sentences " of Peter the Lombard, which had been approved by the Council of 1215, as a true statement of Christian doctrine, and using the philosophy of Aristotle as an absolute revelation of all that reason is capable of accomplishing by itself, constructed a theological philosophy ; which, however, had the fatal defect of assuming the absolute truth at once of the dogmas of the Church and the philosophical conclusions of Aristotle. This is the point of view of Thomas Aquinas (1225-1274), who sought to formulate and defend the ascetic piety, the mysticism, and the belief in the absolute sovereignty of the Church, which constituted the ideal of the Middle Ages. He was the first to put the papal theory upon a reasoned foundation. The two pillars on which he based his whole system were a formal expression of the ideal of Hildebrand : the hierarchy is the Church, and the Church is the Pope. Thomas Aquinas differs from Anselm in regarding faith and reason as independent of each other, and therefore he draws a broad distinction between natural and revealed theology. This distinction runs through the whole of his philosophy. There are truths that can be discovered by reason alone, and truths that transcend its powers ; though, as truth is one, there can be no contradiction between them. The truths that lie beyond the scope of reason are such mysteries as the Trinity, the Incarnation and the Creation of the world. Though reason is limited, it is not confined within the boundaries of the sensible world, but is able to infer the existence of God, as St. Paul says, from " the things that have been made," and thus philosophy becomes the "handmaid of theology." To this distinction between truths of revelation and truths of reason corresponds the distinction between Faith and Knowledge. As the object of Faith is God or the relation of the world to God, and its source is revelation, it involves a surrender of the will to God, since the mysteries of religion cannot be proved; and thus it is higher than knowledge. This is the ground of the distinction between theology and philosophy; for even in the case of truths that are common to both, the former starts from the idea of God and descends to created things, while the latter begins with created things and ascends to God.

The highest way in which God can be apprehended is by intuition. In this conception Thomas does homage to the mystical side of medieval thought. Intuition is not only higher than reason, but as the direct vision of God it is also higher than faith. Such an immediate contact with the innermost nature of God is impossible by the use of man's natural powers, and therefore it implies a supernatural illumination of the soul by God—an illumination which in this life is rare and fitful, because of the resistance of the body and the consequent limitation of intelligence to the forms of sense. Lower than intuition is faith, which is not a direct vision of God, but a conviction based upon revelation of those doctrines that cannot be demonstrated by reason. Lowest of all is knowledge, which can only be attained by the slow and tentative operation of reason, and which, though it is able to prove that God exists, cannot determine his inner nature, as expressed in the doctrine of the Trinity. Since reason cannot of itself give us a knowledge of God, Thomas denies the validity of the ontological argument, as maintained by Anselm, on the ground that reason can only advance from the nature of the cosmos to the existence of a first cause. No doubt it can also demonstrate that the world has been created by God; but it is only by faith in revelation that we know this creation to have taken place at a definite time. An important thesis of Thomas is his contention that, in his will to produce finite things that are an image of himself, God has created man as a free agent. Hence, while the providence of God extends to the minutest detail, it is realized through the free activity of man in subordination to the good of the whole; and the good of the whole demands the subordination of the less to the more intelligent. The world, however, cannot be said to be absolutely perfect; for, as God's power is infinite, he must be capable of creating other worlds than ours; what we must say is that our world has been formed in the best and most perfect way. If it is objected that evil is not consistent with divine providence, Thomas answers that it proceeds from that freedom which alone is compatible with the goodness of God. How, then, is the sin of man to be explained? Thomas answers that, as originally created, the sensuous nature was subordinated to reason, but, seduced by the devil, man disobeyed the command of God, and the proper balance of his double nature as rational and sensuous was destroyed. The equilibrium can only be restored by God himself, and indeed by God becoming man. Not only was the death of Christ the most fitting means of redemption, but the satisfaction offered by him was more than sufficient, his suffering having an infinite value.

In his doctrine of the sacraments, Thomas seeks to establish the sovereignty of the Church, which is identified with the mystical person of Christ. There is contained in them " a certain instrumental virtue for conveying grace." Thus the sacraments reduplicate the redemption of Christ. The State by its ordinances tends to secure the common good, but it cannot demand obedience when its laws are in conflict with the higher commands of God. This higher or divine law is laid down by the Church as the earthly representative of God, and the mind of the Church is expressed by the Pope. This is a necessity, because there can only be one Christian faith, and therefore to the Pope, as Head of the Church, supreme authority in all matters of faith must be delegated.

In Thomas we have a defence of the medieval conception of life that is in its own way perfect. Granting the fundamental assumption of an absolute opposition between faith and reason, philosophy and theology, Church and State, it is difficult to see how a more reasonable doctrine could well be constructed. The conception of faith as higher than reason is the counterpart of the idea of a supernatural revelation, and a supernatural revelation must necessarily be accepted on authority. Thus we have at once the absolute contrast of the Church as the custodian of the "mysteries" of faith, and reason as finding its highest exercise in reconciling to the intellect those truths that are common to faith and reason. And as the Church is the custodian of all truth, it follows as a matter of course that the State must be subordinate to it. Moreover, as the Church is the representative of God on earth, the sacraments are naturally conceived to possess a mysterious efficacy, just because they are not only symbols of spiritual truth, but the means by which the Church repeats the sacrifice of Christ, and secures that regeneration which is impossible through any other channel. The only point in which Thomas partly frees himself from this mechanical idea of an external authority, which forces men into submission to itself, is in his mystical doctrine of the immediate intuition of God. Mysticism, in fact, is the manner in which men have sought to escape from the pressure of authority and tradition, and to come into direct contact with the divine. Thomas, however, is careful to limit the exercise of this power very narrowly, and indeed he teaches that it cannot exist at all, except under condition of the acceptance by faith of the divine mysteries, of which the Church is the Custodian. Thus the whole system of ideas of which he is the powerful exponent is based upon the idea, that reason is impotent to penetrate to the truth. The basis for this assumption is theologically the preconception of a supernatural revelation, and, philosophically, the absolute limitation of reason. These restrictions the new movement of the modern world has swept away, and with them the whole medieval conception of life. Meantime, it will not be uninstructive to dwell a little on that imaginative construction of the universe which we find in Dante, the great poet of medievalism.

LECTURE FOURTH.

DANTE'S THEOLOGY AND POLITICS.

The Middle Ages may not inaptly be regarded as the period in which a preparation was made for the wider and freer life of modern times by the gradual appropriation of the culture of the past, as illuminated and transformed by the spirit of Christianity. When we consider the complexity of the material, we cannot be surprised that the process of assimilation was incomplete. Judea, Greece and Rome may each be said to have concentrated itself on a single task, whereas it was the problem of the Middle Ages to combine into a whole the religion of Christ, the philosophy of Greece and the law and polity of Rome, and to harmonize these various elements with the individuality and love of freedom characteristic of the Germanic peoples. The imperfect fusion of these factors is shown in the series of antagonisms, which rule the whole of medieval thought: the future life is opposed to the present, the sacred to the secular, faith to reason. But it was the Church, and the Church alone, which preserved the germs of a speculative view of the world, and made possible the rise in due time of modern philosophy. In the dissolution of the old order of society, and while a new order was gradually shaping itself, it developed from the invisible beginning of a small religious community into a compact and powerful organization. In its office of teacher of Europe, the Church employed the system of doctrine which received its final form at the hands of Augustine, its great speculative genius, and in that system the dualism of the present and the future life, the Church and the world, faith and reason, is already stated in its most uncompromising form.

Now Dante is the champion and exponent of this dualism, and yet he seizes it at the moment when it is passing away. His theology is Christianity speaking in terms of Neo-Platonism and Aristotelianism. His passion for political freedom is Germanic, but it utters itself in the language of imperial Rome. His impassioned zeal for the regeneration of society is half concealed in his vivid picture of the horrors of Hell, the expiatory punishments of Purgatory, and the glories of Paradise. The spirit of the coming age speaks through him, but it clothes itself in the forms and the language of the past. In coming to the study of such a writer we must seek to do justice both to what he explicitly affirms, and what he unconsciously suggests. The spell of Dante's genius is so potent that there is danger of our attributing to him ideas beyond his age. This danger we must endeavour to avoid, but we must also beware of the more serious mistake of narrowing down the large suggestiveness of his poetic intuitions to the Procrustean bed of his explicit logic. What Goethe says of Byron is in some degree true of every poet, that " when he reflects he is a child." This is especially true of Dante, who, like all medieval thinkers, proceeds from preconceptions which we cannot accept, and moves to his conclusions by a method of ratiocination which to us seems almost childish. To do him justice we must fix our attention upon the perennial truths which these preconceptions and artificial forms of reasoning merely indicate. Much of the interest of Dante lies in the conflict between the old and the new, a conflict which was on his part largely unconscious. By the force

THEOLOGY OF DANTE

of his genius he holds together discrepant elements which can only be reconciled in a higher synthesis. The movement towards a more comprehensive view of life, which he never himself explicitly reaches, is partly indicated by the way in which he makes Bonaventura and other mystics supplement the deficiencies of Thomas Aquinas. He follows the great schoolman as far as the critical intellect enables him to give a clearly formulated theory, and when he is seeking to express the Unity of all things as summed up in God he falls back upon the mystics. Within the limits of medieval thought Dante's sympathy is wide and flexible: he combines Bonaventura with Aquinas; he enters with the same warmth of appreciation into the stern conflict with error of St. Dominic as into the loving ministrations of St. Francis. His catholicity is perhaps nowhere more clearly shown than in his placing Averroes among the throng of philosophers who surround the " Master of those who know." This is the same Averroes against whom the Synod of Paris had fulminated as the greatest corrupter of the faith. Dante simply calls him " Averroes who made the great commentary." Notwithstanding these and many other instances of independence and breadth of view, Dante is a true son of the medieval church. Liberality in the modern sense he does not possess. Carlyle is quite right in saying that he " does not come before us as a large, catholic mind, rather as a narrow and even sectarian mind "; though we must not forget that his narrowness and sectarianism are rather in his formulated creed than in the spirit which informs the free creations of his genius. One is tempted to discount the intellectual narrowness of the first great Christian poet, and dwell only upon the permanent element in his " criticism of life "; but I doubt if this method is as valuable as that which takes him as he is, in his weakness as well as his strength; and I shall therefore begin with the explicit creed which forms what may be called the philosophy of Dante.

The opposition of faith and reason which rules all the thought of the Middle Ages is accepted and defended. The truths of faith rest upon the revelation of God as contained in " the old and new scrolls." They are not only beyond the power of human reason to discover for itself, but they are incapable of being comprehended even when they have been revealed. God is indeed partly manifested in created things, but the infinite riches of his nature is revealed only in his Word, and even then the human mind must in this life be contented to accept what is revealed, without seeking to penetrate the mysteries of faith. " Be content, race of man, with the *quia*; for if you could have seen all, what need was there that Mary should be a mother?" In the future life, indeed, man will see God as he is. This is expressed by Dante in his pictorial way when he represents Beatrice as fixing her eyes on the vast circling spheres of heaven, and finds himself drawn upwards by her eyes, being like Glaucus " transhumanized " or raised above the limits of the finite intellect. How weak human reason is of itself is shown by the errors into which we fall when we trust to our senses. Mere human knowledge is as far from divine knowledge as heaven is from the earth. The proper attitude of man towards the revelation which God has given of himself is therefore that of implicit faith. Having accepted the truths so revealed, human reason may then draw inferences from them, but it can never discover them for itself. Yet faith is not contrary to reason, but only beyond it; when man is at last admitted to the beatific vision of God, he will then directly contemplate what he can now only accept in faith. Moreover, the human mind partly bears the impress of its divine Original, and hence it cannot be altogether without some apprehension of God;

it discovers the divine nature dimly, as the eye sees the bottom of the sea at the shore, though it cannot penetrate the unfathomable depths of the ocean. Philosophy prepares the way for theology by proving the Scriptures to be the veritable word of God. The evidence is mainly that of miracles, but one of the strongest proofs, as Dante follows Augustine in maintaining, is the miraculous conversion of the world to the true faith. "If the world turned to Christianity without the supernatural guidance of God himself, this would be the greatest of all miracles."

The contrast of faith and reason is one with which we are all familiar, and it may be doubted if modern writers have added anything substantial to the doctrine as Dante presents it. Even the distinction of what is above but not contrary to reason he clearly expresses. The contrast is one which draws its support from various considerations. To Dante and all medieval thinkers it implied an identification of the contents of the Holy Scriptures with the dogmas of the Church. To us it is perfectly plain that such an identification rests upon a confusion between the fundamental truths expressed by the sacred writers and the interpretation put upon them by thinkers who brought to them forms of thought borrowed from later Greek philosophy. I do not say for a moment that the effort to express the Christian view of the world in terms of reflection was not a legitimate and necessary problem; on the contrary, it arose from the healthy instinct that Christianity was based upon an impregnable basis of truth; but the inevitable result of the attempt to extract a theology from the letter of Scripture by the use of dualistic categories was to distort to some extent the essential ideas of Christianity. It is thus obvious that the claim which Dante makes for faith is really a claim for the implicit acceptance of the dogmas of the Church, themselves the product of an inadequate historical criticism and an inadequate form of philosophy.

There is, however, another element which contributes to the conviction of the opposition of faith and reason. The religious consciousness rests upon the idea of God, as the absolutely perfect Being in whose presence man becomes aware of his weakness and sinfulness. This consciousness, though in an imperfect and undeveloped form, is found in even the lowest races of mankind, and indeed is inseparable from the consciousness of self. To a man like Dante, coming at the close of a period when the Christian idea of life had been proving its potency by transforming the whole life and thought of men, teaching them to rise above the transient things of sense and to view all things *sub specie aeternitatis*, the consciousness of human weakness and sinfulness was the central truth of the universe, in comparison with which all other truths seemed comparatively insignificant. What attitude but that of faith is becoming to finite man in the presence of the infinitude of God? Now, in so far as Dante by "faith" means this consciousness of dependence upon God, he is only expressing the natural attitude of every religious spirit. But it must be observed that "faith" in this sense is to be contrasted, not with "reason," but with the irreligious spirit of self-assertion, and with that limited and inadequate view of existence which never rises about the finite. The Christian religion above all others, in bringing home to man the consciousness of the infinite perfection of the divine nature, destroys the very root of self-righteousness, making him feel that "after he has done all he is an unprofitable servant." But such a faith is not the opposite of reason, but the very essence of reason; it is the revelation of the true nature of man as capable of finding his life only in losing it; it is a faith which fills his whole being and is the informing spirit of all that makes his life divine. Dante, however, in the usual medieval manner, confuses this living practical faith with that formulation of Christian ideas which had been stereotyped in the creed of the Church. Thus he virtually identifies religion with theology. But, so far from being identical, the one may be widely apart from the other. It is not the "heart" that makes the theologian, except when theology brings to adequate expression what is implicit in the "heart." When faith is opposed to reason on the ground that the former contains truths incomprehensible by the latter, we are assuming a certain formulation of religious truth to be ultimate, and contrasting with it the irreligious view of the world. We forget that our theology may itself be inadequate. Now, a theology which is based upon a supposed absolute limit in human reason is necessarily inadequate, because it rests upon a fundamental contradiction. We can contrast a lower and higher form of reason, but to assert an absolute opposition of reason with itself is to make all our judgments, and therefore our theological judgments, unmeaning. A faith which is opposed to reason must be irrational. Theology, in so far as it expresses in terms of reflection what is implicit in the highest religious consciousness, is knowledge; is, in fact, the philosophy of religion; and hence there can in this point of view be no valid opposition between truths of faith and truths of reason.

There is, however, another complication which gives countenance to the opposition of faith and reason. Faith, it is thought, rests upon truths directly revealed by God himself, whereas the truths of reason are the product of the natural and normal exercise of the human mind. Now, in so far as this means that there have been men who were lifted above the divisive consciousness which is immersed in the finite and particular it is undoubtedly true. But surely it cannot be meant that God is present in some operations of the human mind and not in others, or that man can be man without having some consciousness of the Infinite. The holy men of old who spake as they were moved by the Holy Spirit were indeed inspired, but their inspiration consisted in realizing the divine meaning of the world with a power and vividness that ordinary men never reach, or reach only in their best moments. And what is thus revealed in them, the truths with which they are inspired, are not unintelligible mysteries. They speak as they are moved, but what they utter is the highest knowledge and can seem unintelligible only to those who are unable to enter into the fulness of its meaning. Hence faith must consist in elevation to the point of view of the elect of the race, and failure to reach this point of view must make our faith inadequate. To commend faith because it blindly accepts what is declared to be unintelligible, is to degrade not to elevate it. The faith which is higher than knowledge can only be knowledge in its highest form. Like all medieval thinkers Dante holds that human reason is by its very nature conditioned, and therefore unable to comprehend the "mysteries" of faith. But a true faith can contain no "mysteries" that are irrational, but only those which seem irrational to the mind that operates with inadequate ideas. It is, therefore, the task of philosophy, or theology, to prove that they are rational, and this can only be done by showing that in the knowledge of the finite the knowledge of the infinite is tacitly presupposed, though it is not brought to clear consciousness. Dante himself admits that reason can prove the existence of God, though he adds that it cannot comprehend the inner nature of God. But to prove the existence of God is to show that he is manifested in all forms of existence, and a being so manifested cannot be unknown, much less unknowable. It is instructive to see how in modern thinkers the doctrine of the absolute limitation of the human intellect has by an inevitable dialectic issued in a thinly-veiled scepticism. Sir William Hamilton argued that, as to think is to condition, the Absolute is unthinkable. His follower, Mansel, went on to show that, whatever predicate we attach to the idea of God, it breaks down in contradiction. Thus for us God becomes the Being of whom we can predicate nothing. Herbert Spencer is therefore only drawing the legitimate inference from this doctrine when he maintains that of the Absolute we can only affirm pure being. But an Absolute of whom we can predicate nothing is for us nothing, and thus the very idea of the Absolute vanishes away, and the only reality is the Relative. The doctrine of the opposition of faith and knowledge is a perilous weapon to handle, and invariably wounds the hand which wields it. If theology is to be a real defender of the faith, it must concentrate its efforts upon a purification of the traditional creed, and the elevation of it into a science that like other sciences will need no external support. The medieval separation of faith and reason virtually received its death-blow at the Reformation, and if we are wise we shall abandon all attempts to retain it, and direct our efforts to the really fruitful task of exhibiting the essential rationality of the Christian conception of life.

We have seen how Dante draws an absolute distinction between faith and reason, maintaining that by the former we are carried beyond the limits of knowledge, and have therefore to be contented with a simple acceptance of truths which remain for us incomprehensible. How impossible it is consistently to maintain such an opposition becomes apparent from Dante himself, when he goes on to define the nature of God, *i.e.* to make intelligible what he has declared to be unintelligible. God, he tells us, is one and eternal; himself unchangeable, he is the cause of all the changes in the universe. In the perfect mirror of his intelligence all things are reflected as they really are, but he is not himself perfectly reflected in any. He is thus the absolute concentration of Truth. The "good of the intellect" is to know him, for to know him is to know the Truth. He is the supreme Good, and all good contained in other beings is a reflection from Him, and is therefore finite and limited. Hence all created beings, in so far as they comprehend the good, strive to realize it, and in so striving they are seeking after God. In lower forms of being the yearning after God takes the form of a blind desire, in the higher creatures it is expressed as love. As the sun illuminates all things, so the glory of God suffuses the whole universe in varying degrees of completeness. The love of God is revealed in all things, but it shines most clearly in the higher intelligences. In God knowledge is absolutely complete: in the "great volume" of his intelligence all is perfectly known, and therefore in his mind there is no process. In him there is no "here" or "there," no "before" or "after"; all is an eternal "now." As God is infinitely perfect, there is in him an absolute harmony of knowledge, will and power, just as heat and light perfectly interpenetrate and coincide in a ray of sunlight. Though God is absolutely one, he is in three persons. "In the profound and glorious substance of the high Light there appeared to me three circles of three colors and one potency: and the one seemed reflected by the second, as rainbow by rainbow, and the third seemed fire, which from one to the other is breathed forth in equal measure." In this imperfect symbol Dante seeks to give some faint indication of the incomprehensible mystery of the Trinity,

THEOLOGY OF DANTE

for of more no human mind is capable. "Mad is he who hopes by reason to travel over the boundless way which holds one Substance in three Persons."

The creation of the world proceeded from the eternal Love of God. For, as nothing can add to the perfection of God, the act of creation is the spontaneous outflow of Love, which ever seeks to reflect itself in new loves. Before creation there was nothing, not even formless matter, but form and matter flashed into being together in a single instantaneous act of creation. Contemplating the whole hierarchy of forms in the Logos, the Creator knew all things ere they were created, and loved them with the Son in the Spirit. Thus there came into being the nine heavenly spheres, in which his glory is most perfectly expressed, and by gradual descent the various orders of being, immortal and mortal, until at last it almost fades away in mere accidental and transitory peculiarities. Every created thing is therefore a more or less perfect reflection of the Divine Being, and hence he who apprehends the order or scale of being cannot be altogether ignorant of God. The only beings which are indestructible are the heavens, the angels and the rational souls of men ; the first because they have a peculiar matter of their own, the others because they are pure forms. On the other hand, all things composed of the elements, as well as the soul in its lower forms as nutritive or vegetative and animal, imply the temporary union of matter and form, and are therefore destructible. Dante's view of matter and the relation of the various orders of being to God as the goal of all their striving is summed up as follows. "The whole sum of things displays an order or scale of being—a 'form' which makes the universe a reflection of God. Herein the higher creatures see traces of the eternal goodness, and this is the end for which the orderly arrangement of beings has been made.

According to their rank in the scale of being all things tend by a path more or less direct to their primal source, moving onward through the vast ocean of being to different ports, in harmony with their peculiar nature." Not only has divine Love fixed this scale of being, but it brings all things to their appointed goal, and were it not so, the whole universe would fall into chaos. Yet, though God foresees and orders all things, man as a rational being is endowed with freedom or self-determination.

Even this imperfect statement of Dante's conception of God, and of the relation of the various orders of being to God as their beginning and end, is enough to indicate the substantial truth of his doctrine. To the man who lived in such a faith life could not be otherwise than earnest and noble. Nevertheless, the theology of Dante is nowhere put to so severe a strain as in its effort to express the nature of God and his relation to the world of finite beings. This was inevitable, because the Christian idea of God seems to combine conceptions which the understanding in its ordinary use regards as mutually exclusive. Thus Dante tells us that God is absolutely one and indivisible, while yet he contains in himself three absolutely distinct Persons. He is absolutely complete in himself before the creation of the world, but the infinite Love which forms his very essence must express itself in the creation of finite beings towards whom his love is manifested. God orders all things, and yet man has absolute freedom of action. Nor can the union of such apparently opposite predicates in a single conception be regarded as a mere attempt to do violence to all the laws of our intelligence : it is the expression of an idea to which the human mind has been forced in its effort to frame an adequate theory of the universe ; and unless we can justify it, we shall have to fall back in despair upon the virtual scepticism which denies that we can comprehend God at all, and thus leaves us with a conviction of the illusive character of all that we call knowledge. It is therefore of supreme importance to look beneath the form in which Dante expresses his thought to the permanent and universal truth which it embodies. That his thought is inadequate in form is indicated by the fact that he continually takes refuge in a mystical symbolism; for symbolism is just the expression of a truth which is felt rather than comprehended.

The inadequacy of Dante's theology, like that of his master Aquinas, of which indeed it is mainly a summary, arises from his attempt to express the Christian idea of God in Aristotelian, Neo-Platonic and Jewish formulae. He adopts the Aristotelian conception of God as the " unmoved mover " : the Being who, existing apart from the world in isolated self-completeness, acts upon it from without, and is thus the " first cause " of all its changes. The importance of such a conception as a first step towards the true idea of God is not to be denied. When we contemplate the changes of finite things, we inevitably seek for an explanation or cause of them, and a final explanation can never be found by simply going back along the series of changes, since each of those changes again requires a new cause to account for it. Yet this is the point of view from which the scientific consciousness regards the world, and hence it is not unfair to say that science as such can never give a final explanation of things. This is virtually confessed by Herbert Spencer, when, having argued that our solar system has been evolved from a primeval nebular matter, he tells us that we can go no further, but must simply accept this primeval matter as a fact. We may accept it as a fact, but we cannot accept it as a final explanation; and, unless we can satisfy ourselves with Spencer's " inscrutable mystery," we are forced to seek for a more adequate explanation than he has given us, or any scientific theory can furnish. When, therefore, it is maintained that the true explanation of the changes in the world presupposes a cause which is not itself one of those changes, the reasoning is undoubtedly sound. A cause which is uncaused, or a self-active being, is a conception which the inadequacy of the ordinary idea of cause compels us to adopt. This idea, in fact, is the basis of all purely monotheistic religions, which seize the truth that the explanation of the world must be sought in a Being whose nature is self-determined. But, while we admit that a self-determined Being is the necessary presupposition of all changes in the world, we must observe that such a Being is a cause only as he is active in the production of those changes. And this is what Monotheism, working with the conception of causality, actually affirms. So long, however, as we do not see all that is involved in the conception of a self-determined Being, we inevitably separate absolutely between that Being and the effects it produces. In other words, the conception of cause and effect from which we started presupposes their separation. Hence we conceive of the self-determined Being as complete both before and after the effects which it produces, or, what is the same thing, we separate God from the world, and having done so, we can only affirm their relation without being able to comprehend it. Yet our feeling of their relation cannot be extinguished, and we attempt to satisfy ourselves with analogies which suggest a relation that explicitly we have denied. This is what Dante does. To supplement the imperfection of the idea of God as the "unmoved mover," acting externally upon the world, he falls back upon the Neo-Platonic idea of successive emanations proceeding from God and yet leaving him alone in his isolated self-completeness. The various orders of being are thus figured, not as manifestations of God, but after the analogy of reflections or images in a mirror. But a reflection or image has no substantial reality. Such a metaphor merely conceals the unsolved contradiction involved in the conception of a Being who is self-determined in the sense of being self-complete apart from the activity which he exercises. If we are really to find God in the world we must be prepared to admit that the world is not something accidental, which might or might not be, but is the necessary manifestation of God.

It is not only, however, the Aristotelian conception of an " unmoved mover " which hampered the theology of Dante, but also the conception of creation, which he found in the Old Testament, and which, as a faithful son of the Church, he never dreamt of questioning. For Dante, as for all medieval thinkers and for those who are still at the medieval point of view, the revelation of God was not a series of ever fuller revelations, but a dogmatic statement of different aspects of one unchanging system of truth given at different times. Starting from this preconception, he failed to see that the revelation of God which is given in Christianity transcends the idea of creation and substitutes the more adequate idea of the world as the self-manifestation of the divine nature. The Jewish conception of creation rests upon the idea that God is complete in himself apart from the world, and that the world rather conceals than reveals him. Nor did Dante even see that the conception of God as creator is not identical with the idea of an " unmoved mover " which he had borrowed from Aristotle. The Aristotelian idea is merely that of a being who directs the movements or changes of a world which already exists. In his continual use of the Aristotelian metaphor of the wax and seal, Dante shows that he is not clearly aware of the distinction between a First Cause, or Former of the

World, and a Creator, a confusion which may be readily explained by considering that they agree in conceiving of God as complete in himself apart from the world.

There is however another side to Dante's thought. Like Aristotle he finds among finite beings a graduated scale of existence. All contain a spark of the divine nature, and are continually striving towards their primal source. Now, if we fix our attention upon this aspect of Dante's thought, it becomes obvious that it cannot be reconciled with the conception of God as purely external to the world. If in all beings there is a tendency towards the divine, it must be because the divine is immanent in them, unless indeed we suppose that this tendency is only apparent. From the point of view of an external Designer, or even Creator, finite beings can only be regarded as a dead mechanical product; whereas beings whose very nature is to tend beyond themselves, ever seeking for union with God, must contain in themselves, in more or less adequate form, the principle of Unity which is the very essence of existence. In other words, the idea of the immanence of the divine nature in all things, which Dante expresses in a pictorial way as a reflection in them of the glory of God, is compatible only with the idea that they are in some sense self-determined beings. This idea is most explicit in the contention that man is a free being, for a free being cannot be the passive medium or instrument of any other being. At the same time Dante insists, and rightly insists, that there can be no freedom which is exclusive of the infinity of God. But, as the idea of God as an external Artificer or Creator still survives in his mind, he is again forced to take refuge in metaphors which merely conceal the unsolved contradiction of his thought. The only conception which can at all adequately express the true relation of the finite and infinite is that of an organic or

THEOLOGY OF DANTE 115

spiritual unity, in which the same principle that is present in God as the unity of the whole is also present as the ruling principle in each of the parts. From this point of view we can see that the world is no arbitrary product of the divine nature, but the expression of what that nature essentially is, and we can allow at the same time for the various degrees in which the different orders of being realize the principle of the divine. All beings contain the same essential principle, but only those that not only contain it but are capable of comprehending what it is can properly be said to be identical in their nature with God. And this conception also enables us to allow for the gradual process by which man attains to the consciousness of his unity with God. For, only as he comes to the consciousness of the divine principle which is working in him does he truly understand himself. And as that principle essentially is the identity of all beings in their inner nature with all others, and therefore with God, man can find nothing absolutely foreign to himself; every step in the comprehension of nature, every phase in the development of society, art, science and philosophy, is a fuller revelation of the perfect nature of God. The point where Dante comes nearest to this idea is when he seeks to express the Christian conception of God as Love. For it is of the very essence of Love to go out of itself and find itself in another. An absolutely self-centred Being, complete in himself apart from all other beings, cannot be defined as Love. That conception Dante cannot entirely get rid of, but he virtually transcends it in his interpretation of the doctrine of the Trinity, where he tells us that God brought finite beings into existence in order to find objects in which his own nature should be reflected. If God's very nature is Love, he would not be himself were there no object in which his love is manifested; in other words, the world is the necessary self-revelation of God, not the arbitrary product of his mere good pleasure.

> " Freundlos war der grosse Weltenmeister,
> Fühlte Mangel, darum schuf er Geister,
> Sel'ge Spiegel seiner Seligkeit.
> Fand das höchste Wesen schon kein Gleiches,
> Aus dem Kelch des ganzen Wesenreiches
> Schäumt ihm die Unendlichkeit."

We have seen how Dante, finding in all finite beings traces of the divine workmanship, yet regards man as in a peculiar sense made in the image of God. Following Aristotle, as interpreted by Aquinas, he maintains that while man is a being composed of soul and body, he differs from all other beings in the possession of reason. In virtue of this faculty he can make the essence or form of things an object of thought, and thus he is enabled, ascending from lower to higher phases of knowledge, at last to reach an assured knowledge of God. With the faculty of reason is connected the power of free volition, the greatest gift of God to man, and that which makes him most like God. The first man was directly created by God in immortality, holiness and righteousness, but in his pride or self-will he disobeyed the command of God, and involved in his fall the whole of his posterity, whose representative he was.

It is significant that, while Dante accepts the Augustinian doctrine of original sin, he does not hold that the fall of Adam has destroyed the desire for goodness or the freedom of the human will. According to Augustine the human race has been so corrupted by the fall that it cannot do otherwise than sin (*non posse non peccare*), whereas Dante maintains that man has a natural desire for truth and goodness, and falls into error and sin only because he is

THEOLOGY OF DANTE

led astray by "some vestige of that, ill recognized, which shines through them." Freedom of will, again, which seems to him the indispensable condition of moral responsibility, he seeks to justify by the Aristotelian conception of the rational soul as a "substantial form, independent of matter and yet united to it." By a "substantial form" is meant an independent reality, containing within itself a store of energy, which it exhibits in its effects. Like God and the angels, man is self-active, though unlike them he is united to a body which is the instrument of the soul. Because of this union there are certain primitive desires which do not proceed from the man himself, though, when he becomes conscious of them, the free inherent energy of his own nature enables him to choose between them. Hence arises his moral responsibility for the evil which he does.

In this modification of the Augustinian doctrine Dante shows the influence of the free spirit of the Germanic peoples, and of that conception of a rational human life which was due partly to the influence of Aristotle. But this is not the full explanation of the change; for, in recognizing the freedom of man, with its corollaries of moral responsibility and sin, Dante is the exponent of ideas which are inseparable from the Christian idea of life. It was Christianity that first brought to light the infinite importance of the individual soul. In the pantheistic religions of the East the higher life is conceived to consist, not in the active realization of the true self, but in the annihilation of will. The natural man is under the illusion that his own personal fate is of supreme importance, and the first step in the higher life is to get rid of this illusion. Blessedness is to be found only in liberation from all personal desires. The Greek conception of life, again, fails to recognize the importance of individual freedom for another reason. In the objective institutions of society man finds his true good, and so long as the state is secure the life of the individual is in itself of no importance. This is the doctrine to which Plato has given expression in his *Republic*, though no doubt we may see in his ideal state a virtual recognition of the inadequacy of the Greek conception. Christianity, on the other hand, affirms the supreme importance of the individual and his responsibility for his own acts. In this sense we may say that prior to Christianity there was no clear consciousness of sin as the act of the individual. Of this consciousness Dante is one of the most powerful exponents. His whole conception of life is dominated by it, and his pictures of the future life, as he tells us himself, are at the same time a presentation of the spiritual condition of man in this life, as by the good or ill use of his freedom he becomes worthy of reward or punishment.

But, while he recognizes the freedom and responsibility of the individual, Dante is also aware that the individual cannot be separated from the race; and hence he insists upon the doctrine of the Church, that evil came into the world by the original sin of Adam, and has descended to all his posterity. Thus in the doctrine of the Fall he seemed to find the complement or correction of the truth that the individual is purely self-determined. It can hardly be said, however, that Dante gives us any reconciliation of these opposite aspects of truth; he rather sets them down side by side than attempts to reconcile them; nor indeed can they be reconciled without going beyond the external and mechanical form of the doctrine of original sin and grasping the essential truth to which it points. That doctrine as held by Dante draws its support largely from an uncritical reading of the Pauline epistles, and especially of the classical passage in the Epistle to the

Romans, in which a contrast is drawn between Adam and Christ. The passage has been understood in a way that misses the central idea which the Apostle is seeking to enforce. In various parts of his writings St. Paul draws a distinction between the man who is dead in sin, the man who is conscious of sin, and the man who is delivered from sin. This distinction, in the Epistle to the Romans, he applies on a large scale to the course of human history, mainly with the object of proving to his countrymen the necessity of the new revelation of the nature of God as manifested in Christ. In the opening chapters he shows, by an appeal to notorious facts, that the heathen world was sunk in wickedness, although it was self-condemned when tried even by its own imperfect standard of goodness. The source of this moral degradation he finds in a perverted conception of the divine nature. The necessity of a new principle to lift the heathen world out of its religious and moral degradation is, he argues, too plain to need elaboration. But can we say the same of the Jews? Practically the Jew assumes that, because in the Law he has a clear revelation of the divine nature, no further revelation is needed. He fails to observe that the possession of the Law has not brought him into a right relation to God. In truth the Law was never meant to produce righteousness, but only to create a vivid consciousness of sin. This is manifest from Scripture itself, as where we read that " there is none righteous, no not one." The only way in which man can be brought into a right relation to God is by faith, as indeed is repeatedly affirmed in the Scriptures themselves. Having thus argued that all mankind, Jew as well as Gentile, are by nature sinful, that all are more or less clearly conscious of their guilt, and that only by faith can they come into communion with God, the Apostle divides the history of mankind into three great periods. The first period extends from Adam to Moses, the second from Moses to Christ, the third from Christ to the end of the world. The first man was sinful without being clearly conscious of his sinfulness. To the objection that as the Moral Law had not yet been revealed there could be no transgression, the Apostle answers that if there had been no sin, there would have been no death. In the second period there was the clearest consciousness of sin, because the Law had defined in plain terms wherein sin consisted. In the third period begins the supreme revelation of the infinite grace or love of God, and of faith as the only source of righteousness, *i.e.* of the right relation to God. The main idea, therefore, which the Apostle has in his mind is the natural sinfulness of the whole human race from the very beginning of its existence. It is in this connection that he is led to refer to Adam. What he wishes to show is that all mankind are by nature in alienation from God, and can come into union with him only by a new birth of the spirit. The coarse juridical notion of a punishment imposed upon the human race because of the sin of the first man is due to the false interpretation of minds familiar with Roman Law, who did not distinguish between sin and crime. This conception, first formulated by Augustine, was naturally adopted by Aquinas, from whom Dante received it. It was subsequently made a central idea by Calvin, whose mind was in many respects akin to that of Augustine, and it survives even to the present day.

Dante's conception of salvation is the logical complement of his doctrine of original sin. There are two ways in which man might conceivably be liberated from sin: either God might pardon him out of pure mercy, or man might expiate his sin by a humility correspondent to its magnitude. The former conflicts with the justice of God, the latter is impossible because man could not undergo a humiliation proportionate to the self-assertion implied in disobedience to the will of God. Hence God offered up his Son in man's stead, thus reconciling infinite justice with infinite mercy. We shall in vain seek to comprehend the mystery of the Incarnation ; yet divine illumination enables us to obtain a glimpse into it ; for we can see that it was the work of the eternal Love, the Holy Spirit, and that, although there is in the " Word made flesh " a union of the divine and human, the two natures yet remain distinct.

This doctrine has the same fundamental defect as the medieval conception of original sin. As in explaining the origin of the world God is conceived to be a divine Architect or an external Creator; as in accounting for the ascending scale of being he is conceived to be the Final Cause towards whom all things tend ; so now he is regarded as a Judge before whom a criminal is brought to receive sentence. A Judge has no power to tamper with the law, his function being simply to administer it ; and hence God is conceived as bound by the immutable law that every offender must be punished in exact proportion to his offence. The sin of man, however, is infinite, because it consists in his seeking to equalize himself with God, and therefore the only adequate punishment is eternal death. On the other hand, God is not merely a Judge, but also a merciful Father, and therefore disposed to forgive the sinner from pure Mercy. But as this would conflict with his Justice, divine Wisdom conceived, and divine Love realized, the vicarious punishment of man in the person of the Son of God.

Now, it is impossible to state this highly artificial doctrine without seeing that it is the product of conflicting ideas, which are not reconciled but simply set down side by side. The starting-point is the conception of personal sin, one of the central ideas of Christianity. Dante, powerfully impressed, like all the thinkers of his day, with the conception of immutable law as the corner-stone of all social order, naturally enough identifies sin with crime, and therefore conceives of God as an inexorable Judge. But sin is not crime, nor can God be conceived as a Judge. Crime is the violation of the personal rights of another; it is an offence against the external order of the State, and must be expiated by an external punishment. Sin, on the other hand, is not the violation of the rights of others, but the desecration of the ideal nature of the sinner, the willing of himself as in his essence he is not. Hence sin requires no external punishment to bring it home to the sinner; it brings its own punishment with it in the destruction of the higher life, the realization of which is blessedness. In man, by virtue of the divine principle in him, the consciousness of God is bound up with the consciousness of himself, and he cannot do violence to the one without doing violence to the other. Hence God is not a Judge, allotting punishment according to an external law, but the perfectly holy Being, by reference to whom man condemns himself. No external punishment can transform the spiritual nature. The criminal, after undergoing punishment, may be more hardened in his crime than ever, and yet society must punish him, because its function is to preserve the social bond, which by his act the criminal has assailed. But religion has in view, not the preservation of social order, but the regeneration of the individual; it deals with the inner nature of the man, not with the result of his act upon society; and hence, unless it transforms and spiritualizes him, it fails entirely of its end. It is for this reason that the medieval Church in inflicting external punishment for heretical opinions violated the very idea of religion.

When Dante says that the sin of Adam consisted in pride,

or the attempt to equalize himself with God, he strangely intermingles truth with falsehood. The truth implied in his view is, that in so far as man seeks to realize his true self in separation from God, and therefore wills his own good in isolation from the good of his fellow-men, he brings upon himself spiritual death. This idea Dante grasped with marvellous clearness; it is, indeed, the principle by the application of which he peoples his *Inferno*. But this truth is obscured by the vulgar notion that the sin of man was pride, or an attempt to equalize himself with God—a notion obviously based upon the conception of God as a Ruler whose majesty must be asserted. This pagan conception, drawn mainly from the idea of Caesar as the representative of order and law, is entirely foreign to the Christian idea of God. Dante himself virtually denies this false conception of God, when he speaks of the Incarnation as proceeding from the infinite love of God. Here at last we come upon the only purely Christian idea in the whole doctrine. Stripped of its artificial form, it affirms that the very nature of God is self-sacrifice; that, loving his creatures with an infinite love, he can realize his own blessedness only in them. This is the essential idea in the new way of salvation. Man can be saved only as he realizes in himself the spirit of Christ. In taking upon himself the burden of the race he lives a divine life. This is the secret which Christ revealed, and to have made this secret practically our own is to be justified by faith.

If there were the least doubt that Dante was a faithful son of the Catholic Church, the place which the Virgin Mary occupies in his theological creed would be enough to set it at rest. She pervades the whole of the divine comedy with her benign influence. So great is Dante's reverence for her, that in the *Inferno* she is never mentioned by name. When the poet shrinks from the awful task of entering the spiritual world, he receives courage to undertake it by being told that "a noble Lady in Heaven" has such sympathy with his irresolution that she "breaks the stern judgment there on high." Mary is thus the representative of that divine mercy from which the whole work of salvation proceeds. In the *Purgatorio* she appears as the compassionate helper of repentant souls. When Buonconte, flying wildly through the night from the battle of Campaldino, falls by the shore of the Archiano, he calls on the name of Mary, and his soul is snatched from the Evil One by an Angel of God. In the valley of the Princes the souls who had delayed repentance sit, singing *salve Regina*, on the grass and flowers. On the second terrace the souls who are expiating the sin of envy, cry "Mary, pray for us!" In the fifth circle the souls lying prostrate, purging themselves of the sins of avarice and prodigality, cry "Sweet Mary," like a woman in travail, and recall how she was so poor that "in a hostelry she laid down her sacred burden." Her humility is shown in the picture of the Annunciation, sculptured on the rock of the first circle: "There was pictured she who turned the key to open the love of God." In a vision Dante sees her in the third circle as the embodiment of patience, "with the sweet gesture of a mother, saying: 'My son, why has thou so dealt with us? Behold thy father and I were seeking thee sorrowing.'" The slothful recall how Mary "ran with haste into the hill-country." The intemperate remember that "Mary thought more how the marriage-feast should be honourable and complete than of her mouth, which now answers for you." The two Angels who guard the valley of the Princes from the evil serpent "came from the bosom of Mary." In heaven her praise is celebrated by all the Saints, who circle around her. When, at the close of his vision, Dante sees the white rose of Paradise, Mary is seated

THEOLOGY OF DANTE

on high, " her face most resembling Christ." " I saw upon her," says the poet, " such gladness shower . . . that all I had yet seen held me suspended in no such wonder, nor showed me such likeness of God. And Love which first descended thereon, singing *Ave Maria, gratia plena*, in front of her spread out his wings. To the divine song responded on all sides the holy choir, so that every face grew more serene." To paint her divine beauty is impossible : " had I as great power of speech as of imagination, I should not dare to attempt the least of her sweetness." St. Bernard addresses to her the following prayer, which is the very essence of supplication :

"O Virgin Mother, daughter of thy Son,
    Lowlier and loftier than all creatures seen,
    Goal of the counsels of the Eternal One,
Thyself art she who this our nature mean
    Hast so ennobled that its Maker great
Designed to become what through it made had been.
In thy blest womb the Love renewed its heat,
    By whose warm glow in this our peace eterne
    This heavenly flower first did germinate.
Here in Love's noon-tide brightness, thou dost burn
    For us in glory ; and to mortal sight
    Art living fount of hope to all that yearn.
Lady, thou art so great and of such might
    That he who seeks grace yet turns not to thee
    Would have his prayer, all wingless, take its flight ;
Nor only doth thy kind benignity
    Give help to him who asks, but many a time
    Doth it prevent the prayer in bounty free.
In thee is mercy, pity, yea sublime
    Art thou in greatness, and in thee, with it,
    Whate'er of good is in creation's clime.
He who stands here, who, from the lowest pit
    Of all creation, to this point has pass'd
    The lines of Spirits, each in order fit,

> On thee for grace of strength himself doth cast,
> So that he may his eyes in vision raise
> Upwards to that salvation noblest, last."[1]

At the close of this prayer, " the eyes beloved and reverenced of God, fixed on him who prayed, showed us how pleasing to her are devout prayers. They to the Eternal Light were then directed, into which we may not deem that by a creature the eye is able so clearly to penetrate." Mary is thus from first to last the mediator between man and God.

Nowhere is Dante more obviously the exponent of the medieval mind than in the reverence he shows for " the Virgin Mother, daughter of her Son." It is not hard to understand the depth of devotional reverence which gathered about her name, though it would be difficult to disentangle the various elements which contributed to it. She is the living symbol of that humility, gentleness, alacrity in kindly offices, renunciation of wealth and charity, which is the medieval ideal of the womanly as distinguished from the manly type of character, and which was embodied in the gentle unworldly life of the monastic saint. Such an ideal exercised a purifying influence in an age when strong and ungovernable passion was only too prevalent. It sprang from the same root as the chivalrous devotion to women which expressed itself in the lays of the troubadour, but it was associated with the deeper religious consciousness which Christianity had introduced. In this aspect of it we can see how it helped to give vividness and reality to the abstractions of a dualistic theology. The separation of God from the world led to the idea of his incomprehensibility; the conception of him as a stern Judge who inexorably punished sin plunged man in despair; and though this idea was partly transcended in the doctrine

[1] Plumptre's translation.

of the Incarnation, yet the self-sacrificing earthly life of Christ was so overshadowed by his transcendent heavenly life, that its power to awaken love and imitation was almost gone. The love of God, which in theory was affirmed, had lost its practical influence. The repentant sinner, touched with the keenness of remorse, did not feel that that love had any definite bearing on his own life. Thus Mary came to take the place which Christ occupied in the heart of the Christian of an early age. Her soft sympathy he could understand, while yet she was removed from the ordinary sphere of his everyday life, and was thus able to appear in his imagination as the living symbol of divine Mercy. It may be added that the same movement of the mind, which found in Mary the concrete presentation of the mercy of God, led to the creation of the host of Saints who figure in the Catholic calendar. Just as Christ had more and more ceased to be human, so Mary became more and more divine, and her place was supplied by Saint after Saint, who seemed to be nearer to humanity. Such a process was necessarily endless, and, in fact, it is but an expression of the inherent contradiction involved in the primary separation of the divine and the human, the sacred and the secular life; for where the divine is not found in the human but above and beyond it, the process of trying to bring them together necessarily leads to an infinite series. The Reformers were therefore justified in rejecting the Mariolatry and Saint-worship of the medieval Church, and insisting that the " eternal womanly " is to be sought in the ordinary life of the wife and mother.

When Dante goes on to speak of the Christian life he separates, as we should expect, the natural from the theological virtues. The highest point reached by philosophical reflection, as it appears in Plato, Aristotle and Virgil, cannot satisfy the innate desire for truth. The noblest minds of antiquity are represented as consumed by a fruitless longing, and this indeed constitutes their only punishment. In a pathetic passage,[1] Virgil, after referring to the sad state of " Plato, Aristotle and many others," " bowed his head, said no more, and remained disquieted." No one has ever ascended to Paradise " who did not believe in Christ, either before or after he was nailed to the cross." Faith in Christ is thus the precondition of righteousness. Nor is it enough to possess this faith, but it must be openly professed. Statius, convinced by the unconscious prophecy of Christianity contained in Virgil's picture of the return of righteousness and of the first age of man, accepted the Christian faith, but was " through fear a Christian only in secret, for a long time making outward profession of paganism," and for his pusillanimity he was confined to the fourth circle of Purgatory for more than four centuries. Faith must manifest itself in act, or the heathen will put Christians to shame. " Many cry, Christ, Christ, who in the judgment shall be far less near to him than those who had no knowledge of Christ ; and such Christians the Ethiop shall condemn, when the two companies shall be separated, the one rich to everlasting, the other poor." Faith is " that precious jewel, on which all goodness rests." It is the " entrance to the way of salvation " by which the kingdom of heaven has been peopled. Heresy, which is the opposite of faith, often springs from pride, as in the case of Sabellius and Arius, who first swerved from the true path and were then too proud to acknowledge their error. All light is from above, darkness is the shadow of the flesh. The false doctrines of heretics are like swords which cut and disfigure the scriptures, and therefore in the *Inferno* the heretics are imprisoned in burning tombs. With Faith is closely connected the virtue of Hope, which

[1] Purgatorio, 3, 43.

is "the sure expectation of the glory that shall be, and comes from divine grace and foregoing merit." God is the object of the Love of all the saints. Both reason and revelation teach us that the more we know him as he is, the more must love be enkindled in our hearts. And he who is possessed by the love of God will also love his creatures. Without these three virtues no man, however blameless his life, can enter into the kingdom of heaven.

The cardinal virtues, which are all reducible to the Platonic virtues of Temperance, Courage, Wisdom and Justice, prepare the way for the theological virtues, which only came to earth with the advent of Christ. The Christian life assumes two forms, the contemplative and the active, the former consisting in the intuition of divine truth, the latter exhibiting itself in outward activity. The contemplative life, so far as it existed prior to Christianity, is typically presented as Rachel, the active life as Leah ; the Christian life of contemplation is symbolized by Beatrice, the active life by Mathilda. By a special vow the Christian may dedicate himself to the practice of good works, which are not essential to salvation. Thus he gives up his free will, the most precious treasure which he possesses. The Church may liberate the individual from his vow, but not without substituting something else in its stead. Dante has the highest reverence for the religious orders, which he regards as specially instituted in the providence of God for the salvation of the Church ; and hence he depicts with especial sympathy the lives of St. Francis and St. Dominic. These self-sacrificing men seemed to him perfect types of the ideal life.

The contrast of the cardinal and the theological virtues, and of the contemplative and the active life, is another instance of the dualism which pervades the whole of Dante's thought. He admits, indeed, that the virtues of

Temperance, Courage, Wisdom and Justice, which constitute the natural virtues, assume a new form under the influence of the theological virtues of Faith, Hope and Love; but this does not prevent him from regarding the contemplative as higher than the active life. Now, we need not repeat what has already been said as to the confusion between faith as the informing spirit of the Christian life and faith as the acceptance of a particular formulation of doctrine. Taking faith in the former sense, we see at once that it cannot be separated from the natural virtues without losing its meaning. As Dante himself admits, faith must realize itself in action; in other words, only he who finds his life by losing it in others is possessed of a saving faith. But the so-called "cardinal" virtues are just the form which that faith assumes in actual life. Wisdom is the wise adaptation of means to ends in so far as it makes for the social good, and thus it implies the pursuit of all those sciences by which the welfare of the whole is realized. To have a genuine faith is to discharge faithfully our special function in the social organism. Thus we can see how the Christian idea of faith spiritualizes the physical and moral sciences by employing them as the means for the development of an ideal humanity. To conceive of them as purely secular is to separate what elsewhere Dante himself joins together, namely, the love of God and the love of man; and the separation inevitably leads to the false and pernicious doctrine, that the social well-being may be left to take care of itself. How otherwise than by the exercise of practical wisdom is the true means of promoting the common good to be discovered? And what has been said of Wisdom is of course equally true of the other cardinal virtues; indeed these are simply aspects of the same thing. Justice, as the means of preserving and promoting social order, is wisdom applied to the sphere of politics; Temperance is the wise self-restraint which is essential in the discharge of all social functions ; and Courage is the moral heroism which shrinks from no danger that has to be faced in the discharge of one's duty, though for historical reasons it is apt to be limited to the military profession. Thus all the natural virtues are the expression of an active practical faith.

As the natural virtues all spring from one principle, so the three theological virtues are merely different aspects of that principle. Hope is that attitude of the religious mind in which the individual lives in the practical conviction that the soul of the world is good. It is thus the antithesis of all pessimism. In the consciousness that all things work together for good, man is lifted above the anxieties and disappointments of his everyday life, and sees already fulfilled in idea what in actual fact is only in process of fulfilment. Hope, in short, as a form of the religious consciousness, is the conviction that evil must be overcome by the irresistible power of goodness. And, finally, Love is manifestly the expression of faith and hope ; it is the Christian spirit realizing itself in the Christian life through all the channels by which the ideal of humanity is advanced.

Now, although Dante has not entirely neglected this practical aspect of the Christian life, he cannot get rid of the medieval idea that the contemplative is higher than the active life. If this only meant that it is the religious consciousness which gives meaning to life by presenting it as the process in which the individual is enabled to view his own petty efforts as contributing to the triumph of goodness, there would be nothing to object. But, viewed in this way, the opposition of the contemplative and the active life is meaningless. The true life of man is neither in reflection nor in action, but in both ; in other words, it is not the special function which a man fulfils, but the spirit in which he fulfils it, that makes his life divine. Dante's contrast of the contemplative and the active life does not correspond to the life of the thinker as distinguished from the life of the practical man, but to the sequestered life of the monk or nun as compared with the everyday life of ordinary humanity. But, in admitting that the active life is compatible at all with the life of faith, he has practically surrendered the opposition of secular and sacred. If the contemplative life, as he understands it, is higher than the active, the latter must be essentially inconsistent with the Christian ideal; the logical inference from which is, that all should take upon themselves the vows of poverty, celibacy and obedience, *i.e.* that society and even the race itself should cease to exist.

How strong a hold this idea of the religious life, as something apart from the secular life, had upon Dante's mind is shown by his maintaining that there are good works which are not essential to salvation. No greater contradiction of the Christian ideal of life could well be conceived. For that ideal throws into relief the inadequacy of any actual realization of the supreme good; and it is the contrast between the ideal and the real which is the source and inspiration of all spiritual progress, whether in the individual or the race. Only an external and mechanical conception of the religious life can permit anyone to imagine for a moment that a man may claim merit for anything that he can do. With all his fine insight and strong religious spirit Dante here shows in the most unmistakable way the limitations of his time. In a sense, no doubt, he was a " Reformer before the Reformation," but only in the sense in which all the best minds of the Middle Ages might be so named. Theoretically he has not grasped the principle which lay at the very heart of the Reformation, the principle that works are not the source of merit, but only the outward manifestation of the life of the spirit.

The Politics of Dante is determined by his assumption that the free operation of reason in the citizen cannot create the best form of the state. To Dante it seemed almost a truism that anarchy and faction can be suppressed, and the highest good of man secured, only by the subjection of the whole world to the enlightened and unselfish rule of a single monarch. The first proposition, therefore, which he seeks to establish in the *De Monarchia* is, that, whatever be the subordinate organs of society, there must be " a Prince who is over all men in time, or in those things which are measured by time." This at once gives his conception of the state and prescribes its limits. There must be a single Ruler over the whole human race, and his jurisdiction must not extend beyond the concerns of the present life and the temporal welfare of man, while all spiritual interests must be committed to the guidance of the Pope as the divinely appointed head of the Church. In seeking to establish this thesis, Dante gravely advances arguments which we can hardly read without a smile ; and indeed we should find it hard to understand how they could ever have carried conviction to any rational being, were it not apparent that beneath the highly artificial form of his reasoning there glows a strong enthusiasm for humanity, a keen perception of the evils of his time, and a permanent substratum of truth.

To show that there ought to be a single Ruler, Dante appeals in regular scholastic fashion to " the Philosopher," *i.e.* to Aristotle. In the Politics of Aristotle it is pointed out that " where a number of things are arranged to attain an end, it is fitting that one of them should regulate or govern the others, and that the others should submit." Therefore, argues Dante, we have the support of Aristotle for our contention, that all mankind should be subject to a single Ruler. It need hardly be said that Aristotle never contemplated for a moment the possibility of a world-wide empire. In the passage to which Dante refers, what he is seeking to show is that nature intended the Barbarian to be a slave, the Greek to be master. We have here, therefore, a good instance of the uncritical way in which the medieval thinker read and appealed to the authority of Aristotle, as he read and appealed to the authority of scripture. But, even supposing Aristotle had meant to argue from the analogy of the rule of the soul over the body, and of the reason over the appetites, to the rule of the Monarch over all men, we should now say at once that such an analogy proves nothing. The Greek thinker, feeling his way to an adequate conception of the state, tried to assimilate the body politic to a work of art, in which a given material is formed by the shaping intelligence of the artist. The analogy prepared the way for a deeper comprehension of society, but manifestly no valid inference can be drawn in this way in regard to the form which a perfect state ought to assume. Some of Dante's other proofs are even more external and superficial. What shall we say of a writer who argues that, as the whole movement of the heavens is regulated by one God, the whole human race should be under control of one Ruler ? We feel how far we have travelled from this " high priori road " of superficial analogy. So, when we are asked to admit that the Empire is the only perfect form of social order, because man being made in the image of God, and God being one and the human race one, there must be one Ruler, we simply answer that the unity or solidarity of the race does not involve its subjection to a single Monarch, unless it can be shown that in that way the unity of the race is best realized.

Passing from this outer framework of Dante's thought, let us see what is the kernel of his political doctrines. The true life of man, he maintains, consists in the exercise of his rational powers, *i.e.* in the comprehension of the highest principles and their realization in the lives of men. Now this end cannot be attained unless the social order is fitted to secure peace and tranquillity. But how can there be peace without submission to a supreme authority? The individual man is at war with himself when his passions are not subjected to the authority of reason; the family is a scene of discord when the authority of the father is set at naught; the village community must have its chief, the city its podesta, the nation its king. But if we take the family, the village, the city, or even the nation as the ultimate unit, we shall never have a stable social order. Perpetual strife is inevitable if we stop short of an all-comprehensive unity. So long as the territory of one people is limited by that of the other, the selfish tendency of men will lead them to grasp at unlimited sovereignty. Who is to settle the disputes which inevitably arise? If there is no supreme authority to whom appeal can be made, wars and conflicts will be unending, and man will never attain the end of his being. Hence we must have one supreme arbiter of national disputes, *i.e.* the Emperor.

Again, society exists not only in order to preserve peace, but to secure justice to all men. Injustice is a violation of the rights of individuals, and all such violations proceed from the evil influence of the passions, which war against reason. What is wanted in the perfect Ruler is that he should be guided by reason, and therefore free from all merely personal desires. But where shall we find such a Ruler except in a universal monarch? A limited monarch will always be subject to the desire for conquest, and to other selfish desires which disturb the exercise of even-handed justice; but the Emperor can have no temptation to wars of conquest, since the only territorial limit to his dominions is the sea, and he can have no other interest to engage his affections but the good of his subjects; hence he is the ideal Ruler, whose reason is stimulated by that pure love for others, which is the true incentive to justice.

Lastly, a universal monarchy is best fitted to secure the third great end for which society exists, namely, the preservation of freedom. True freedom consists in living a noble and rational life. It is one of the characteristic marks of man as distinguished from the animals that he can control his desires by reason, instead of being controlled by them. Such a rational freedom is the greatest gift of God to man; it is the necessary condition of all well-being here, and of eternal happiness hereafter. Now, freedom in this sense, Dante contends, is best secured under the government of a single Emperor, while "democracies, oligarchies and tyrannies, drive mankind into slavery, as is obvious to anyone who goes about among them." The Emperor, seeking only the good of his subjects, will prescribe laws which allow men to live the life of freedom. Dante distinctly insists that the Emperor must be the servant of all, and that the citizens do not exist for the good of the ruler, but the ruler for the good of the citizens; and it is because a universal monarch can have no temptation to seek his own personal good, that the empire seems to him essential to the welfare of the world. In thus maintaining the necessity of a supreme legislative authority, Dante does not mean that all legislative power is to be in the hands of the emperor, but only that cities, nations and kingdoms shall be " governed by a rule common to them all, with a view to their peace." In this way, he thinks, harmony will be secured between the constituent parts of the human race, all moving together with one will. In support of these general considerations, Dante appeals to the testimony of history. From the fall of man to his own day, he contends, the world has never enjoyed tranquillity except during the rule of the " divine Augustus." " How the world has fared since that ' seamless robe ' has been rent by the talons of ambition, we may read in books : would that we might not see it with our eyes ! Oh, race of mankind ! what storms must toss thee, what losses must thou endure, what shipwrecks must buffet thee, as long as thou, a beast of many heads, strivest after contrary things. Thou are sick in both thy faculties of reason ; thou are sick in thine affections. . . . Not even the sweetness of divine persuasion charms thy affections, when it breathes into thee through the music of the Holy Ghost : ' Behold how good and how pleasant a thing it is for brethren to dwell together in unity.' "

Having thus sought to prove that the only cure for the miserable political condition of man lies in a return to universal monarchy, Dante's next step is to show that this monarchy must be Roman. There was a time, he says, in which he himself ascribed the supremacy of Rome merely to its superiority in arms, but deeper reflection convinced him that its success was due to the guidance of divine providence. He does not hesitate to apply to Caesar the words which he regards as originally spoken of Christ : " Why do the heathen rage, and the people imagine a vain thing ? The kings of the earth stand up, and the rulers take council together against the Lord and against his anointed." But he will do what in him lies to " break their bonds asunder and cast away their yoke," and therefore he will show that both reason and revelation unite in establishing the sacred mission of Rome.

The right of the Roman people to universal empire is proved, in the first place, by the noble ancestry of their founder, Aeneas. "Our divine poet, Virgil, and Livy both testify, that in his veins flowed the best blood from every part of the world." Secondly, the Roman Empire was helped to its perfection by miracles, which are an attestation of the will of God. Thirdly, the Roman Empire was based upon right; for, neglecting their own interest, the Romans sought to promote universal peace and liberty. Their government, as Cicero says, "might have been called, not so much empire, as a protectorate of the whole world." The same spirit animated the individual Roman citizen. "Shall we not say that they intended the common good, who by hard toil, by poverty, by sacrifice of their lives, endeavoured to build up the common weal?" It is thus obvious that the Roman people assumed by right the dignity of the empire. That the Roman people attained to universal dominion by the will of God is shown by their success: "that people which conquered when all were striving hard for the empire of the world conquered by the will of God." The Assyrians, Egyptians, Persians, Greeks, all strove for the prize but failed; the Roman people succeeded, as St. Luke testifies, when he tells us that "there went out a decree from Caesar Augustus that all the world should be taxed." But not only is the claim to empire of the Roman people proved by their right and their providential success, but it may be established by arguments drawn from scripture. For, if the Roman Empire did not exist by right, Christ in being born under it sanctioned what was unjust; nor can the sin of Adam have been punished in Christ, for Christ would not have suffered a just punishment, if he had not been condemned to death by a duly appointed judge.

So strongly was Dante convinced of the necessity of the Roman Empire to the well-being of the race, that he has with difficulty suppressed his indignation against those who

POLITICS OF DANTE

countenance the unrighteous interference of the Church with secular concerns, and towards the close of the second part of his treatise it bursts forth in fiery invective. " It is those who profess to be zealous for the faith of Christ who have chiefly 'raged together' and 'imagined a vain thing' against the Roman Empire; men who have no compassion on the poor of Christ, whom they not only defraud as to the revenues of the Church, but the very patrimonies of the Church are daily seized upon; and the Church is made poor, while, making a show of justice, they yet refuse to allow the minister of justice [*i.e.* the Emperor] to fulfil his office." And again: " Let those who pretend to be sons of the Church cease to insult the Roman Empire, when they see that Christ, the bridegroom of the Church, sanctioned the Roman Empire at the beginning and at the end of his warfare on earth." After this outburst he goes on more calmly to examine the claims urged by its supporters in favour of the temporal power of the Church, and to give his reasons for stripping it of all its usurped authority.

For those who deny that the authority of the state comes directly from God mainly from zeal for the power of the Church Dante has a certain respect, and he will therefore endeavour to show that their view is untenable. One of the arguments upon which they rely is that as the sun and the moon typify the Church and the Empire respectively, it is plain that the Empire receives its authority from the Church, just as the moon receives its light from the sun. But, answers Dante, both were directly created by God, and therefore the Empire, no less than the Church, receives its authority directly from God, while yet the Church ought to shed its gracious influence upon the Empire. Other arguments from scripture are similarly disposed of, but the whole method of reasoning is so foreign to our ways of thinking that we may pass them over as irrelevant. By such a method anything may be proved or disproved, the whole process being what Carlyle calls "endless vortices of froth-logic."

The main argument relied upon by the champions of the Church is that based upon the Donation of Constantine. Dante's reply is that Constantine could not alienate the dignity of the Empire without destroying its essential function, and therefore destroying the source of his own authority. Moreover, the argument proves too much, for if one emperor may alienate part of the jurisdiction of the Empire, why should not his successors alienate the whole of it? And finally, it is contrary to the very idea of the Church to receive temporal power from anyone, for the Church is expressly forbidden to possess gold and silver. Another argument for the temporal power of the Church is that Pope Hadrian bestowed the imperial dignity upon Charles the Great, and hence all his successors owe this dignity to the Church. But, replies Dante, the Pope could not confer a dignity which was not his to bestow. Besides, the same line of reasoning would prove that the Church receives its authority from the Empire, since the Emperor Otto deposed Benedict and restored Leo.

Let us now see the positive reasons for maintaining the independence of the Empire and the Church. It is manifest that the Empire did not derive its authority from the Church, for the simple reason that it possessed authority before the Church existed. Nor can the Church have any power to grant authority in secular matters, since Christ expressly affirms that his kingdom is not of this world. And if we consider the ends for which the Empire and the Church exist, it is plain that each has its own independent jurisdiction, and draws its authority directly from God. Man alone of all created beings has a two-fold nature; and,

POLITICS OF DANTE

corresponding to these, there are two distinct ends, the happiness of the present life, which consists in the exercise of his natural power, and the blessedness of life eternal. The former end he may attain by the use of his reason, the latter can be secured only by transcending reason and exercising the theological virtues of faith, hope and love. Hence man has need of two guides for his life : the Supreme Pontiff, to lead him to eternal life, in accordance with revelation, and the Emperor, to guide him to happiness in this world, in accordance with the teaching of philosophy. Both powers are directly ordained of God. " Yet we must not deny that in certain matters the Roman Prince is subject to the Roman Pontiff. For that happiness which is subject to mortality in a sense is ordered with a view to the happiness which shall not taste of death. Let therefore Caesar be reverent to Peter, as the first-born son should be reverent to his father, that he may be illuminated with the light of his father's grace, and so may be stronger to lighten the world over which he has been placed by Him alone who is the ruler of all things spiritual as well as temporal." The Empire, in a word, is paramount in its own sphere, but it ought to be the protector of the Church, and to receive with all humility the teaching of the Church in all spiritual matters. Thus neither can come into collision with the other, while the temporal and eternal happiness of mankind will be effectually secured.

I have thought it well to give such a statement of Dante's *De Monarchia* as should convey some idea of its form as well as of its content. The form is purely medieval and scholastic, and is totally inadequate to express what Dante had in his mind. For, beneath all this barren display of school logic, there burned an almost fierce fervour of patriotism, or rather cosmopolitanism, which it would be unfair to overlook and impossible to overestimate. What

Dante longed for was that Astraea should return, bringing with her the reign of peace, justice and freedom; and the separation of the Empire and the Church seemed to him the only means by which that consummation could be attained. How impossible and even undesirable was such a return to this ideal of the past, a mere glance at the course of Italian history is sufficient to show.

The politics of Italy was determined for centuries by the failure of the Lombards to conquer the whole peninsula. Venice, Ravenna and the five cities of Romagna called Pentapolis were left by Alboin, their leader, in the hands of the Greek emperors. Rome remained independent. In Southern Italy they failed to get possession of Bari, Amalfi and Naples. Thus Italy at a very early period was divided into distinct political units, which were never fused into one till our own day. Now this fact had the closest connection with the relations of the Church and the Empire. It was only after the tenth century that the Popes exercised a direct influence upon the political development of Italy. Purified by the efforts of Henry III., the Church came to the consciousness of its power, and by the mouth of Gregory VII. advanced the claim to dominion " over all creatures." Thus began that conflict between the Church and the Empire, which ultimately proved fatal to the latter. Meantime the cities of Upper Italy were quietly laying the foundations of their independence; and when Frederick I. asserted his claim to dominion over the whole of Italy, they were able, by the aid of the Pope, to extort a recognition of their freedom. And as the power of the Communes grew, so the people gradually gained an ascendancy over the nobles. In the conflicts of Emperor and Pope the Communes of Northern Italy naturally allied themselves with the Pope, in order to preserve their political independence. The triumph of the papacy, however, only prepared the way for their subjection to Tyrants, who often presented themselves in the guise of demagogues. The loss of freedom in the Italian cities was due chiefly to their want of cohesion ; to hereditary feuds, faction and bad government ; and to the imperfect fusion of the noble families with the burghers. In Dante's day the elements of discord and disruption were in full activity, and we can therefore understand how he should have sought for an escape from the evils, which he not only witnessed but of which he was the victim, in a return to the Empire. His ideal was not new : it was the form which the consciousness of the unity of the race, first distinctly enunciated by Christianity, naturally assumed under historical conditions. The conception of the separate jurisdiction of Emperor and Pope had struck root as early as the fifth century, and it never ceased to haunt the medieval mind. But, in the beginning of the thirteenth century forces were at work which were destined to intensify these divisions and destroy the ideal bond of unity that had held them together. The distinct formation of independent nationalities, the growth of modern languages and literatures, and the rise of a third estate antagonistic to the nobility, all led to a new conception of society. The cosmopolitan spirit of the knight was unintelligible to the plain burgher, and we are not surprised to find the chivalrous lays of the time full of laments for the glory of a vanished past. In the beginning of the fourteenth century, the old ideal of a single race, ruled by one Emperor and one Pope, had lost its fascination, and on its ruins the new ideal of nationality was rising into view. In the faction-ridden Communes of Northern Italy this new ideal seemed a mere dream, and we cannot be surprised that Dante should turn back to the ideal of the past.

The remedy of Dante for the evils of his time, as it need hardly be said, was based upon a false conception of the past and a defective foresight of the future. Not only is the universal Roman Empire a mere "magni nominis umbra," but it involves a false conception of the true relation of the individual to society. The highest form of the state is inseparable from nationality. No ruler is so wise as the whole people. Dante's idea of an Emperor who should be the embodiment of pure reason is contradicted by all that we know of the rule of an absolute monarch. But, even if such a monarch could be found, a universal empire, such as Dante imagined, has the fundamental defect, that it shuts out the citizen from the education which comes from personal participation in the government of the state. The end of the state is not simply to secure the prosperity of the people, but to develop the spiritual powers of every citizen, and in this development training in citizenship is a necessary factor. Dante did not see that even the discord and faction of his day were the confused expression of the struggle towards self-government. No doubt the selfishness of Guelf and Ghibelline, of Bianchi and Neri, was destroying the freedom of the Communes, and Italy had to pay dearly for its want of union and patriotism; but it is none the less true that the inextinguishable desire for freedom was behind it all. The political problem which the Middle Ages were trying to solve, was to unite the free spirit of the Germanic people with that reverence for law which was the great heritage bequeathed to the race by the Roman people, just as its ethical problem was to combine the spirit of Christianity with the desire for intellectual freedom; and the former problem can be solved only by the independence of the citizen, even when that independence is accompanied by the evils of faction and self-seeking. The reason implicit in a people will assert itself if it is only allowed free play.

We must not fail to observe, however, that if Dante would sacrifice the independence of the political community, it is because only in this way, he believes, can true freedom be found. The universal peace which the Empire is to bring back to earth is the condition of justice and freedom; and by freedom he means all that makes for the development of the higher powers of man. Though Dante cannot rid himself of the idea that the contemplative is higher than the practical life, he practically says that the only life worth living is that of the active citizen, who is at the same time interested in all the things of the mind. The production of wealth he does not regard as unspiritual, but only the selfish accumulation or expenditure of wealth; and his ideal embraces all the arts by which man is lifted above sense. We do not find in him, as in Plato, a reluctant renunciation of art as an " imitation " of the sensible; he views it as a medium through which the highest truth may be conveyed. This is manifest from the delight which he felt in music, from the value he attaches to architecture, sculpture and painting, as well as the interest he shows in even the form of poetry. The full development of all the powers of the mind is his ideal of a worthy human life. So long as this end was attained it seemed to him a small matter that men should receive their laws and institutions from a supreme authority; nay, this end, he thought, could be attained in no other way. In this as in all else Dante is the exponent of all that is best in medieval thought. Greece had bequeathed to Christendom not only the desire and means of intellectual culture, but it had also handed on its special gift of art, although mainly in its imitative Roman form. It is well to remember, as Dr. Bosanquet points out, when we speak of the " Dark Ages," that the period from the fifth to the fifteenth centuries was the great building age of the world; nor should we forget that the Church was the great patron of sculpture and painting; and that in Dante the two streams of chivalric and religious poetry were united, as Giotto his contemporary combines close and accurate study of nature with reverence for sacred themes. The modern world has gone far beyond the medieval conception of the state and the church, but the problem of combining culture with intellectual and political freedom is very far from being solved.

There is another thing which we should do well to bear in mind. Dante's ideal of a universal empire was no doubt a dream, but it was one of those inspired dreams of a great mind which are unconsciously prophetic. For, though there cannot be a universal emperor, there ought to be, and we trust will yet be, a universal people. Dante failed to estimate the importance of nationality as the necessary step to a wider unity, for nationality has been the great political educator of the race. Yet he was not wrong in regarding national hate as of the same essence as faction. The highest progress of the race demands, not a "spirit of watchful jealousy" between nations, but a spirit of active co-operation in all that concerns the well-being of man. No doubt we are very far from the realization of universal peace, justice and freedom, but at least the progress of the mechanical arts, of political science and of philosophy are bringing us approximately nearer to it. If we take Dante's lesson to heart, we shall at least be led to admit that selfishness in a nation is as indefensible as selfishness in an individual. Like all men who fix their eyes on the Eternal, Dante was so enamoured of the ideal that he sought to anticipate at a stroke the slow progress of the ages. As Plato could only conceive of the perfect state as an idealized Sparta, in which the distinction of "mine" and "thine" was abolished by the negation of individual property, and even of the family; as Goethe, in his passion for universal culture, undervalued the principle of nationality, partly confusing it with that spurious but aggressive form of it which is almost indistinguishable from hatred of all other nations; and as Carlyle, in his desire to put the hero at the head of the state, seemed to forget that a hero can in our day only be found among a people politically free; so Dante, in the excess of his idealism, would bring about at once the golden age of the world. In one way these masters of thought were wrong, but in their protest against the narrow and mean ideals of their age, as in the large and liberal spirit by which they were animated, they were undoubtedly right; and we read them ill if we forget the essential nobility of their aims in a perception of the inadequacy of the means by which they sought to realize them.

Of Dante's conception of the Church much the same has to be said as of his conception of the Empire. Like all medieval thinkers he cannot see how the spiritual interests of men can be kept secure without a supreme authority to decide in matters of faith. Freedom of thought in religious matters naturally seemed a contradiction to one who conceived of the Church as the guardian of a body of doctrine which had received its final statement. The free operation of the intellect, he thought, can only mean freedom to fall into error. To us, on the contrary, it seems manifest that, just as there can be no perfect form of society which is not based upon the free consent of the whole people, so there can be no system of religious truth which is not the product of the free and unbiassed exercise of reason. The duty of private judgment is the watchword of the modern world, and no Protestant can be faithless to it without abandoning the central principle of the Reformation.

LECTURE FIFTH.

ECKHART, DESCARTES AND SPINOZA.

SCHOLASTICISM, as we have seen, was essentially a compromise between the traditional conceptions and dogmas of the Church and the free spirit of philosophy. Its problem was therefore an insoluble one; for, unless under presupposition of the absolute truth of the whole system of doctrine, the critical movement of philosophy could not be carried out to its logical issue. A tacit recognition of the impossibility of defending the traditional faith led finally to the express dogmatic assertion, that the doctrines of the Church must be regarded as true even when they are in flat contradiction to the plainest deliverances of reason. Even the idea of Aquinas that reason might be employed to confirm the dogmas accepted in implicit faith was abandoned, and we find William of Occam (1300-1347) going so far as to say that the utmost irrationality of its contentions can in no way affect the authority of the Church, since it is in the absolute power of God to act in contradictory ways. This is virtually a *reductio ad absurdum* of scholasticism. Meantime, there grew up among the laity a form of religion and morality that was independent of scholastic Christianity. The dogmas of the Church were not questioned, but men fell back upon their own inner life, which was supported by popular preaching rather than by learned disquisition. What encouraged this virtual separation was the rise of Christian mysticism,

THE THEOLOGY OF ECKHART

which had come down from one aspect of Augustine's teaching as appropriated and developed by Bernard of Clairvaulx and by Hugo of St. Victor. From the fourteenth century there prevailed a mystical piety, not only among monks and nuns, but even among the laity. The greatest of all speculative mystics was Meister Eckhart (b. *ca.* 1260, d. 1329). The "Godhead," he declares, "is the universal ground or potentiality of being, from which the Triune God proceeds." The universe expresses the whole thought of the Father, so that "before creation God was not God." The Trinity is not an emanation from the Absolute, for without the Son the Father would not be God. The eternal generation of the Son, who is Reason, consists in the creation of the ideal world, which is above space and time. There is no subordination of the second and third person to the first: "the eternal fountain of things is the Father, the image of things in Him is the Son, and love for this Image is the Holy Ghost." When God expresses himself in the intelligible world the phenomenal world arises, but this world, as is usual with mystics, is held to be in itself merely negative. Eckhart's view of evil is that as Good is identical with Being, so Evil is the same as non-being. In the human soul there is a "spark" which is one with God, and through it man holds communion with God. "There is in the soul," says Eckhart, "something which is above the soul, Divine, simple, a pure nothing; rather nameless than named, rather unknown than known. Of this I am accustomed to speak in my discourses. Sometimes I have called it a power, sometimes an uncreated light, and sometimes a Divine spark. It is absolute and free from all names and all forms, just as God is free and absolute in Himself. It is higher than knowledge, higher than love, higher than grace. For in all these there is still distinction." What Eckhart calls "reason," and other mystics " intuition," is the highest of all faculties ; it " cannot rest content with goodness or wisdom, nor even with God himself, but must penetrate to the Ground from whence all goodness and wisdom spring." This is " the way of the Godhead," which is open only to the mystic. No doubt he must first tread " the way of the Manhead," but only as a means by which the soul may penetrate into the " Divine darkness " underlying the manifestation of the Trinity. On the other hand, Eckhart seems also to teach that contemplation is but the means to the active life of love.

In the successors of Eckhart mysticism assumes a practical and devotional aspect, in which communion with God is regarded as a fact of personal religious experience. The effect of their teaching was to undermine sacerdotalism, and in a sense to prepare the way for the Reformation, though none of them struck at the root of the medieval view of the Church as the only and the necessary medium through which the soul can enter into communion with God. The medieval world was subjected to a much more effective though less direct attack by the Renaissance. The renewal of sympathy with the free spirit of antiquity was the most effective criticism of the superstition and bigotry of the Church. At the same time this movement, by its revival of the study of Greek and Hebrew, prepared the way for the future regeneration of the Church, by awakening the feeling for a historical interpretation of scripture as compared with the dead mechanical method of forced interpretation that had prevailed for centuries. Men like Colet, More and Erasmus even imagined that there might be a humanistic regeneration of ecclesiastical Christianity, which should lead to the removal of abuses, a moral regeneration of the Church, and an interpretation of the dogmas in terms of ethics. This dream was rudely

THE RENAISSANCE AND THE REFORMATION 151

dispelled by the Lutheran Reformation. When Luther at the Diet of Worms in 1521 refused to retract what he had written, he expressed the principle of the supremacy of the human conscience. This principle cut up by the roots the doctrine that there is a distinction between church and state, clergy and laity, the religious and the secular life. Luther's whole attitude finds its highest interpretation in his doctrine of justification by faith, which meant for him that man needs no external process by which to attain to forgiveness, but is able to see that the inmost nature of God is revealed in the absolute self-surrender of Christ, and therefore that through faith he may share in the righteousness of Christ. Thus the believer becomes one with God, and has the assurance of liberation from sin. Luther's idea of scripture, though he was unable to free himself from the idea that it was an external and absolute authority, is of a large and liberal kind. Scripture he regards as divine, because it contained a record of the highest religious experience. Luther's actual treatment of it shows that he virtually distinguished higher and lower elements in it, according as it did or did not appeal to his own experience. Hence he regarded the Epistles of St. Paul as higher in authority than any of the gospels except the Fourth, while the Epistle of James he characterized as an " epistle of straw," and in the Book of Revelation he could see no trace of real inspiration by the Holy Spirit. To miracles he attached a very subordinate value. " External miracles," he said, " are the apples and nuts which God gave to the childish world as playthings; we no longer have need of them." But, while Luther virtually made an appeal to reason, he was not by nature fitted for a speculative reconstruction of religion, and indeed no such reconstruction was possible until the foundations upon which a religious view of life is supposed to rest have been subjected to the severest scrutiny. For this thorough-going criticism we must look to the philosophers; and to them, in the remaining lectures of the present course, I shall mainly confine myself, beginning with Descartes, the "father of modern philosophy."

In the remarkable words in which he characterizes his own age, Kant affirms that rational criticism must be absolutely comprehensive. "When religion seeks to shelter itself behind its sanctity," he says, "and law behind its majesty, they justly awaken suspicion against themselves, and can no longer lay claim to the sincere respect which reason yields only to that which can bear the test of its free and open scrutiny."[1] For criticism of this wide and impartial type Descartes was not prepared, or at least for it he professes not to be prepared. Though his philosophy begins in a doubt that claims to be absolute, and though, like Luther and Bacon, he starts with a determination to free himself from the yoke of tradition and to grant no unproved assumptions, the limitations of his time, and possibly a certain defect in moral courage, prevented him, as it prevented his great predecessors, from applying the principle of private judgment in its complete generality. While he admits that no state is perfect in its constitution, as is sufficiently proved by the variety of discrepant constitutions, he has no sympathy with those restless and busy meddlers, who, called neither by birth nor fortune to take part in the management of public affairs, are yet always projecting some new reform. And if the subject of Louis XIV. naturally shrank from enquiring into the foundation of the state, a tenderness for so sacred and tender a plant, and possibly a wholesome dread of the Inquisition, which had but recently silenced Galileo, led him to speak even more guardedly of religion. The ordinances of religion, he

[1] Kant's *Kritik der reinen Vernunft*, 1st ed., p. vi. note.

THE CARTESIAN PHILOSOPHY 153

says, have been directly instituted by God, as a means of conducting man to heaven ; but, as the way thither is as open to the simple as to the most cultivated, it would be an evidence of irreverence and presumption to subject religion to the feeble test of human reason. The truths of revelation are more certain than anything reached by the use of reason ; for faith, which is their foundation, as in all that is obscure, is an act, not of the intellect, but of the will. It is true, Descartes holds, following the usual distinction of the schoolmen, that there are truths of faith, such as the existence of God and the immortality of the soul, which may be confirmed by reason, unlike the " mysteries " of the Trinity and the Incarnation, which are accepted only by faith. No doubt, as theologians are agreed, the latter are not contrary to the light of reason, but the former are not only in harmony with reason, but are demonstrable by reason. Guarded, however, as Descartes was in his attitude towards the state and the church, the inherent contradiction of an absolute doubt, from which the most important concerns of life were excluded, begins to reveal itself the moment an attempt is made to confine it within such arbitrary limits. The free spirit of the modern world was not thus to be fettered, but must needs expand until it has subdued all to itself.

Having made these inevitable concessions to the spirit of the times, Descartes goes on to apply his rational test to the mass of ideas that he finds in his own mind. It must seem strange, he says, that after the enormous labours of past generations, no clear and certain knowledge has been reached, notwithstanding the fact that good sense or reason, which is the distinctive mark of man as compared with the animals, is so equally distributed. It must be because knowledge has not been sought in the right way ; and therefore until we have discovered the true method of knowledge, we must provisionally reject all the beliefs that have come to us by hearsay and tradition. This method is certainly not that of the traditional logic, which gives no help in the discovery of new truth, however useful it may be in the exposition of truth already obtained. In mathematics alone Descartes found clear and certain reasons for the statements made, and the method of mathematics is to begin with the simplest and most general elements and to advance in regular order to the more complex. This method, then, may be expected to be universally applicable. Now the intelligence is the unity on which all knowledge depends, and hence we must first enquire into its nature and limits. To get a satisfactory solution of this problem, the mind must be freed from all confused and doubtful ideas, and therefore that which is merely probable or has been received upon authority must in the first instance be rejected. Nothing can be accepted as true which is not perfectly clear and certain; either because it is directly revealed by the natural light of reason or is deduced from self-evident principles. Now, the apparent reality of the objects of sense cannot be admitted, for confidence in the senses results in self-contradiction, and therefore we cannot in the first instance admit that even our own bodies have any reality other than that of dreams. Nor, setting aside the sensible properties of things, can we admit the existence of extended being, which is the object of geometry and arithmetic; for, clear and certain as the propositions of mathematics seem to be, extended being itself may be an illusion produced in us by God, if there is a God, or, if not, by the deceptive character of our faculties. Thus no part of our consciousness of the world is beyond doubt. But when we fall back upon consciousness itself, we at last reach a proposition that cannot possibly be doubted. For though it is possible to doubt that what we think has any objective existence, it is not possible to doubt that we actually think it. Even the doubt that we have knowledge of reality cannot extend to consciousness itself, and therefore the proposition that *I who think exist* is absolutely certain. Thus in the very centre of doubt we have found something that is indubitable.

It is important to observe that all that is asserted in the *Cogito ergo sum* is that *the thinking subject exists*. Whether the subject is in its existence independent of extended reality is neither affirmed nor denied. To think at all implies an immediate and necessary relation to a self, whereas the reality of that which is thought is not thereby determined. Descartes also, in spite of the *ergo* employed in the formula, declares that the reality of the *I that thinks* is not an inference but an " intuition " ; for, if it were an inference, we should have to start from the judgment, " whatever thinks exists," and go on to reason : " I think, therefore I exist." We must therefore interpret Descartes' first principle as meaning simply that the *individual subject* that thinks exists. For aught that we know at this stage, the thinking subject may be alone in the universe. Nevertheless, the individual thinking subject is aware of one instance in which there is no possible opposition between what is thought and what exists. From the " void and formless infinite " has been won this firm and solid reality, the existence of the individual thinking self. So far, however, we have not advanced beyond Solipsism. How does Descartes seek to establish the existence of other objects and other selves ?

How do I know that I myself exist as thinking ? I know it because I have a " clear and distinct consciousness " of myself as thinking. Descartes himself points out that the faculty by which I know myself is not perception or imagination, but understanding, *i.e.* it is not the mere fact that the self is in a particular state, but the thought or conception of the self, as the subject of various successive states, that constitutes the clearness and distinctness. Without understanding we should have no consciousness of the self as thinking; and indeed we are expressly told that perception and imagination are not essential to the existence of self. The *Cogito ergo sum* must therefore be interpreted to mean: " I think of myself as conscious, and therefore I exist."

Descartes, however, gives to this proposition a meaning that seems to me quite illegitimate. Finding it possible to doubt the existence of external reality, but not the existence of himself as thinking, he came to the conclusion that he was " a substance whose whole essence or nature consists purely in thinking, and which in order to be has no need of any place, nor is dependent on anything material." Hence, " this I, *i.e.* the soul, by which I am what I am, is entirely distinct from the body, and though the body were not, the soul would not cease to be all that it is." Or, as he expresses it in another passage, " It is very certain that the knowledge of my existence does not depend upon things the existence of which is not known to me." Here Descartes has fallen into a fatal confusion of thought. Granting that I may doubt whether there is any external reality corresponding to my ideas, how can it possibly be inferred that I am entirely independent of everything material? The only proper inference is that I cannot tell whether I can or can not exist apart from the material world, because I do not know whether that world exists, and if so, whether my existence is bound up with it or not. What Descartes should have said is that as the knowledge of his own existence was true whether or not the material world existed, the knowledge of his own

THE CARTESIAN PHILOSOPHY 157

existence was not dependent upon a knowledge of the material world; instead of which, by an extraordinary μετάβασις εἰς ἄλλο γένος he argues that his existence cannot depend upon "things the existence of which is unknown to him." Obviously, ignorance of dependence cannot be a reason for affirming independence.

Descartes, however, attempts to prove that the thinking subject is independent of all external reality by other considerations. There are in my consciousness ideas of sense, which do not belong to me as a purely thinking being, (1) because my thought is independent of them, and (2) because they often arise in my mind without my own consent. These ideas, though as ideas they have the reality of all facts of consciousness, are yet representative of something external to me. My ideas of change of place, occupation of different situations, etc., cannot be attributed to me as a purely thinking being, because their clear and distinct conception implies extension but not intelligence. Thus I must distinguish between corporeal and thinking substance, neither having any except accidental relations to the other. Is there a real substance corresponding to my conception? The answer can only be given by considering the Cartesian proofs of the existence of God.

In my consciousness there are ideas of corporeal substances, of animals and of men like myself, but none of these necessarily implies a cause higher than myself, and therefore they do not compel me to affirm the existence beyond me of objects corresponding to them. But there is in my consciousness one idea of which I cannot possibly be the cause—the idea of God, as a Substance, infinite, eternal, unchangeable, self-dependent, omniscient, omnipotent, the Creator of all things; for, though I can explain the presence in my mind of the idea of Substance from the fact that I am conscious of myself as a thinking substance,

I cannot in this way obtain the conception of an infinite substance. This idea can be produced in me by nothing short of a substance itself infinite. To the objection that the idea of God may be derived from my knowledge of myself, since the infinite is nothing but the negation of the finite, Descartes answers that the idea of the infinite is not negative but positive, representing not less but more reality than the idea of the finite. "Let it not be supposed," he says, "that the idea of the infinite is not the idea of reality, but merely the negation of that which is finite, in the same way as rest is conceived by the negation of motion, and darkness by the negation of light. On the contrary, it is manifest that there is more reality in infinite substance than in finite substance; nay, that in some sense I have in me rather the conception of the infinite than of the finite, *i.e.* the idea of God than the idea of myself. For, how could I know that I doubt and desire, or, in other words, that there is some defect in me which prevents me from being perfect, if I had no idea of a Being more perfect than myself, in contrast to whom I recognize the defects of my own nature? Nor can it be said that the idea of God may be false, and may therefore have no representative value; for it is perfectly clear and distinct, and as representing the highest possible reality is beyond all suspicion. The idea of the infinite comprehends all my ideas of perfection. No doubt I cannot conceive all that it involves, but this only proves that the cause contains in it more than I who am finite and limited can grasp." If it is further objected that, though the idea of the infinite is positive, it need not imply the existence of a being distinct from myself, but may be simply my ideal of what I might myself become, Descartes answers, in the first place, that the idea of a being who is only potentially infinite is not the same thing as the idea of a being who is actually infinite;

THE CARTESIAN PHILOSOPHY

secondly, that as perfection must always remain an ideal unattainable by us, we are not even potentially infinite; and, lastly, that in any case the actual existence in our minds of the idea of the infinite cannot be produced by us, inasmuch as, even if we are capable of becoming infinite in the future, we are admittedly at present only finite.

Another form of the argument from causality is based upon the fact that I exist. If I were self-produced, I should have endowed myself with the perfection which I regard as in the highest degree desirable. But as I am not perfect, I must conclude that I have not the power to make myself perfect, much less to create myself. Nor can this conclusion be avoided by supposing that I have always existed, for the conservation of a substance requires the same power as its creation, and indeed conservation is just continuous creation. Nor can any other finite cause account for my existence. Thus I am forced to conclude that my existence must be attributed to God, as a Being containing within himself all perfection.

This idea of God as involving all perfection is elaborated in the second argument of Descartes—that usually known as the ontological. I find in my mind a great number of ideas, which are not mere negations, though there may possibly be no reality corresponding to them. Thus, when I imagine a triangle, I find that it has a certain immutable nature, form or essence, which is no invention of mine. Now, I am just as certain that I have the idea of God as an absolutely perfect being as that I have the idea of a triangle. And, just as the idea of a triangle is clearly and distinctly, and therefore necessarily, connected with the idea of its three angles being equal to two right angles; so the idea of God is clearly and distinctly, and therefore necessarily connected with the idea of his actual and eternal existence. The existence of God is therefore at least as

160 ECKHART, DESCARTES AND SPINOZA

certain as the truths of mathematics. Descartes admits that at first sight this argument seems to be sophistical. In all other cases we assume that there is a distinction between existence and essence, and hence we naturally suppose that we can conceive of God as having no actual existence. But it is not really possible, Descartes argues, to separate the existence from the essence of God. We can no more conceive of an absolutely perfect being as wanting in existence, *i.e.* wanting in perfection, than we can conceive a mountain without a valley. Thus the thought of God is absolutely inseparable from the thought of his existence. It will of course be objected, that, admitting the necessary connection in my thought of the essence and the existence of God, it does not follow that God actually exists. My thought, it may be said, does not impose any necessity upon things. Because I can imagine a winged horse, it does not follow that such a horse actually exists. Similarly, I may attribute existence to God, although no God exists. But this objection, Descartes replies, rests upon a fallacy. It is quite true that my thought does not impose any necessity upon things; but for that very reason the absolutely indissoluble connection between my thought of God and my thought of his existence shows that it is the necessity of the existence of God that determines my thought of his existence. I can perfectly well imagine a horse without wings, but I cannot conceive of God without including existence in my conception. It may be said, however, that, admitting the assumption of an absolutely perfect being, it no doubt follows that he exists, but it is not necessary that such an assumption should be admitted. If I grant that all four-sided figures may be inscribed in a circle, I must also grant the inference that a rhombus can be inscribed in it. But the original assumption is false, and therefore the inference

THE CARTESIAN PHILOSOPHY

is also false. This objection, however, is not really apposite. The idea of an absolutely perfect being is not an arbitrary supposition. Just as there is a necessary connection between the idea of myself as thinking and the idea of myself as existing, so there is a necessary connection between the idea of a Supreme Being and the idea of his infinite perfection. I am, therefore, entitled to deduce from the idea of a Supreme Being all the predicates necessarily involved in or connected with it, and therefore the predicate of existence. This necessary connection of ideas is what distinguishes conceptions that belong to me by the very nature of my intelligence from conceptions that connect ideas in an arbitrary way. The conception of God is of the former kind, as is evident from these among other considerations: that God is the only being whose nature necessarily involves existence; that it is impossible to conceive of more than one such being; that, granting his existence now, I see clearly that he must necessarily have existed from all eternity, and will exist to all eternity; and, lastly, that I cannot conceive of him as subject to change.

Having established the existence of God, as he believes, Descartes' next step is to advance to the existence of the world. As God is an absolutely perfect being, among his perfections is included absolute truthfulness, and from him I have received the faculty of distinguishing between truth and falsehood. The truthfulness of God, indeed, does not demand that I should never fall into error, but only that I should never fall into error except by a misuse of the faculties with which God has endowed me. Now, the persuasive force of our first principle lies in its absolute clearness and distinctness; and therefore we conclude that we cannot fall into error except by giving our assent to what is not clear and distinct, but obscure and confused. Such assent is an act of will or free choice. The understanding makes no affirmation in regard to reality, but merely shows the relation of ideas to each other; the acceptance or rejection of this relation as holding true of reality is our voluntary act. I cannot make or unmake my ideas, or their relation to each other, but I can give or withhold my assent from the ideas presented to me until I have satisfied myself that I am accepting only those that are perfectly "clear and distinct." Hence error does not proceed from God, but from myself; and if I am careful to limit the assent of my will to absolutely clear and distinct thought, I shall never fall into error.

When I examine the ideas of external or material things that I find in my mind, the idea of continuous magnitude, *i.e.* of that which is extended in length, breadth and depth, is perfectly clear and distinct. Such a magnitude is therefore possible, for nothing is impossible except that which is unthinkable. Now, there is in me a certain passive faculty of perception, which does not belong to me as a thinking being; and therefore my ideas of sense must be referred to some substance other than myself, which is sufficient to account for their *representative* character. That they are not directly produced by God we must conclude, because otherwise he would deceive us by the apparently representative character imparted to them; and hence we must conclude that they are caused by corporeal things. Of course it does not follow that corporeal substance or matter corresponds to our perceptions, so far as these are obscure and confused, but only that it corresponds to that clear and distinct conception of an extended magnitude which is the object of mathematics.

There are, then, three kinds of being: thinking substance, extended substance and absolute substance, or God. Now, we have no other idea of substance, taking the term

THE CARTESIAN PHILOSOPHY 163

in its strict sense, than that it is that in which there exists objectively that which is in us an idea. The substance in which thought immediately resides is mind ; the substance which is the immediate subject of local extension and the accidents that presuppose local extension—such as figure, situation, and motion—is body. Now, we clearly conceive mind without body, and body without mind ; hence mind and body are really distinct, or are capable of existing separately. But, while mind and body are substances in the sense of being independent of each other, they are not substances in the sense of being self-existent. There is but one self-existent substance, namely God ; for no created thing could exist for a single moment without being sustained and conserved by the power of God. Hence the schoolmen rightly said that the term substance does not apply "univocally" to God and his creatures. Mind and body are called "substances" because they are independent of each other and depend for their existence only on the "concourse" of God. The only way in which we come to know that thinking and extended substances exist is through their attributes ; and in each kind of substance there is one attribute that constitutes its nature and essence, and upon which all the others are dependent. *Extension* constitutes the fundamental attribute of body, *thought* the fundamental attribute of mind ; the other attributes being modes of extension or of thought. As "modes" are the changing forms assumed by the essential attribute of a substance, they are found only in created substances ; for God is absolutely unchangeable, and therefore possesses only attributes.

The philosophy of Descartes bears the closest relation to the attitude of Luther. As the latter set aside all the traditions of the Church as despotic over the religious consciousness of the individual and yet affirms that man can only find his true self in direct union with God, so the former, generalizing the whole problem, carries doubt of all preconceptions to its ultimate result in a provisional rejection of all knowledge, and, finding in the nature of the consciousness of self the one indubitable foundation of all truth, he advances to the proof of the being of God. Descartes has therefore sought to give a reasoned basis for the right of private judgment and the necessity of submission to God as the prius of all reality.

The *Cogito ergo sum* may therefore be regarded as the principle upon which is based the demand that nothing should be accepted that is not established on rational grounds. When we examine this principle more closely, it becomes evident that it contains an ambiguity which prevents Descartes from constructing a philosophy that carries out its own aim of admitting nothing that is not established by reason. Is the *Cogito* to be interpreted as meaning, " I as a particular self think," or does it mean, " I as a universal self think " ? The distinction is by no means unimportant. Descartes tells us that, in the effort to reach a first principle, he assumed provisionally that none of his ideas was true, and that after supposing that the whole of his ideas might be no more real than dreams, he found that, whether that which he thought was reality or illusion, he could not doubt that he did think and therefore was not himself an illusion. And the ground for this proposition was that to think and to be were inseparable, since he could not think without being. Descartes' presupposition therefore is, that in self-consciousness he came into direct contact, without any mediation, with himself as a thinking being. The first principle, however, is regarded by him as only establishing the existence of his own particular self, for he tells us that it still remained doubtful whether there was anything real but himself.

Now, it may be readily shown that this assumption of the reality of the particular thinking being cannot possibly serve as the basis upon which an edifice of knowledge can be erected. Let it be granted that in self-consciousness the particular self is directly aware of his own existence; and the question still remains, whether this is more than an unfounded belief. The individual man may have the most undoubting assurance of his own existence as thinking, but if it is assumed that this assurance is peculiar to himself, or at least that it cannot be shown not to be peculiar to himself, he has not reached a proposition that will bear the weight of a true system of knowledge. It is thus evident that, only if the *Cogito* of Descartes is interpreted to mean, "I as a universal intelligence think," can it be the presupposition of all truth. For, unless the *Cogito ergo sum* means: "In virtue of my reason I know that in thinking I am," there is nothing to hinder us from denying that the proposition is more than a natural, but perhaps untrue, conviction. Hence the first principle of Descartes must be interpreted to mean, that the only possible ground upon which any knowledge whatever can be based is that the particular self, in thinking, is thinking as every possible intelligence must think. No intelligence, in other words, can possibly be conscious of thinking without recognizing that this implies the existence as thinking of the being that thinks. So interpreted, the first principle of Descartes may be taken to express the doctrine that the presupposition of all knowledge is the existence in every self-conscious being of an intelligence, which under the same conditions operates in the same way. The counterpart of this truth, that nothing can be real that is not intelligible, we shall immediately see.

Now, I do not think that Descartes rejected this principle —the principle that all intelligences are identical in their essential nature; indeed, it seems to be implied in his view of " innate ideas," *i.e.* ideas that must be accepted by every one who understands their meaning; but it yet is true that his want of explicit recognition of this principle has led him into fundamental error. Thus his interpretation of the *Cogito ergo sum*, as equivalent to the doctrine that the thinking subject is a substance existing independently of the body and of the whole material world, is obviously due to a confusion between the particular and the universal self. For, the first principle, on any tenable interpretation, does not establish the reality of a purely spiritual substance, but only shows that, whatever may be the object of thought, there exists a thinking subject. Whether this thinking subject could exist in independence is not determined by the first principle.

At the same time the first principle of Descartes may be regarded as implying that the thinking subject is at once particular and universal. For, though its author did not discriminate between these two senses, what was working in his mind undoubtedly was the principle that the particular thinking subject is capable of reaching a conclusion in which every thinking subject must agree. Thus the thinking subject is self-active and yet its self-activity must conform to the universal laws of all intelligence. It was, however, just as natural for Descartes as for Luther to accentuate the particular aspect of the self, in contrast to the enslavement of the individual from which the modern world had to free itself; and therefore it is not surprising that he thinks more of the self-activity of the individual than of the universality of intelligence which it implies. The subsequent course of philosophy will therefore, as we may expect, first bring into prominence the aspect of universality that he has neglected, and then endeavour to reconcile the self-determination of the particular self with the universality of his intelligence. The one extreme naturally gives rise to the other; and hence, just as the freedom of the individual man as affirmed by Luther was immediately followed by the unqualified assertion of his absolute subjection to the sovereignty of God, so the individualism of Descartes was followed by the universalism of Malebranche and Spinoza.

The inadequacy of the Cartesian formula, when it is interpreted as referring only to the particular thinking self, is virtually confessed by Descartes himself, when he goes on to give a demonstration of the existence of God.

In his first argument, as we have seen, Descartes starts from the principle of causality, which he regards as an "intuition" of reason. In other words, we have in the idea of the inseparable connection of anything real with its ground or cause, a principle that is just as immediate, and just as absolute, as the *Cogito ergo sum*. If this is true, the principle of causality must be one that is not peculiar to this or that thinking being, but must be recognized by every possible intelligence. Descartes, therefore, in making the assumption that the judgment of causality is absolute, has virtually affirmed that the thinking subject as thinking is beyond the limits of his finite individuality. It is only on this principle that the Cartesian proofs of the existence of God can be regarded as in any sense valid. When Descartes tells us that " the conception of the finite in some sense presupposes the conception of the infinite," he admits, though with some hesitation, that in the consciousness of self there is involved the consciousness of a universal intelligence. What prevents Descartes from recognizing that the knowledge of the infinite is the necessary condition of the knowledge of the finite is his assumption that the human mind cannot come into direct contact with the infinite, and must therefore "represent" it by more or less inadequate symbols. Hence, though it is true that the thought of the finite is inseparable from the thought of the infinite, yet the infinite remains beyond direct knowledge, and must therefore be inferred from the knowledge of the finite. It is for this reason that Descartes employs the principle of causality as the medium between the finite and the infinite. The idea of the infinite, he argues, cannot be produced by the finite subject; therefore, it must be due to God, who alone is infinite. On the dualistic basis from which Descartes starts, the argument is open to the objection of Kant, that the conception of the infinite cannot be identified with the infinite, and that there is therefore no way of advancing from the conception to the objective existence of a Being corresponding to the conception. But, while this is a valid criticism of the dualism of Descartes, it does not do justice to the principle that really rules his thought. That principle is, that what thought by its very nature cannot but think must be a determination of real existence. This is the principle, as we have seen, that really gave force to the *Cogito ergo sum*. In the present case, granting its truth, the conclusion that the infinite is presupposed in the finite will follow from the impossibility of attaching any meaning to the finite except as presupposing the infinite. It must be observed, however, that with this interpretation of the Cartesian argument, the dualistic basis of his doctrine disappears. The independence of the thinking subject can no longer be maintained, when it is seen that apart from the infinite neither it nor any other finite reality could exist. If the infinite by the necessary law of intelligence is the prius of all reality, not only must the finite thinking subject involve the infinite, but both it and the external world must be alike related to the infinite, and therefore to each other. The infinite cannot be separated from the finite without

THE CARTESIAN PHILOSOPHY 169

itself becoming finite; and the finite, if it has no reality except through the infinite, cannot be opposed to the infinite. Hence the Cartesian doctrine that the infinite is the presupposition of the finite raises the whole question as to the relation of the one to the other. This was the main problem of Spinoza, and indeed of all succeeding philosophers. Descartes could not possibly give a satisfactory solution of the problem because not only does he never get rid of the dualism from which he started, but he is entirely deficient in any comprehension of the relative value of the categories of substance and causality, which he employs in his proof of the being of God. The category of causality, as Kant has shown—and the same thing is true of " substance "—is necessarily of a divisive character, since it separates between an effect and its cause. It is indeed only by employing the term causality in the unusual sense of self-cause that Descartes is able to make his demonstration march at all; and self-cause is at bottom the Absolute interpreted as self-determining. Hence the cosmological argument, as he employs it, really presupposes the ontological; while this again gets its meaning and force from the principle that the Absolute is self-determining.

When he advances from the idea of God to the world, Descartes argues that to regard matter as illusory is to suppose that our intelligence is in its intrinsic nature incapable of arriving at truth, and therefore that in its creation God has violated his essential nature. The principle here involved is again that which we have seen to be implied in the two first principles; namely, that the intelligence of man is essentially identical in nature with universal intelligence. Descartes, indeed, admits that we are so constituted as to fall into error, but only because we weakly give the consent of our will to that which is not clear and distinct to the intellect. The whole of this reasoning is pervaded by the idea that the individual mind can only obtain an indirect knowledge of anything but itself. It is for this reason that Descartes, in order to give a certainty to our beliefs that does not belong to them in their own nature, falls back upon the idea of God, as the only warrant for the reality of that which is not directly known to us. In truth there can be no consciousness of self or of God that is not mediated by a consciousness of the world. Unless it can be shown that, in knowing the cosmos, we are, in Kepler's language " thinking the thoughts of God after Him " we can have no knowledge whatever. In this sense, and only in this sense, can it be said that the truthfulness of God is the only guarantee of the reality of the world. Knowledge, in fact, is a system of ideas, in which each involves all the others ; so that the consciousness of self is inseparable from the consciousness of the world, and both from the consciousness of God.

From what has been said it is evident that there is in the philosophy of Descartes a confusion of principles. The main source of this confusion, as I have argued, is due to the want of discrimination between the particular self and the universal self, leading to the notion that in knowledge the subject is separated both from the world and from God. The over-emphasis of individuality in Descartes naturally led to the over-emphasis of universality in Spinoza, though in the former we have already the germ of all that becomes explicit in the latter.

In making doubt the necessary presupposition of knowledge Descartes was virtually affirming that reason or intelligence is the only foundation of truth. To this principle, however, as we have seen, he was so far untrue that he expressly excepted from its operation the dogmas of the Church and the sovereignty of the State. Spinoza displays none of this inconsistency. There is for him no authority but reason, and philosophy, as the systematic formulation of the true nature of things, is not the handmaid of theology but a substitute for it, just as it is the sole guarantee of society and the State. This enlarged conception of the province of philosophy as independent of all external grounds gave to Spinoza's effort to get at the ultimate truth of things a depth of interest that it could not have for Descartes. In the view of Descartes man is unable to break through the self-enclosed circle of his ideas, so that all other objects but himself are matters of faith, vouched for by the absolute truthfulness of God ; Spinoza saw that, to make the possibility of knowledge depend upon the existence of that which in itself is unknown is suicidal, since that which falls beyond the circle of knowledge cannot be shown to exist. The only knowable reality is therefore that reality which is comprehended by reason, and the truth so comprehended cannot be a mere assemblage of fragments, but must be an organic whole. It must therefore be possible to show that the true order and connection of ideas is identical with the order and connection of things. Descartes held that in the order of our knowledge the consciousness of self precedes the consciousness of God, while in reality the existence of God is the presupposition of the existence of the self. This opposition between the *ratio cognoscendi* and the *ratio essendi* Spinoza rejects. If the self cannot exist apart from God, it cannot be known in its true nature until we have obtained a knowledge of God. We must therefore start from the idea of God and proceed to derive all reality from that idea in an order corresponding to the true nature of things ; and therefore the object of Spinoza's *Ethics* is to give a systematic statement of existence in its totality and in the true subordination of its parts.

The philosophy of Spinoza may be regarded as a consistent

development of that aspect of the Cartesian philosophy in which it is maintained that God is the one absolute Substance or Reality. Just as Descartes expressed in terms of philosophy the fundamental ideas which governed the thought of Luther, so it is not fanciful to say that the *Ethics* of Spinoza is the philosophical counterpart of the theology of Calvin, with its faith in the absolute sovereignty of God, and the absolute impotence of man or any finite being to escape from the predestinated order and connection of events instituted by the divine will. Spinoza therefore refuses to accept any of the compromises by which Descartes sought to preserve the independence and freedom of man. There is for him no " substance " but God ; for no being but God can be defined as " absolutely independent " or self-complete. There is no " substantiality " whatever in any finite thing, considered in itself, and therefore we must discard the illogical conception that finite things are substances relatively to one another, but not substances relatively to God. " Substance," says Spinoza, " is that which exists in itself and is conceived by itself," and that which does not answer to this definition has no reality of its own whatever. This one Substance is the necessary presupposition of all finite modes of being ; and as itself absolutely permanent or unchangeable, it consists of unchangeable or permanent attributes. Of these attributes—" that which the intellect perceives of Substance as if constituting its essence " (Def. V.)—two are known to us, namely, Extension and Thought ; and Spinoza agrees with Descartes in maintaining that they are mutually exclusive of each other, both in reality and in our thought of them. They are mutually exclusive in reality, because each is infinite or complete in itself ; for nothing can be added to the totality of extension or to the totality of thought ; and they are mutually exclusive in conception, for the addition of thought adds nothing to the conception of extension, or the addition of extension to the conception of thought. Now, a Being that contains in itself all the reality implied in thought and all the reality implied in extension must be more real than one which contains only the reality of thought or the reality of extension. But Substance is that which contains in itself all reality, and therefore it is at once infinite in thought and infinite in extension. Spinoza, however, is not content to define Substance as that which at once involves the totality of thought and the totality of extension, but goes on to maintain that this one Substance, since it is absolutely real, must possess an infinite *number* of attributes. In this last step he has unwittingly introduced a principle that cannot be reconciled with the rest of his system. The attributes of extension and thought fall within the range of human experience, and therefore in ascribing them to the one Substance, Spinoza does not transcend the limits of verifiable experience; but, when he contends that the one substance must contain an infinite number of attributes, he has on his own admission transcended the limits of all possible knowledge, and based his conclusion upon an *a priori* conception that for us has no definite content. Only in this doctrine does Spinoza give countenance to the point of view of Mysticism, which is widely different from the Pantheism on which the rest of his doctrine is based.

It will help to make clearer Spinoza's conception of God, whom he defines as " Being absolutely infinite or substance consisting of an infinity of attributes, each one of which expresses eternal and infinite essence " (Def. VI.), if we consider his criticism of the followers of Descartes, who like their master conceived of God as a purely thinking being, and therefore separated him from the extended world, to which he was conceived to be related only as an external Creator and Preserver. In support of this view, they argued that whatever is extended is finite, and therefore that God as infinite cannot be extended. The assumption here is, says Spinoza, that extended being is made up of finite parts; which is as absurd as to say that a line is made up of a number of points, a surface of a number of lines, and a solid of a number of surfaces. It is no doubt true that imagination so presents extended being; but the moment we attempt to think it, we perceive that it is one infinite and indivisible. Hence there is no valid reason for denying that extension is an attribute of God. No doubt the world is continually assuming new forms, but these in no way affect the absolute persistence of extended being. Nor can it be admitted that the world came into being at a particular time by the creative act of God. That doctrine rests upon an opposition between the intellect and the will of God, and the consequent dualism of God and the world. It is supposed that God, in human fashion, first had in his mind an idea or plan of the world, and subsequently willed it into existence. In support of this view, it is said that the world cannot be a complete manifestation of the power of God, which as infinite is inexhaustible, and therefore we must suppose that in creating the world God had in his mind an idea of that which he did not create. To this argument Spinoza answers that to suppose God to possess infinite power without being able to exercise it for fear of its exhaustion is an absurdity, based upon the assumption that God may think what he does not will. In an infinite being there can be no opposition between the possible and the actual. This is virtually admitted by the Cartesians when they declare that God has foreordained all things from all eternity; for what is this but to say that God is absolutely unchangeable and that all things follow necessarily from the infinite perfection of his nature?

Spinoza therefore concludes that the world cannot be separated from God, but is in fact a complete expression of his absolute nature. No doubt it is not the only expression of that nature, since in mind and in the other attributes of God his essence is also expressed; but it is an absolutely complete expression of it. Hence Spinoza uses the terms God, Substance, and Nature interchangeably. When he speaks of God he is thinking mainly of the absolute unity of all existence; when he calls God Substance, he is emphasizing the eternal and unchangeable character of God; and when he employs the word Nature, his thought is directed to the manifestation of God in the visible and the spiritual world.

The infinity of God, then, is implied both in the world of nature and the world of mind. But the one is manifested in the form of motion and rest, while the other is manifested in what Spinoza calls the "absolutely infinite intellect." In contrast to Descartes, who attributed the motion of bodies to the external action of God upon them, Spinoza holds that bodies are not by nature inert masses, but exist only in virtue of the activity which they possess as modes of the attribute of extension. The world must therefore be conceived as in eternal motion, and as this motion includes that of all the bodies constituting the world, it is "infinite." And as motion and rest presuppose extended being, of which they are modes, Spinoza calls them "infinite modes." The world is thus not only eternal and unchangeable in its extension, but in all its changes in the way of motion and rest no increase or diminution of its activity as a whole can arise; indeed to suppose any such increase or diminution is incompatible with the infinite and eternal nature of God as expressed in the visible universe.

In his conception of "absolutely infinite intellect"

Spinoza betrays the influence of that mystical tendency to which reference has already been made. "Intellect" is mind making an attribute of God its object; and as there is an infinite number of attributes, we must suppose that "absolutely infinite intellect" is that which has as its object this infinite number of attributes. It is true that the only attributes which are the object of intellect as known to us are extension and thought, but, as Spinoza looks upon these as only two out of the infinite number of attributes in which God expresses himself, we must suppose that in its totality intellect has all these attributes as its object. Thus in a curious way Spinoza is led to maintain that there is an infinity of minds corresponding to the infinity of objects which they think. The thought of God is one, but it is fully expressed in the absolute totality of ideas which are present in the infinity of minds constituting the "absolutely infinite intellect." Yet this intellect is only a "mode," because it is not identical with the complete thought of God, but is only a form in which that thought is expressed. It is, however, an "infinite" mode, because it is not affected by the infinite mode of extension or any of the other modes. And, lastly, it is an "absolutely infinite" mode, because it comprehends the infinite totality of ideas.

When he goes on to consider the nature of man, Spinoza drops all reference to any attributes or modes except the attributes of extension and thought, and the modes corresponding to them. In considering the nature of man as at once body and soul, he refuses to admit with Descartes that animals, and man on his animal side, are mere automata, maintaining, in consistency with his general system, that nothing exists which is not at once extended and thinking (II. 13, Schol.). It is true that things differ very much in the character of their ideas, but the difference is one of

THE PHILOSOPHY OF SPINOZA

degree, not of kind, and exactly corresponds to the greater or less complexity of the body. This is the first suggestion of a doctrine afterwards elaborated in a modified form by Leibnitz. It is not further developed by Spinoza, because, as he tells us, his object in the *Ethics* was not to give a complete system, but only to consider the nature of man, so far as that was necessary for a comprehension of the conditions of his higher life.

Man, as conceived by Spinoza, cannot be said to be *composed* of body and mind; for, at bottom, mind is simply in idea that which body is as extended. The series of affections constituting the human body are mirrored or represented in the series of ideas constituting the human mind; and there never is an idea that has not its counterpart in the body. There is, however, this difference between mind and body: that the former is not only an idea of a bodily affection, but involves an idea of that idea; in other words, there is in man not only consciousness but self-consciousness. It must not be supposed, however, that there is any "substance" of mind, as distinguished from the series of ideas and the consciousness of these; the human mind is nothing but the series of ideas itself, or those ideas as abstracted from their particular content.

The ideas, then, which constitute the first form of human knowledge follow one another in the same inevitable way as the series of bodily affections of which they are the mental counterpart. But the human mind is capable of a higher kind of knowledge. In its first form knowledge is imperfect both in the ideas themselves and in the order in which they arise. In themselves they are only a partial representation of an affection of the body, itself the result of a partial relation to other things, and they are confused and obscure; and as in their order they correspond merely to the successive changes in the body, not to the real connection of things, they follow one another by perfectly arbitrary association. Thus Spinoza, while he agrees with the empirical psychologists in holding that every idea has its correspondent bodily counterpart, differs from them fundamentally in denying that sensible perception is the criterion of reality, and that succession and simultaneity are the only bonds of connection between ideas. Hence he goes on to explain how an advance is made from *experientia vaga*, the first form of knowledge, to a truer view of things.

The first step out of the partial and confused view of the world is taken when the mind penetrates to the universal relations which are implied in immediate experience, and is thus enabled to see that a deeper order and connection of things underlies and is presupposed in the merely external order of association by succession and simultaneity. In the first stage of knowledge, for example, we observe that water extinguishes and oil nourishes flame, and we are satisfied with knowing this mere fact; in the second stage we seek to discover the cause or reason of the fact. When the cause or reason is discovered, the knowledge thus obtained is common to all men, and hence Spinoza tells us that it consists of " common notions or adequate ideas of the properties of things." These " common notions " are the laws of motion and the laws of mind. They must not be confused with either abstract or transcendent ideas, which are produced, not by reason, but by imagination. The product of imagination is an abstract or partial image, and as the mind can only have a limited number of distinct images, anything beyond this is blurred and confused. We can easily picture an octagon, but not a chiliagon. Transcendent ideas, again, are even more abstract and inadequate. Nothing can be less fitted to give us a true knowledge of things than such ideas as " being," " thing," " somewhat," since they are devoid of all determinate content. Quite different are the "common notions" of reason, which may be called "universal individuals," since they constitute real elements or relations and are identical for all men. They are the foundations of reason, and from them all our adequate ideas are derived. Through them we learn that nature and mind are determined by necessary and inviolable laws. At the first stage of knowledge the most incongruous elements may be associated; we can imagine trees walking, men changed into stone, and an infinite number of other impossible things. For the imagination is abstract, in the sense that it abstracts from, or does not discern the relations of things. Rational knowledge, on the other hand, frees us from all such faith in the impossible by "thinking things together" or in their necessary relations. Spinoza applies this principle to the conscious life as well as to external nature. When we are yet at the first stage of knowledge, we imagine, for example, that there is a faculty of will which originates our actions independently of law; at the stage of reason, we see that this supposition is due merely to our ignorance of the causes from which our actions proceed, and vanishes with the discovery that these causes are as certain and invariable in their action as the laws which govern the fall of a stone or the revolutions of the planets.

Even with the ascent to rational knowledge, however, the highest stage has not been reached. No doubt all things are under the dominion of inviolable law, but, in order to comprehend reality in its true nature we must contemplate all things from the point of view of the absolute unity and perfection of God. In this highest stage of knowledge the material world is seen to be the form in which the infinite extension of God is displayed, and the human mind to be a mode of the infinite thought of God.

From the "intuitive" point of view we see that all things involve God, and that God is present in all things; and only when we have risen to this serene height of contemplation, in which all merely personal desires have vanished away, do we attain to that blessedness which is the true aim of philosophy.

It is natural to object to this doctrine that it seems to make the "blessed life" consist in a purely intellectual contemplation of existence. This objection, however, overlooks the fact that Spinoza maintains that the active life undergoes a development corresponding to that of the intellectual life. As the first stage of knowledge is *experientia vaga*, so the first stage of activity is passion or feeling. All things exhibit the two aspects of motion and idea. The former aspect implies that in all things the activity of the one Substance assumes a particular form. Not only men, but animals, plants, and even organic things " by their very nature strive to continue in existence." This inherent activity, however, is checked or destroyed by the counteractivity of other things, and hence there is no mode of being in which pure activity is manifested, but only activity limited and counterbalanced by contrary activity. This general conception of all things as essentially active Spinoza proceeds to apply to man. Outwardly the activity of man manifests itself in the movements of his bodily organs; inwardly, in the passions or emotions which are their counterpart. And just as the body is subjected to a thousand influences from without, so the mind as simply the idea of the body is similarly limited. Nevertheless, the effort to continue in existence is not destroyed, but manifests itself on the conscious side as appetite, desire or will. Consciousness does not originate anything, but merely reveals the existence of the effort to continue in existence. When this effort is in process of realization, there is a

THE PHILOSOPHY OF SPINOZA 181

feeling of pleasure; when its realization is checked, there is a feeling of pain; and the degree of pleasure or pain is proportionate to the degree of realization or limitation.

The effort to realize his own being must in man take an inadequate form so long as the true nature of things is not understood. In passion man is acted upon by something external to himself, which presents itself to him as pleasurable, and with which he identifies his good. Coming from without, that which he regards as his " good " is, in this case, variable and inconstant, changing with the individual temperament, with accidental relations to outward things, and with nearness or remoteness in time and place. At this stage there is no universal good, but, on the contrary, a conflict of passions and a continual struggle between opposite ideas of the " good." Moreover, as external goods are limited, their appropriation by one excludes others from their possession, and hence arise envy, jealousy, anger, hatred and other disturbing passions; so that to live the life of passion is to be " like a wave of the sea, driven to and fro, and tossed by contrary winds."

Man, however, has the power of liberating himself from this bondage to passion, and indeed the natural effort to realize his own being of itself tends towards such liberation. The first step out of bondage is taken when reason learns the meaning of passion. Man must seek his own good, but he can only find it when he sees wherein it really consists. The good of the individual is inseparable from the good of others, and therefore the foundation of society consists in the contract by which men agree to submit to reason as the only means of realizing their own good. In a life which is devoted to universal ends passion is annihilated, and with it the unrest that necessarily accompanies the consciousness of energy unrealized. The objects which the reason declares to be good are eternal, *i.e.* they are universal and inviolable laws. The life of reason is not the passionless tranquillity of self-negation: it contains all the energy of passion, no longer misdirected, but devoted to the realization of universal ends. The rational life is not one of self-mortification. Including all that ministers to well-being, it lifts a man above mere sentimental pity for the sufferings of others, above all fear of death, and above all ambition that springs from the mere desire for the pleasure of approbation. Thus while the result is peace, it is a peace that comes from self-affirmation, not from self-negation. The rational man does not waste his energy in remorse, but learns to avoid the causes which lead to remorse by a better comprehension of the laws of the universe. His repentance is no vain regret over the inevitable consequences of his own action, but consists in devotion to universal ends. Self-sacrifice in any form is, for Spinoza, a weakness, due to imperfect liberation from the power of the passions.

Though the life of reason frees man from the tyranny of passion, it is not the highest stage of morality. The perfection of man consists in the " intellectual love of God " (V. 33). He who reaches the highest stage of knowledge—that in which he contemplates all things from the ultimate point of view, and in all his actions is determined by it; he who, as we may say, occupies the religious point of view—is liberated absolutely from the power of passion, and even rises above the stage of reason to that intellectual love of God in which emotion is perfectly rationalized. What precisely is meant by this " intellectual love of God " ?

In the last section of the *Ethics* Spinoza begins by reminding us that memory and imagination imply the existence of the body, since the ideas which form their content are the mental correlate of certain bodily affections; therefore, with the dissolution of the body, memory and imagination become impossible (V. 21). "Nevertheless," proceeds Spinoza, "in God there necessarily exists an idea which expresses the essence of this or that human body under the form of eternity" (V. 22). In other words, any given human body must, from the highest point of view, be regarded as but a transient form which arises and disappears in the unbeginning and unending process of nature. When, therefore, any individual human body is dissolved, mind, as the intellectual counterpart of the body, must also be destroyed. As Spinoza himself puts it, " we cannot ascribe duration to the human mind except while the body exists "; in other words, the succession of ideas which constitutes the conscious life of the individual man endures only as long as the succession of affections which constitute the existence of the body. Spinoza, therefore, as I understand him, denies personal immortality. No doubt, he adds that "something pertaining to the essence of the mind will necessarily be eternal" (V. 23), but this "something" can only be the eternal and unchangeable nature of mind, *i.e.* the intellectual activity which constitutes the essence of mind. This cannot be destroyed, because its destruction would mean that God himself would cease to exist. And as the intellectual activity of God has no existence except in some finite mind, Spinoza must mean that, while the individual mind perishes with the individual body, conscious life is eternal. Now, when man succeeds in freeing himself from the illusion of imagination, he is able to view his own mind as a transient phase in the eternal process of the cosmos, and thus to contemplate his own being as objectively and dispassionately as the being of others (V. 25). Entirely freed from the influence of passion, he has reached the consummation of that striving after completeness which constitutes his nature, and therefore he experiences complete satisfaction (V. 27). This is what Spinoza calls the "intellectual love of God." It is "intellectual" because it presupposes that comprehensive view of the universe which sees "our noisy years as moments in the eternal silence," and it is an intellectual "love" because it involves the perfect transcendence of the individual self. Even death itself from this comprehensive point of view is not an evil, for the "intellectual love of God" destroys selfish desire by showing that death is but an incident in the eternal process of nature (V. 38). Thus disappears the false idea that blessedness is the reward of virtue. The only reward of virtue is virtue itself. He who loves God has no desire that God should love him in return, for in love to God consists his perfect satisfaction. "If the way to this life of blessedness," concludes Spinoza, "is hard and steep, it yet is not impossible of attainment. Hard it must be, or it would not be followed by so few; but all that is of great value is as difficult as it is rare" (V. 32).

In the philosophy of Spinoza emphasis is laid upon the absolute necessity of the relation between the Absolute and the finite modes of reality, in which it is manifested and from which it is inseparable. For Descartes God is complete in himself in entire independence of the world, and therefore he is unable to explain consistently how a Being already complete in himself can create a world distinct from himself without adding to his completeness. Spinoza does not fall into this inconsistency; for, holding that the world never began to be but is eternal, and affirming that its changes are absolutely determined by the unchangeable nature of God, he maintains that whatever exists is necessary from the very nature of the Absolute, and therefore that nothing has any separate and independent being. In thus referring all modes of existence to a single principle, and denying that any of these modes can exist in independence of it, Spinoza has undoubtedly made an advance that can never be rescinded. That there is but one ultimate principle, a principle inseparable from the universe, is the presupposition of all knowledge, all morality, and all religion. If this is denied and it is supposed that there may be a plurality of universes, we are landed in a phenomenalism from which there is no possible escape. For, supposing it to be true that there are various universes, it directly follows that none of these can have any relation to the others, and must therefore have an entirely different nature. What underlies that idea therefore is, that there are intelligences which differ from one another so absolutely, that whatever is affirmed by the one can have no meaning for the other ; and such an opposition necessarily leads to the destruction of all valid judgments. Spinoza, then, is right in maintaining that there can be but one absolute principle, and that this principle is not separated from any mode of existence, but is manifested in it. The real question is not whether " all is One," but whether Spinoza has succeeded in expressing the true nature of the One.

It is obvious that the success of Spinoza's philosophy depends upon his ability to show that nature and mind cannot be absolutely opposed to each other, since, if they were so opposed, they could not possibly be an expression of an absolute Unity. But Spinoza does not question the opposition of extension and thought which he inherited from Descartes, but on the contrary he contends that that which is extended has nothing in common with that which thinks. For while he goes on to say that nature and mind are each a complete expression of the Absolute, yet this mere affirmation does not remove the fundamental difficulty that two abstract opposites cannot possibly be united. The doctrine of Spinoza therefore leads to an insoluble contradiction. If the Absolute is completely manifested in nature, there can be no reason for declaring that it is also completely manifested in mind. Here, in fact, Spinoza is open to the same objection as applied to the Cartesian doctrine of a God who is complete in himself apart from the world and no more than complete after the creation of the world. Spinoza is no doubt right in holding that God is manifested in nature as well as in mind, but, still retaining the abstract opposition of nature and mind, he is forced to conceive of God simply as the Unity in which mind and matter are combined. But such a Unity can only be conceived as that which somehow, we know not how, combines irreconcilable opposites; it is a Unity not really manifested in the opposites, but one that is beyond the opposites; in other words, it is a Unity that does not reconcile differences but merely evades their reconciliation. Spinoza seems himself to have had an uneasy feeling that all was not well with his idea of the Absolute, when he suggests that the abstract opposition of nature and mind does not exist for the Absolute but only for us. But this only leads to a new difficulty; for he thus violates his fundamental principle that what intelligence must think necessarily exists. For, if nature and mind are for our intelligence irreconcilable opposites, their reconciliation in the Absolute must mean that from the ultimate point of view they are not irreconcilable opposites. Thus our human intelligence must be in irreconcilable antagonism with itself, now affirming an absolute opposition of nature and mind, and again denying that opposition. But when contradiction is introduced into the intelligence itself, our latter state is worse than the first. The philosophy of Spinoza thus leads to the insoluble dilemma : if nature and mind are absolute opposites, they cannot be united in the Absolute ; if they are united in the Absolute, they cannot be absolute opposites. The only possible escape from these alternative contradictions lies in the demonstration that nature and mind are not complete in themselves apart from each other, but mutually imply each other; in other words, that the distinction between them is not absolute but relative.

In his denial of a fundamental opposition in God between intellect and will, Spinoza was undoubtedly on the right track. To conceive of the will of God, after the manner of the Cartesians, as independent of his intellect, and therefore as an arbitrary exercise of power, is a doctrine that strikes at the roots of any rational conception of the universe. But Spinoza does not mean merely that intellect and will are inseparable, but that in the Absolute their distinction is meaningless. To this conclusion he was led by his antipathy to anything like anthropomorphism. From the ordinary point of view, he argues, in which an idea is conceived to precede its realization, intellect and will are in us separated, while in God there can be no such separation, because in him that which must be is. Now, Spinoza is no doubt right in denying that intellect and will can be separated; but it does not by any means follow that they cannot be distinguished. When their distinction is denied, the activity of God can only be conceived of as a blind necessity. In truth the denial of the distinction of intellect and will must lead to the abolition of self-conscious intelligence. Hence in this denial we have another instance of Spinoza's tendency to abolish all distinctions in favour of an abstract unity, instead of showing that all distinctions are ultimately combined in the Absolute without being abolished.

Since all distinctions are absorbed in the Absolute, Spinoza consistently maintains that the teleological view of the world is a survival of anthropomorphism. Now, one may admit that the popular conception of teleology, which is based upon the idea of an external adaptation of means to ends, and especially an adaptation that is intended to subserve the particular ends of man, is an untenable doctrine, without admitting that all teleology must be discarded. The whole question is whether the universe is a manifestation of reason or exhibits nothing but the blind play of mechanical forces. Spinoza everywhere insists, and rightly insists, upon the inviolability of law; but he seems to assume that this inviolability is incompatible with any divine purpose which expresses itself in and through it. But it may fairly be contended that if the universe is the expression of a single Unity, and if that unity is manifested in mind as well as in nature, either there is an irreconcilable dualism of mind and nature, or nature must involve mind, and therefore must be at bottom rational. We must therefore, I think, regard Spinoza's denial of teleology as but the inverse aspect of his separation of mind and nature. If we are really earnest in contending that the universe is intelligible, we must also admit that it is an organic or rational whole, and this is the same as saying that it is not only a mechanical but a teleological system.

In his endeavour to give an explanation of existence that would harmonize with the assumed opposition of matter and mind, and yet be consistent with the reduction of all forms of existence to the unity of a single principle, Spinoza was led to maintain (1) that finite things have no individual reality, but are merely modes in which the Absolute is manifested, (2) that in God there is no self-consciousness, (3) that as a consequence there is in the universe no manifestation of intelligent purpose, but all things follow by inevitable necessity from the eternal nature of the universe, (4) that the survival of personal consciousness is impossible because of the indissoluble relation of soul and body. All of these propositions seemed to Leibnitz highly questionable, and we may regard his philosophy as an attempt to defend the individuality of finite beings, the self-consciousness of God, the providence of God as displayed in nature and in human life, and personal immortality. It was perfectly clear to him, however, that none of these theses could be established on the basis of the dualism of Descartes. With the Cartesian defence of human personality and the conception of nature as a system of inviolable law, Leibnitz had the deepest sympathy ; but he was just as clear that no synthesis of individual personality with the self-conscious intelligence of God, and no reconciliation of mechanism and teleology, was possible on Cartesian principles. There must, therefore, it seemed to him be a mode of conceiving the relation of finite and infinite, of matter and mind, of the world and God, that would avoid at once the abstract individualism of Descartes and the equally abstract universalism of Spinoza. The principle which he finally fixed upon as supplying this eirenicon was the conception of the Monad, which he believed to unite in itself the seeming opposites of individuality and universality.

LECTURE SIXTH.

LEIBNITZ, LOCKE AND THE ENGLISH DEISTS.

In attempting to explain the nature of things, Leibnitz begins by pointing out the defect in the Cartesian conception of body as pure extension. The mere presence of a body in a certain place does not explain how it comes about that every body offers resistance, that it is impenetrable by any other body, and possesses inertia, in virtue of which it can only be set in motion or brought to rest by the expenditure of a definite amount of force. If the essence of body consisted in mere extension, when a body A encountered another body B, which was at rest, both bodies would move on together at the same rate of velocity as that of A previous to the encounter. Extension or presence in space is, therefore, not the fundamental nature of body, but merely the result of the "original force" with which it is endowed. What is properly meant by the substantiality or reality of a thing is the active force that it possesses. And this active force must belong to it as a simple or individual being, or what Leibnitz calls a "monad," because a mere aggregate is not a true unity, but only an *ens rationis*. Now this active force, which constitutes the real individuality of things, must be of the same fundamental nature as that which we experience in ourselves as mind or soul. Hence we must regard the world as consisting of spiritual beings, each of which is a real unity and possesses something of the nature of consciousness. As these monads are the only true beings, and constitute the ultimate elements of all things, they cannot be derived from anything else or resolved into anything else; but can only originate by creation and be destroyed by annihilation. Since matter is divisible to infinity, and each of its parts therefore implies as many monads as the real beings presupposed in them, the number of monads must be infinite. Moreover, no two monads can be absolutely identical, because that which is indistinguishable from something else is necessarily identical with it. As perceptive beings each monad is involved in perpetual change from one state to another, and this change must be purely internal, or self-originated. All the changes through which monads pass must be already implicit in them from the first.

The perceptions of monads, internal as they are, are a representation of all that is: they are a "living mirror" of the universe, so that the eye to which all that is present in them was transparent could read in each the whole order and course of the world. Each monad, however, differs from every other according to the clearness and distinctness with which it mirrors the whole. Hence there are infinite degrees in the perceptions of monads. For perceptions are not always so clear and distinct that they rise into consciousness, and therefore we must distinguish between "perceptions" or unconscious mental states and "apperceptions," *i.e.* those that involve consciousness. When we hear the confused noise of the sea, we are not conscious of the separate tones of which it is composed. The degree of perfection of a monad is, therefore, determined by the distinctness with which it represents the universe.

As each monad is absolutely excluded from all external influences, the question arises, how it comes about that monads nevertheless have a knowledge of one another, and that the knowledge of one is in harmony with that of the other. Leibnitz cannot admit any real influence between monads, and therefore he falls back upon the idea that the harmony of all monads with one another has been predetermined by the divine will. That harmony is not immediately produced by God, but results from the original nature with which they have been endowed. The independent development of each monad thus results in a harmony of their ideas with one another.

But, though they are harmonious, the monads differ in the degree of their mental life; and this again is determined by the degree of force which each possesses. For the degree of force is in each limited, and upon this limitation depends the clearness and distinctness of its representations. Leibnitz explains the differences in monads on the principle that God has imparted to each that measure of force which is compatible with the perfection of the whole. In this way he accounts for the existence of bodies, which are simply complexes of monads, combined by their common relation to the soul, the control and controlling monad. There are no bodies without soul, and when we speak as if there were, it is only from the inadequate point of view of sense. "Matter," in the sense of dead unliving masses, has no real existence. Nevertheless, in the explanation of particular phenomena we must not have recourse to the divine activity or to the action of spirit. " I am as corpuscular," he says, " as any one can be in the explanation of particular phenomena. All special phenomena can be explained mechanically, and in no other way can the causes of material things be understood." Leibnitz even criticizes Newton's theory of gravitation on the ground that it assumes the action of bodies on one another at a distance, which to him seems to involve a perpetual miracle. At the same time in order to explain the world as a whole we must, he maintains, interpret mechanism from the point of view of teleology.

According to Leibnitz, then, there is no contrast between organic and inorganic beings, but only between more or less perfect organisms. Wherever there is an aggregate of monads or a body there is a central monad or soul. The connection of soul and body is only that of their pre-established harmony. The changes always going on in the body have correspondent changes in the soul because of the universal harmony of the world.

There is an essential difference in the nature and fate of monads. All possess perception and impulse, but the lowest of all monads—the " naked monads," as Leibnitz calls them—live in a perpetual slumber, and never reach even the stage of sensation. This is the condition in which plants exist. But, when a monad has organs of sensation, it rises to the distinctness of sensation and even of memory. This is the condition of the animal. Lastly, when a soul reaches the stage of reason, as is the case with men and beings higher than men, the stage of spirit is attained. This constitutes a difference, not merely in degree, but in kind, between man and lower forms of being. Man alone of all earthly beings is capable of apprehending eternal and necessary truths, and he alone is capable of self-consciousness. Hence, man is not merely a mirror of the world, but he is capable of a close and intimate communion with God, in whose image he is made. Leibnitz also holds that death is at the most merely an interruption of self-consciousness; man never loses his physical or his personal identity, and therefore he differs from the animals, who at death sink back into the condition of slumber characteristic of the lowest monads.

The theory of knowledge of Leibnitz is in accordance

with his monadology. As there is no influence of external things on the subject, the empirical view represented by Locke is untenable. It is true that sensible perception precedes and is essential to thought, but sensible perception is itself but a lower stage of thought, the former being confused and the latter distinct. As in all its operations the subject is self-active and self-determined, it can receive nothing from without. No doubt there are no "innate ideas" in the sense objected to by Locke, but there are "innate ideas" in the sense that all ideas are developed from the indistinctness of perception to the distinctness of thought by the activity of the subject.

Corresponding to the distinction of perception and thought is Leibnitz' well-known opposition of contingent and necessary truths. The former deals with the individual, the latter with the universal. Being self-evident, the one class are unconditionally necessary, and their denial would be self-contradictory. At the same time, they are hypothetical in nature, since they merely express what is true under the supposition that there are real things corresponding to them. Hence the truths of reason only declare that which is possible, and to pass from possibility to actuality involves a complete knowledge of the whole world in all its relations, and indeed a knowledge of all possible worlds. Such knowledge is therefore the prerogative of God alone, while man can only learn the laws of the actual world from experience. Contingent truth therefore depends upon the representation of the external world in the individual mind, and for this reason our ideas assume the confused form of sensible impressions.

To the distinction of rational and empirical knowledge correspond respectively the principle of Identity or Contradiction and the principle of Sufficient or Determinant reason. The former affirms that nothing can contain in itself contradictory attributes, and therefore expresses the essential harmony of everything with itself. The latter affirms that nothing can exist without a sufficient reason for its existence, and therefore expresses the necessary harmony of a thing with all other things. The truths of reason are discovered by an analysis of our fundamental conceptions; the contingent truths or truths of fact we understand only by the discovery through experience of their ground. The fundamental truths of experience are the facts of inner experience of which we are immediately conscious; and from them we derive our knowledge of external things. The distinction between fact and fiction therefore depends, not upon the mere vivacity of our perceptions as compared with the faintness of our ideas of imagination, but in the connection and harmony of the former as compared with the latter. Still, systematic and harmonious as our ideas may be, they can never give us more than a high degree of probability.

The active nature of man is the other side of his knowledge. Our volitions are therefore the expression of our inner nature. The supposition that there is such a thing as liberty of indifference is due to the fact that our motives do not always come into clear consciousness; nevertheless, every act of will presupposes a motive, or the law of sufficient reason would be overthrown. Our volitions are just the inevitable development of our individual nature. Man is nevertheless free, for he is not acted upon by anything external to himself.

We have seen, then, that in the conception of the world as composed of an infinity of self-determined beings or monads, each of which reflects the whole, and the nature of which is determined by regard for the whole, Leibnitz looks for a reconciliation of the claims of individual beings with the demand for a rational universe. The ultimate proof, however, of these propositions is given in his arguments for the existence of God, and in his conception of the world as the best of all possible worlds. As to the former, he regards the ontological argument of Descartes as valid, under condition that the conception of God is not self-contradictory. He also regards the cosmological argument as confirming the ontological, inasmuch as it argues, and rightly argues, that, as no contingent being can be self-existent, no possible existence is conceivable except under presupposition of an absolutely necessary being. The argument, however, to which Leibnitz attaches greatest weight is that which starts from the idea of the pre-established harmony, and advances to the idea of the world as forming a teleological system. Events as known to us in experience are no doubt necessary, in the sense that they presuppose a sufficient ground for their existence; but it is impossible, by any regress from effect to cause, to show that the whole series of events is unconditionally necessary. Hence, in order to reach the ultimate ground for the existence of the world, we must go entirely beyond the world itself, and posit as its cause a Being distinct from the world. Now, the doctrine of the pre-established harmony is alone consistent with this argument; for, if things can actually influence one another, it is not necessary to go beyond the world in order to explain events. On the other hand, if nothing really acts on anything else, it is necessary to suppose that the harmony of the numberless beings composing the world is due to a Being of infinite intelligence. There can only be one such Being, for the connection of all things in the one cosmos proves that the cause is one; and this Being must not only possess infinite intelligence, but also infinite power and infinite goodness: the former to realize the harmony of all

PHILOSOPHY OF LEIBNITZ

things, and the latter to will it. Now, nothing is unconditionally necessary but the logical, metaphysical and mathematical truths, and therefore all facts of experience together with their laws are only conditionally necessary. Numberless worlds are possible, and that which actually exists must be that which is the most perfect possible. Thus the final cause of the world is the moral necessity by which God selected out of all possible worlds that which was most perfect as a whole.

If this is the best of all possible worlds, it may be asked how Leibnitz explains the presence in it of imperfection, misery and sin. His answer is, that the world, notwithstanding the evil it contains, is more perfect than any other conceivable world. Evil is inseparable from finitude, and besides it is the means of a higher good than could otherwise be attained. We may distinguish between metaphysical, physical and moral evil. The first is inseparable from the very nature of the finite, which is inconceivable without numberless degrees of perfection and therefore of imperfection. The second is necessary in beings that have a bodily organism, and this again is essential to the order and beauty of the whole. The third, again, Leibnitz explains as in its own nature want or privation, proceeding from confusion of thought and a concomitant perversity of motive. Moral evil, in fact, is inseparable from created beings, which are necessarily limited, and therefore it is not to be regarded as contrary to the will of God, but as a means of greater good. Leibnitz holds, however, that evil exists only in order to be transcended, or at least gradually lessened. This indeed is a logical necessity, for a being absolutely evil would be devoid of all disposition to good and would therefore be morally irresponsible.

While Leibnitz imagines that he has got rid of the pantheism of Spinoza by his doctrine of the monads as self-determinant beings, there is one aspect of his theory which seems to lead logically to pantheism. Finite beings owe their whole existence as active forces to the creative activity of God, and therefore it would seem that their whole nature is determined by the power of God as operating in them. Leibnitz himself repeatedly declares that the conservation of the world is a continual creation; and that the monads originate from one moment to another by continual fulgurations from God. It is difficult to distinguish this doctrine from the view of Spinoza that the finite has no being of its own, but is merely a manifestation of God in a particular mode. No doubt Leibnitz regards his doctrine as differing fundamentally from that of Spinoza, but it may be doubted whether he has really got rid of the pre-suppositions that led to the pantheism of Spinoza.

Religion is for Leibnitz essentially practical, but it is possible only under definite theoretical presuppositions. In its essence it consists of love to God, the only Being who is perfect in power, knowledge and goodness, and who is the source of all order, harmony and beauty. In love to God consists true piety and happiness. To love God, however, we must know him, and the more distinctly we realize his true nature, the purer and stronger will be our love to him. No one can truly know God without loving him, and no one can love him without doing his will. Religion is not the obligation to fulfil the divine will in order to obtain a reward, but the free conformity to it for its own sake; it consists in clearness of thought and purity of will.

The philosophy of Leibnitz may be said to move between two great poles: the idea that the universe is the expression of an absolutely perfect intelligence, and the idea that it involves the independent activity of its parts. In virtue of the former conception, he denies that the mechanical explanation of the world is more than the outer or superficial appearance of its true nature as a rational organism; in virtue of the latter conception, he affirms that nothing can be real except that which has an inalienable nature of its own. The former contention was directed mainly against Descartes, who maintained that the limitations of human knowledge preclude the human mind from comprehending the purpose of God in creation, and that we must therefore abandon the search for final causes. To detect the end God has in view in any given case, it would be necessary, he argues, to have a comprehensive view of the whole universe, and such completeness of knowledge is manifestly beyond our reach. "All God's ends," as Descartes expressly says, "are hidden in the inscrutable abyss of his wisdom." This denial of any knowledge of final causes is involved in the Cartesian doctrine, that, while we have a direct or intuitive knowledge of our own existence, our assurance of God's existence does not imply that we directly know God, but only that we must infer his existence as the only explanation of our own existence and of the idea of God that we find in our consciousness. Descartes, indeed, while he denies that we can truly be said to know God, yet assumes that we know that which he has produced. Though he refuses to admit that we have any knowledge of final causes, he still assumes that as the world is the expression of the creative activity of God, it is a rational system, all the parts of which conduce to the realization of the divine purposes, though we only know it as a mechanism. So far as Descartes, in thus limiting knowledge of the world to the necessary connection and interdependence of its parts, is protesting against the importation of final causes into the explanation of nature, and especially against the assumption that all things must be intended to minister to the satisfaction of human needs, he is the spokesman of the whole scientific movement of the modern world. But this is a very different thing from maintaining that it is impossible to establish the existence of rational purpose in the universe. One of the congenital defects in the Cartesian philosophy is its uncritical assumption of the categories by which meaning is given to our knowledge. Such conceptions as mechanical causation on the one hand, and final cause on the other hand, are regarded by Descartes as " innate ideas " of which no further account can be given. Hence it does not occur to him to ask whether these categories are not related as less and more developed forms of the same fundamental thought, namely, that the universe is rational. Now, it can hardly be said that Leibnitz instituted any inquiry into the subordination of categories to one another in a rational scheme of the universe, but he undoubtedly seeks to show that the category of mechanical causation is no complete and satisfactory determination of reality, and must be supplemented by the idea of final cause. Hence he refuses to admit that human knowledge is limited to an observation of the orderly movements of nature. To assign in explanation of a motion another motion of the same kind, no doubt suggests the interdependence of all movements upon one another, but no ultimate explanation can be reached by this method, since we are launched upon an endless series, and an endless series cannot be a whole. The conception of the movements of nature must therefore rest upon a deeper conception. This deeper conception must be sought in mind, and mind is meaningless apart from the idea of purpose or final cause. The whole nature of things must therefore be explained as forms in which mind is manifested. The laws of motion are just the manner in which at a lower stage of knowledge we represent the universe ; and when we advance to a higher stage we see that those laws are really the ways in which the reason of God operates.

Leibnitz has two ways in which he seeks to show that we must interpret the universe from a teleological point of view. In the first place, each monad by its very nature is ever striving towards the end of a complete evolution of that which is obscurely present in it from the first. This assumption seems to him essential to any ultimate explanation of things. For, unless we get back to a real unity, the world must seem to be suspended by a chain that has neither beginning nor end. It is no real explanation of motion to refer it to a prior motion, because until we reach the conception of that which is self-moved or self-determined, the mind is unable to rest. This is a profound truth, which all the great masters of speculation have discovered for themselves independently, but it is perverted by Leibnitz when he assumes that self-movement or self-determination implies absolute separation from all other self-moved or self-determined beings. This may be shown both from the point of view of knowledge and from the point of view of morality. (*a*) If the independent subject is in his knowledge limited to his own ideas, by what process does he learn that his ideas represent a reality beyond himself? Leibnitz tells us that knowledge is merely the process by which the individual comes to have a clear consciousness of what is obscurely present in his mind from the first, and in proof of his doctrine he refers to certain facts which in his opinion prove this contention. But the facts to which he refers do not prove that the individual extracts from his own consciousness all that we call knowledge. The question is not whether the human subject has subconscious states, modes of mind that do not rise above the threshold of consciousness; that is a contention that no one would now dispute; the real point is whether the subconscious states belong to the subject in its separate individuality. That in the process of knowledge the knowing subject passes from a state prior to consciousness to a state in which he is conscious, does indeed imply that he becomes that which he in potentiality is, but it does not imply that he derives his knowledge from the unconscious modifications that precede knowledge. The truth is that Leibnitz, like Descartes and Spinoza, and indeed all the thinkers of the period, assumes that the real must be unchangeably the same; so that any development which takes place must be merely the explicit consciousness of that which is implicit. But this conception of reality and development is obviously untenable. It rests upon the false notion that substantiality or identity means unchangeability; and therefore that the process of thought is purely analytic. The substantiality or identity of the knowing subject does not mean that it undergoes no real development; on the contrary, the only real identity is that which involves a transformation of the subject—a transformation, no doubt, which implies that its identity is nevertheless preserved; and the only real development is that in which elements come into being that never in any form existed previously, though no doubt these are elements that involve the continuity of the developing subject. The transition from blind or unconscious " perceptions " to sensible experience, and from sensible experience to rational knowledge, is not, as Leibnitz contends it is, merely a change in degree; it is a qualitative change, and is practically treated by him as such; and qualitative change is in this case development, or a transition to a new and higher conception of existence.

(*b*) A similar remark must be made in regard to the development of the moral consciousness. Leibnitz, assuming the independent individuality of the subject, holds that all the actions of man proceed from himself in the sense that no influence upon him of the world or of other selves is possible. Such a conception implies that no real process takes place in the transition from the primitive state of man to his more developed state. Man is from the first moral, though he is not aware of it, since morality is merely the distinct expression of that which is already present in an obscure form. Now, this doctrine suffers from the fundamental fallacy that morality is not a transformation of the natural man but merely an explicit recognition of what is there from the first. There is no real development, but only a change that brings to light what is already present. The negative movement of morality, by which the merely natural man is negated in view of the ideal, is entirely overlooked. The result is that any distinction between moral and immoral conduct is logically inconceivable. For, when Leibnitz attempts to explain why a man acts in one way rather than in another, he is forced to maintain that his action is the precise result of his original nature. Here, therefore, we see again the baleful effect of the assumption that absolutely self-centred individuality is the only explanation of the facts of experience. It is no doubt true that without real self-activity and self-determination morality is unmeaning, since in that case all action must be regarded as the resultant of mechanical forces; but it by no means follows that such self-centred existence involves absolute separation from all other existence. "The individual is the real," but certainly not the abstract individual: the real individual undergoes a real process of development in virtue of his power of negating the immediate self and determining himself by reference to the higher self that gradually reveals itself to him through the activity of his whole rational nature. It is not by isolation, but by inclusion, that true individuality is attained.

And this leads us to the complementary defect involved in the conception of the individual subject as "representing," but not really comprehending, the world. The fact which Leibnitz is seeking to explain by his doctrine of the "representative" character of the monads, is the order, law and system which everywhere prevail in the world. Nothing is what it is apart from all other forms of being, and the whole constitutes a unity so differentiated in all its parts, that nothing can exist that has not its perfect individuality and yet its perfect harmony with everything else. Thus the most infinitesimal movement in one part of the world involves a correspondent alteration in all other parts. But, though the totality of changes in the universe precisely corresponds, Leibnitz denies that there is any connection or influence of one being upon another. And no doubt there are certain facts that give plausibility to his contention. The scientific man does not admit that in molecular motion or chemical change there is any action of one thing upon another; what he affirms is that there is a redistribution of the several particles or atoms. Starting from this mechanical conception of nature, Leibnitz goes on to argue that it gives no real explanation of the world, and he finds in mind the only true cause of all motion and change. For mind, he contends, is a real and indivisible unity, and therefore we must conceive all forms of being as of the nature of mind. Now, we may admit that mind is the *prius* of all existence, without accepting the corollary with which Leibnitz burdens his thesis, that every mind is an indivisible unity in the sense that it has no real relations to anything else, whether natural or spiritual. In such a splendid isolation it is not mind or a unity or self-active, or indeed anything but a pure abstraction. A mind conceived in this way is not a unity, because there is no true unity that is not manifested in differences. Nor is it self-active, because self-activity can be displayed only in overcoming that which exhibits counter-activity. The whole conception of mind as involving isolated individuality is untenable. The only true individuality is that in which the subject is related to all other beings, and therefore comes to the knowledge of himself only in and through his comprehension of those beings. Self-consciousness is attained only by self-effacement in the first instance. This is the law of mind, whether we view it as knowing, as feeling, or as willing. Thus mind must not be conceived as an abstract self-centred individual, but as a spiritual organism, in which true individuality implies true universality. It is true that a mind cannot be regarded as deriving its nature from its relations to other modes of being; it is essentially self-active, and without self-activity it is not mind; but, on the other hand, its relation to other modes of being is necessary to its self-consciousness and self-determination. It is the very nature of mind to comprehend the world, and so to find in it nothing alien to itself; and yet in this identification its individuality is not surrendered but realized.

When Leibnitz tells us that each monad represents the world " from its own point of view," he is again the victim of abstraction. The conscious subject, he says, directly represents his own body, and therefore other bodies only indirectly. Now, it is no doubt true that at the stage of perception the world is only known from a partial and inadequate point of view. But the subject who is still at this stage cannot be aware that there is any higher point of view; and it is only because he is capable of determining the principles of reality that he is able to rise above the imperfection of the perceptive stage of knowledge. Any absolute limit must make it impossible for the subject to comprehend the true nature of things, and such an absolute limit seems to be implied in the "passive force" which Leibnitz ascribes to every monad. A "passive force" which is conceived as merely a name for incompleteness of knowledge, is a tenable doctrine; but a "passive force" which shuts out the subject from a comprehension of the true nature of the universe, is at bottom a purely sceptical doctrine.

Though he has not been able to construct a self-consistent doctrine, the philosophy of Leibnitz is full of suggestiveness. Everywhere he states the problem that demands solution, and he never loses faith in the rationality of the universe. Mind, as he rightly holds, is self-conscious and self-determinant, and the universe is no assemblage of inconsistent and mutually contradictory fragments, but a perfect unity. The process of knowledge may be regarded as directed to the end of the rational comprehension of a rational world, and the process of morality as the development in the individual of that reason which is the nature of things. Man must advance from the external determination of the world as co-existent and successive to the conception of it as displaying inviolable law, but the goal of all knowledge is the comprehension of all things as the manifestation of the divine self-consciousness. Hence Leibnitz assumes that man contains in himself, both as knowing and as willing, the principle which constitutes the essential nature of reality.

Leibnitz' second reason for maintaining that the mechanical view of the world is merely provisional and subordinate to the teleological view, is that all monads, independent as they are, harmonize with one another in their perceptions. For, though this concord is not externally produced, but follows from the inner nature of the monads themselves, yet the fact that the monads do harmonize requires explanation, and the only satisfactory explanation Leibnitz finds in the divine will. God has out of all possible worlds chosen the best. The fundamental defect of this mode of thought is that it draws an impossible distinction between possibility and actuality, and while affirming the rationality of the world, virtually denies it. So long as we limit our attention to some particular aspect of existence, it seems reasonable to say that many things are possible that can never be actual. It does not at first sight seem absurd to say that the sun may possibly not rise to-morrow; and indeed there is a sense in which the statement is perfectly correct: it is possible that the sun may not rise to-morrow, *provided that the whole system of things admits of its not rising.* Thus, we never affirm anything to be really possible, without tacitly presupposing that the universe is a connected and rational system. No doubt we may not be certain whether a given thing is possible or not, but our uncertainty does not rest upon any doubt of the fixity of conditions in the universe, but only upon our ignorance of its details. It is therefore essentially absurd to maintain that in a Being of infinite knowledge there can be any opposition between the possible and the actual. Such an idea arises from assuming that possibility, in the sense of ignorance of the particular structure of the universe, is identical with real possibility. Hence, when Leibnitz speaks of God as having before his mind the idea of all possible worlds, he is assuming that the world known to us is not completely rational; from which it plainly follows that we cannot refer it to an absolutely rational Being as its source. If therefore Leibnitz' argument from the pre-established harmony of all things is to have even a measure of validity, we must deny absolutely his contrast of possibility and actuality. Nothing is capable of coming into being that is not consistent with the unchangeable and rational system of the universe.

When we do away with the false distinction between the possible and the actual, it is obvious that there can be no distinction between the conditional necessity of natural law and the absolute necessity of the eternal truths of reason. Conditional necessity can only mean that which is in harmony with all the conditions of the universe, and there can be no absolute necessity which does not involve the same presupposition. What misleads Leibnitz is, as before, his confusion between the two sorts of possibility. Our ignorance of the details of the world does not show that, because we are uncertain which of one or more possibilities is true, therefore any one of them may take place ; were our knowledge complete, we should be perfectly certain that only one possibility can become actual, consistently with the subjection of the world to law. Hence there is no distinction, such as Leibnitz draws, between the conditional necessity of natural law and the absolute necessity of the truths of reason. The events in the world are as necessary as the truths of mathematics, and if we are disposed to distinguish the one from the other, it is only because the data of mathematical truth are simple and may be fully known to us, while the data upon which the laws of nature are based may be too complicated for us, at the stage of relative ignorance which we have not been able to transcend. Leibnitz' attempts to base the old distinction between what transcends reason and what contradicts reason on the distinction between conditional and absolute necessity, is therefore futile and inept. Nothing can transcend reason except that which is contradictory of it or is irrational. What gives plausibility to Leibnitz' contention is a confusion between the process of knowledge in us and the deliverances of reason. It is no doubt true that we cannot show in detail that whatever has taken place, or will take place, is in harmony with the unchangeable constitution of the universe; but this by no means proves that there are truths which transcend reason. The supposed transcendence of reason can at the most mean that we do not possess the data for coming to a definite conclusion in certain particular cases; but, unless we are to deny all rationality to the universe, we must grant that nothing can transcend reason itself except that which is contradictory of the rational system of the universe. When Leibnitz draws this futile distinction, one cannot but suspect that it was only in accommodation to the so-called "mysteries" of faith, which, taken literally, no doubt transcend reason, but only because they contradict it.

One of the main motives by which Leibnitz was actuated was the desire to preserve the independence and self-consciousness of God, in contrast to the reduction of the divine nature by Spinoza to an undifferentiated substantiality, in which all things follow by an unpurposive necessity. He therefore sought to show that God is the Creator of all things, and as such distinct from all other monads. But as he affirms the independence and self-activity of the created monads, and at the same time maintains the infinite perfection of God, it becomes difficult to determine the precise relation between God and other things. Leibnitz himself tells us, that God is not only the Creator of all things, but he is also their Preserver; in fact, Creation is not a single act, but a continuous act. Now, the sole nature of created beings consists in self-activity, and all the modes of this self-activity are pre-ordained by God. It would thus seem that, after all, the so-called self-activity of the monads is entirely due to the creative activity of God, and that if this were withdrawn they must cease to exist. Thus God would seem to be the only original substance, while all other modes of being are, as Leibnitz himself puts it, "fulgurations" of God. No doubt he says that the origination of monads is a free product of the divine will; but, even then, it is hard to see how he can escape from the determinism of Spinoza. The truth seems to be that Leibnitz here, as in the whole of his system, is "in a strait betwixt two": on the one hand, he is seeking to preserve the independence of God and other beings, and, on the other hand, to show that all proceeds from God. No real solution of this problem is possible, so long as it is assumed that the monads can be free and self-determined only if they are entirely separated from one another and from God, and that the self-consciousness of God involves his independent self-subsistence. Under these conditions the attempted solution of the problem in regard to the relation of the monads to one another and to God must be a compromise; for between things that are absolutely isolated no real relation can possibly subsist. If, therefore, the absoluteness of God and the self-activity of other beings are to be preserved, it must be denied that any being, whether God or man, can exist in isolation. The nature of God must involve his relation to the world, and the nature of finite beings their relation to one another and to God. This does not really imply the destruction of the self-activity of either God or his creatures, because true freedom consists not in separation but in union with other beings, and the consciousness of freedom is impossible except in so far as the particular life of each is transcended by the universality of reason. The difference between God and man cannot consist in the originative or creative power of the former and the dependence of the latter, but in the completeness with which God is related to all beings, and the slow and

PHILOSOPHY OF LEIBNITZ

halting steps by which this consummation is attained by man. The goal of all human endeavour is to attain the perfection of union involved in the idea of God, and what religion does is to give the assurance that already in ideal identification with God that goal is in a sense already attained. Lifting man above his weakness and divided life, it assures him that the universe as rational makes perpetual progress in the higher life a reality. The ideal is thus continually realizing itself, and must continually realize itself, not independently of human effort, but as inevitably as man must follow the guiding star of reason. In this sense the providence of God works always for good, and must prevail; but it would not so work or prevail were it not that in his deepest nature man can only will that which appears "under the form of good." Hence, we may say that man always is, and indeed must be, seeking after God. This is the motive-power that lies behind all human endeavour, and therefore, apart from the idea of God, life has no meaning or purpose. That men are not always aware of the goal towards which they are moving, often by what seem very devious paths, is true; but this only shows that man is never fully conscious of what manner of spirit he is. Herbert Spencer somewhere says that man must seek happiness, because otherwise we must suppose that he prefers misery. Put in this way, the doctrine is more than questionable; but, interpreted to mean that the end of all men's striving is the realization of the rational self, which is identical with God, it may be accepted. As Plato says, human life is the undying search for the good, and the good, as he also saw, is ultimately identical with God.

With the philosophy of Leibnitz one of the great movements of modern philosophy comes to an end; for his successor, Wolff, removes from the teaching of his master its large suggestiveness, and drops back into a mechanical system from which all the ideal elements have vanished away. The strength of Descartes, Spinoza and Leibnitz lay in their grasp of the unity of things, and in their persistent attempt to defend the rationality of the universe. The philosophy of Locke and his successors, on the other hand, insists upon the necessity of appealing to experience in support of any proposition regarding the nature of the world, of man or of God. Descartes had indeed claimed to begin at the beginning, but the very fact that he assumed the existence of "innate ideas"—ideas that, as Locke understood him to say, are not derived from experience, but belong to the human mind prior to all experience—shows that he had not really cleared his mind of all preconceptions. Locke is absolutely resolute in his determination to exclude all assumptions, even the assumption that we are capable of any knowledge whatever. "I thought," he tells us, "that the first step towards satisfying several inquiries that the mind of man was very apt to run into, was to take a view of our own understanding, examine our own powers, and see to what things they were adapted. Till that was done, I suspected we began at the wrong end, and in vain sought for satisfaction in a quiet and sure possession of truths that most concerned us, whilst we let loose our thoughts into the vast ocean of being, as if all that boundless extent were the natural and undoubted possession of our understanding, wherein nothing was exempt from its decisions, or escaped its comprehension. Thus men extending their inquiries beyond their capacities, and letting their thoughts wander into those depths where they can find no sure footing, it is no wonder that they raise questions and multiply disputes, which, never coming to any clear resolution, are proper only to continue and increase their doubts, and to confirm them at last in perfect

PHILOSOPHY OF LOCKE

scepticism. Whereas, were the capacities of our understandings well considered, the extent of our knowledge once discovered, and the horizon found which sets the bounds between the enlightened and the dark parts of things, between what is and what is not comprehensible by us, men would perhaps with less scruples acquiesce in the avowed ignorance of the one, and employ their thoughts and discourse with more advantage and satisfaction in the others (Essay I. i. 7). Locke is equally decided in his rejection of all religious preconceptions. While Descartes sought to preserve religion as a sacred enclosure sheltered from the rude assaults of reason, Locke tried to secure the same end by showing that there is nothing in scripture that is in any way incompatible with the demands of reason. The distinction between the two thinkers is characteristic; for, whereas, as a good catholic, the former identifies religion with the dogmas of the Church, the latter adopts the protestant principle that scripture contains the whole body of religious truths. And as we have seen that the cautious and tentative attitude of Descartes soon gave way to the bold speculations of Spinoza, so the guarded criticism of Locke finally results in the outspoken scepticism of Hume.

Discarding all "innate ideas," Locke finds that the individual mind is left facing the world; and the question of philosophy seems to be, to explain how the mind, which is at first absolutely empty, comes to be furnished with ideas, what certainty is possible, and what are the limits within which human knowledge is confined. Philosophy can only deal with ideas; for, whatever may be the nature of things, knowledge must come to us through the operations of our own minds, and it is possible that we may not be able to discover the true nature of reality. "Every one is actually conscious of having ideas in himself, and men's words and actions will satisfy him that they are in others." Truth and falsehood, however, are not in ideas themselves, but only in the judgments by which they are affirmed or denied of things. When we examine our own minds, we find that in it there are complex ideas of possible modes of things, which we regard as dependent on individual substances; of individual substances, as subsisting independently or by themselves; and of relations between substances. These are all compounded of "simple ideas." There are two ways in which we obtain ideas of real things; for either we come in contact with the external world through our senses, or we have a direct perception of the operations of our own minds. Thus the elements of knowledge are derived from the two sources of sensation and reflection; the nature of the world we learn through sensation, and the nature of the self through reflection. Knowledge is no original endowment, but a process by which man learns the nature of things, gradually and imperfectly, under the conditions of his experience.

Locke's treatment of the complex idea of "substance" is of special interest as a test of his derivation of all knowledge from experience. He virtually admits that the idea of substance cannot be presented in sense or imagination, for it is impossible to regard a mere aggregate of sensible qualities, or a mere aggregate of mental operations, as existing by themselves; we are forced by the constitution of our minds to attribute the aggregate in each case to a "substratum wherein they do subsist, and from whence they do result." Locke admits that the only meaning we can attach to the term "substance" is the negative one of "an uncertain supposition of we know not what." This must be regarded as a virtual admission that knowledge cannot be explained by the mere reference to ideas of sensation and reflection, or any combination of them.

PHILOSOPHY OF LOCKE

When he goes on to speak of the "substance" of mind, Locke naturally falls into still greater perplexity; for here he has to account not only for unity, but for a unity that is conscious of itself. As on his own showing there are breaks in consciousness, the difficulty arises to explain "personal identity," and he is forced to fall back on a distinction between the identity of the underlying substance of mind and the identity of the person.

When he goes on to treat of knowledge, Locke tells us that it does not consist in ideas themselves, but in our perception or "discernment of agreements or disagreements" in our ideas. Knowledge, therefore, is always concerned with the relation between a given idea and the idea of reality, and involves assurance of an agreement between them. The relation is one of four kinds: (1) two ideas may be judged to be unlike; (2) they may be in a necessary relation to each other, as when we judge that "two triangles upon equal bases between two parallels must be equal"; (3) one idea coexists with other ideas, or one always precedes or follows another; (4) one of our ideas corresponds to the idea of reality. In regard to the third of these relations—that dealing with the coexistence or succession of phenomena—Locke holds that the conditions on which they depend are so obscure, that he "suspects a science of nature to be impossible." In the case of mathematical judgments it is different, for here, though the conclusion is not based upon intuition, each step that leads to it is so based. "In every step," Locke tells us, "that reason makes in demonstrative knowledge, there is an intuitive knowledge of that agreement or disagreement it seeks with the next intermediate idea which it uses as proof." To the certainties of knowledge the actual perception of a thing as here and now is added. The distinction between such perceptions and mathematical as well as moral knowledge is, that the former are concerned only with this or that individual thing, whereas the object of the latter are abstract and universal propositions.

Besides individual sensible things, Locke holds that each man knows himself to be an individual conscious being, and is capable of knowing the individual existence of God. As to the former, " in every act of sensation, reasoning, or thinking, we are conscious of our own being, and, in this matter, come not short of the highest degree of certainty." The certainty, on the other hand, that God exists is not self-evident, but can only be reached by a process of demonstration. "Though the existence of God be the most obvious truth that reason discovers to us; and though its evidence be, if I mistake not, equal to mathematical certainty; yet to see it requires thought and attention, and the mind must apply itself to a regular deduction of it from some part of its intuitive knowledge." We know that we ourselves exist, and that we have not always existed. "If we know there is some real being," says Locke, "and that non-entity cannot produce any real being, it is an evident demonstration that from eternity there has been something, since what was not from eternity had a beginning, and what had a beginning must be produced by something else." The basis of the argument therefore is that, in the regress from effect to cause, we must ultimately reach a Being who is self-caused, or who, while he contains in himself all the perfections that exist or can exist, must be the cause of all that exists. As I am conscious of myself as mind, this Being must be "what we mean by mind." Locke, however, is by no means clear what "mind" means, when applied to the infinite Being. His perplexity no doubt partly arose from the fact that, in accordance with the principle of causality, as he understood it, there can be nothing in the nature of the effect that is not contained in the nature of the cause; and as there are two diverse forms of contingent being, viz. matter and mind, it would seem to follow that the infinite Being, who is their cause, must be "both material and cogitative." This conclusion Locke was not prepared to accept, mainly because it seemed incompatible with the idea of God as mind. And yet it seems obvious that, if the attribute of thought must belong to the cause inasmuch as it is found in the effect, the attribute of extension, as Spinoza consistently held, must also belong to it for the same reason. The only way of escape from this conclusion would be to reduce matter in some way to mind; and from this method of solution Locke was precluded by his opposition of sensation and reflection as two independent sources of knowledge. Hence he attempts no solution of the difficulty, though he admits that "mind" can hardly be predicated of God in the same sense as of man. "Though I call the thinking faculty in man 'mind,'" he says in a letter to Anthony Collins, "yet I cannot, because of this name, equal it in anything to that infinite and incomprehensible Being, which, for want of right and distinct ideas, is called Mind also, or the Eternal Mind." It can hardly be necessary to point out that this is but another of the contradictions that beset the philosophy of Locke; for, if mind as applied to God does not mean the same thing as mind in ourselves, what becomes of the argument that cause and effect must be identical in nature? Locke does not attempt to meet this difficulty, but contents himself with affirming that the Infinite Being, having supreme power, is able to create matter out of nothing by the bare exercise of his thought; a view which in itself makes a radical distinction between human and divine thought, since the former is not creative of matter. Thus, after affirming the essential identity of cause and effect, and indeed basing upon it his whole argument for the existence of God as an infinite intelligence, Locke goes on to speak of the cause as fundamentally different in nature from the effect, so far as the effect consists of material things. All that Locke can possibly derive from the existence of matter and mind, when these are assumed to be opposites, is a cause of a dual nature, and thus his assertion of the unity of God is destroyed. The truth is that his argument for the existence and attributes of God is plausible only because he overrides the main distinctions upon which his philosophy is based. In his explanation of knowledge, he holds that thought cannot possibly contribute anything to the constitution of the world of experience; that, on the contrary, any addition made to our ideas of things by the "workmanship of the mind" is incompatible with our knowledge of reality; and yet, when he goes on to explain our idea of infinity, eternity, substance, and cause, he virtually assumes that apart from these constitutive ideas no knowledge whatever is possible. In dealing with the idea of God, he therefore maintains that here we have an instance of a reality which is seen through demonstration to be eternally necessary; in other words, that in this case the mind is able to employ the idea of cause as constitutive of the nature of existence. The same thing is implied in his account of the attributes of God. How do we reach the idea of "infinite"? It is an idea, he says, that is obtained by the negation of finitude, as experienced in ourselves and other finite minds. We know from experience that we ourselves and other beings of like nature exist; that we have some knowledge and power; that we are capable of a certain degree of happiness; and, in seeking to understand the nature of God, we enlarge these to infinity. No doubt we do not in this way comprehend the inner essence of God ; but, when we look more closely, we find that we have no knowledge of the real essence of anything, not even of ourselves. Locke's idea of God, in short, is that he is a Being existing beyond the world, and indeed beyond knowledge, whose existence we infer from contingent things. How we can be entitled to assign existence to a Being, whose nature is admittedly for us merely the negation of all determinate reality ; or how the human mind, which is assumed to be limited to experience, can thus transcend its necessary limits ; these things Locke does not tell us. Rigid as he believed himself to be in excluding all ideas except those derived from experience, he was unable to give a plausible account of knowledge without assuming that thought is not only formal but constitutive ; and without the assumption of the categories of reality, substance, and cause, he could not have given even a plausible account of the world, the self and God. Locke has not succeeded any more than Descartes in freeing himself from all preconceptions. No one would now maintain the doctrine of "innate ideas" in the sense in which it is attacked by Locke. The notion that babies are capable of dealing with such abstractions as "being," or that savages are endowed with a primitive idea of God as an infinite, eternal and unchangeable spirit, is too absurd to need refutation, and indeed it seems to us incredible that anyone should ignore the palpable fact that all our ideas have come to us in a process which involves the labours of centuries. But when we have discarded the preconception that we have only to "look into our own minds" in order to discover certain ideas that are inseparable from human consciousness, it does not follow that the individual mind is a *tabula rasa* ; nor indeed that there is any individual mind, in the sense of an independent substance, that would be what it is were there nothing else in the universe but itself. That we are conscious of ourselves as distinct from all other selves is no doubt true ; but this self-consciousness involves the consciousness of a world of which we are only part, and without which we could not be. For Locke the rational constitution of the universe is unintelligible, because he assumes that the mind must passively reflect objects ; not seeing that there can be no objects except in so far as the mind comprehends the rational constitution of the universe, and that no such rational constitution can be known unless in it is expressed the same nature as the knowing subject finds in himself, when he makes a regress upon himself, and contemplates the forms in which his intelligence works. Locke's theory of knowledge could not possibly be satisfactory, because he was entirely oblivious of the tremendous assumptions he was making in positing the existence of separate minds, a world lying apart from them, and a God transcending both. Nor had he more than a passing glimpse of the perplexing problems connected with the ideas of quantity, substance, causality and other categories—problems that were only brought to light by Hume's persistent attempt to carry out the empiricism of Locke to its inevitable conclusion, with the result that all knowledge, morality and religion were dissolved in a universal scepticism. It is no doubt true that Hume does not do justice to certain higher elements in Locke, just as Spinoza ignores the truth in Descartes' conception of the reality of the individual mind ; but this is the inevitable penalty a writer must pay for the enunciation of a principle that he does not consistently carry out to its logical consequences. It is necessary that one aspect of the doctrine of a great thinker should be resolutely and fearlessly stated, if his successors are to recoil upon its other aspects ; and we may safely say that, but for the development of Locke's empiricism in Hume, we should not have had a Kant, with his new method of interpreting experience.

Just as Locke in his " Essay " makes assumptions which he does not attempt to justify, so in his theological writings he makes the plenary inspiration of scripture the foundation of his theology. It is strange to us to find a writer, whose main principle is that nothing can be admitted to be true that is not based upon the facts of experience, accepting scripture in child-like faith, without any effort at historical criticism, and with hardly a consciousness that it is a legitimate problem. To him reason and revelation are co-ordinate authorities, and it never seems to occur to him that they may be in conflict with each other. The case for scripture appeared to his mind to involve the clear-cut problem: either every word of the Bible is inspired, or it is an imposture. That this alternative was by no means exhaustive, and that scripture might be inspired in a very real sense without being infallible, never once struck him. Yet, uncritical in the modern sense as he was, Locke brought to bear upon scripture a method of investigation natural in one who in philosophy had discarded all traditional ideas: he read the New Testament without note or comment, discarding the labours of commentators and divines. The result was to convince him that the teaching of Jesus, when freed from the spurious theology of scholastic divines, was superior to all human wisdom. The substance of that teaching is that there are but two essential articles of faith: (1) Christ is the Messiah, (2) there is but one God. To be a Christian it is therefore not necessary to accept the Athanasian Creed, the thirty-nine Articles, or the Westminster Confession. " Nobody can add to the fundamental articles of faith, nor make any other necessary but what God hath made and declared to be so." But, though he reduces the creed to these two propositions, Locke is not prepared to say that honest doubt of even these is of itself sinful, and he admits that those who lived before Christ must not be held responsible for not believing what had not been presented to them. If it is asked what need there was of revelation, since the one supreme invisible God was discovered without its aid, Locke answers that an authoritative endorsation of religion and morality was necessary for the mass of mankind, who are incapable of following long chains of demonstration ; and that otherwise there would have been no sure and certain hope of resurrection, and no assurance of God's assistance in the dangers and temptations of the world.

Locke's view, then, is that Christianity was intended by its Divine Author to give new authority to the dictates of reason. He admits that it contains doctrines which men could not discover of themselves ; but he says that while he reverences these, he will make no attempt to fathom their mysterious depths. As for the discord of which they had been the occasion, for that he felt nothing but disgust. It thus turns out that after all Christianity contains two sets of essentially different doctrines : (1) those which can be, and indeed have been, discovered by reason independently of revelation ; and (2) those that cannot be so discovered, and indeed are incapable of being understood even after they have been revealed. Manifestly, any one who appreciated the real force of this distinction must seek to get beyond it by reducing the one to the other ; holding either (*a*) that all doctrines alike derive authority from revelation, or (*b*) that all are based upon reason. The latter alternative was chosen by the deists, who denied that there were any doctrines revealed in scripture that cannot be discovered and therefore understood by the human intellect in its normal exercise. This was the thesis formally maintained by Toland, who, not unfairly, claimed to be the legitimate follower of Locke.

In his *Christianity not Mysterious* (1690) Toland does away with the reservation of Locke, that there are doctrines revealed in scripture which are beyond human comprehension, maintaining that there is in the gospel no doctrine that can be called literally a " mystery." All that is meant in scripture by the term " mystery " is a truth which was unknown at any earlier time, or only obscurely apprehended, but is now completely revealed. There is therefore a perfect agreement between Christianity and the religion of reason. As Locke had maintained, by revelation we come to the knowledge of certain truths, but we believe them to be true, not because they are revealed, but because they are rational. Toland admitted that there are religious ideas that cannot be presented to the imagination, such as those of God and eternity, but it by no means follows that they cannot be grasped by thought— a suggestion, which may possibly have been borrowed from Spinoza, but one which in any case shows that Toland was not entirely deficient in speculative subtlety. A doctrine like this, which removed the veil that concealed even from Locke the fundamental discrepancy between " rational " Christianity and the popular creed, naturally gave offence to the champions of the latter. If there are no " mysteries " in Christianity, as Toland maintained, some explanation of the " mysteries " embodied in the creed of the Church must be found ; and the explanation that Toland gave, which would now be admitted to be sound in principle, was one that threatened to abolish all that was conceived to be distinctive of Christianity. That explanation was, that while the teaching of Jesus was perfectly simple and reasonable, it had been overlaid by accretions derived by theologians from Jewish and heathen mysteries and philosophical doctrines. Remove those additions, and we shall lay bare a Christianity entirely accordant with reason. No doubt it must be accepted by faith, but faith is not a blind and irrational acceptance of what is mysterious and incomprehensible, but must be based upon intelligence and knowledge; indeed, strictly speaking, nothing else can be an object of faith. Hence nothing should be believed except that which can be demonstrated. Knowledge, as Locke held, consists in the perception of the agreement or disagreement of our ideas, and it is impossible to tell whether our ideas agree or disagree unless each of them is perfectly clear and distinct. Applying this principle to our theological beliefs, we see at once that we can accept nothing that is "contrary to reason," for what is "contrary to reason" is self-contradictory. Nor can there be anything "above reason." We can no more believe what is incomprehensible than what is self-contradictory. "Could that person," Toland asks, "justly value himself upon his knowledge who, having infallible assurance that something called a Blictor had a being in nature, in the meantime knew not what this Blictor was?" So far all is clear; nothing can be admitted to be true that is self-contradictory or incomprehensible. But what is self-contradictory or incomprehensible? Is the existence of the soul, or of God, or of the Trinity, a doctrine that comes under the ban? Toland gives no clear answer, probably from dread of the consequences. He does indeed maintain that, while we know the "nominal" essence of a thing, we may not know its "real" essence. This, however, does not mean that the object is a "mystery" in the technical sense of the term; for, as Locke has shown, we have no knowledge of the "real" essence of anything. Toland would therefore deny that God or the soul, and apparently even the Trinity, are really mysterious. No more than his

THE ENGLISH DEISTS

master Locke does he see that the limitation of knowledge to the "nominal" essence of things, so far from abolishing all "mystery," introduces "mystery" into the simplest object of knowledge. It was impossible to establish the reasonableness of Christian doctrines by what was essentially a sceptical reduction of all knowledge to mere appearance.

Toland's advance on Locke consisted in his refusal to exempt from reason any of the doctrines contained in the New Testament. This principle, however, he did not consistently apply in criticism of the Creed of the Church, nor was he consistent in assuming, without proof, that the doctrines of Christianity were certified by miracles. Tindal, in his *Christianity as Old as the Creation*, is not open to the same charge of inconsistency. He will have no doctrines that cannot be established by reason. Nor does he even admit that a revelation was necessary, in order to anticipate truths that otherwise might not have been discovered for ages; on the contrary, he virtually makes revelation superfluous, by maintaining that natural religion is written upon the hearts of all men. The unassisted reason of man is quite able to discover the few and simple truths of genuine religion. These truths are in content identical with morality: for religion is simply morality viewed as an expression of the will of God. As God is infinitely wise, good, just and immutable, while human nature is fundamentally the same in all ages, it follows that the law which God lays down for men must be also immutable. God, as the Almighty Creator and Ruler of mankind, cannot be supposed to have selected a small and barbarous tribe as the sole recipient of his favour, or even to have granted special favours to mortals like ourselves. He must distribute his favours equally and impartially among men. Hence all arbitrary enactments are the inventions of priests. Whatever deviates from the law of nature is mere superstition, the source of which is to be found in the attempt to gain the good will of God by particular services and performances. There is but one all-sufficient principle, obedience to nature. " Whoever so regulates his natural appetites as will conduce most to the exercise of his reason, the health of his body, and the pleasures of his senses taken and considered together, may be certain he can never offend his Maker ; who, as he governs all things according to their natures, cannot but expect his rational creatures should act according to their natures."

As he rejects all doctrines that go beyond the light of nature, so Tindal declares that miracles prove nothing, because they may be adduced to prove anything. The only test of truth is therefore agreement with the teaching of reason. " It's an odd jumble," he says, " to prove the truth of a book by the truth of the doctrines it contains, and at the same time to conclude those doctrines to be true because contained in that book."

To show that the principles of religion are common to all men, Tindal was forced to eliminate all the ideas and practices which were peculiar to this or that people. We must, he argues, discard all the superstitions found in various religions, which are the inventions of priests, in order to reach the fundamental truths, which constitute the original unpolluted religion. This is what Christianity does ; for Jesus did not promulgate a new religion, but merely republished the original natural religion that had been overlaid with superstitious accretions. This indeed is the *rationale* of that allegorizing method, by the application of which theologians try to get rid of what is obviously irrational when understood literally. Among the things that are inconsistent with the law of nature are those ascetic practices which are incompatible with the nature of God, who can take no pleasure in the self-torture of his creatures. Nor can we even accept a number of the doctrines common to almost all Christian Churches ; such, *e.g.*, Tindal somewhat obscurely hints, as the doctrine of the Incarnation. Especially for the positive precepts contained in the Old Testament he expresses the greatest contempt, *e.g.* the practice of circumcision, which he says was borrowed from the Egyptians, and the whole theory of sacrifice. Even in the New Testament he finds erroneous statements, as when the speedy return of Christ is prophesied, a prophecy that has never been fulfilled. Dr. Clarke had insisted upon the clearness, immutability and universality of the law of nature, arguing that morality, like mathematics, is based upon the " eternal and necessary differences of things." To deny the golden rule is as unreasonable as to " affirm one number or quantity to be equal to another, and yet that other at the same time not equal to the first." Tindal asks why, if the law of nature is so clear and sufficient, there was any need for supplementary revelations, such as Clarke contended for.

The main contention of Tindal, that the immutability of God and of human nature proves that there can be but one unchangeable religion, seems to us hardly worthy of refutation, so familiar are we with the idea that religion passes through various stages of development, in accordance with the progressive evolution of ideas. But, when we turn our attention to the defenders of the faith contemporaneous with Tindal, we are at once struck by the fact that they accept his premises while trying to evade his conclusions. The answer they give is not drawn from the inevitable development of religious ideas, but from an assumption inconsistent with it—the assumption of a primitive religion, revealed to man and only lost by the Fall. The contradictory nature of this assumption, based as it is upon the myth of an original state of innocence—

which is exactly the reverse of the truth—Tindal had no difficulty in showing. What it really amounts to, he argued, is that man is accountable to God for not possessing a religious knowledge which he could not possibly have.

An advance is made beyond Tindal by Thomas Morgan, who is the first to make some attempt to apply historical criticism to the Christian sources. His theory is crude enough, but it indicates a desire to go beyond the abstractions current among previous deists. He still believes that false religion was due to the intrigues of the priests, but he makes an attempt on this basis to account for the superstitious accretions with which natural religion was overlaid. The primitive natural religion was in his view corrupted by a sort of fetishism, which, under the pernicious influence of the Egyptians, ascribed every event to the direct interposition of the divine power. The religion of the Jews consecrated brutal ferocity. Jesus discarded this superstitious growth and taught the pure religion of nature. After his death St. Paul was " the sole representative of true Christianity, the great free thinker of his time, and brave champion of reason against authority." Morgan points out the difference between St. Paul and the Jewish Christians on the question of the Law, very much after the manner of later criticism. He may be regarded as marking the transition from constructive to critical Deism. The identity of Christianity with a body of abstract truths had ceased to be credible, and the problem was shifted to the field of history. The result was that great emphasis was laid upon the external evidences of Christianity, and especially upon the evidence from prophecy and miracles.

Anthony Collins begins his *Discourse of the Grounds and Reasons of the Christian Religion* by arguing that the one valid argument for Christianity is the argument from the fulfilment of prophecy. Both Jesus himself and the

THE ENGLISH DEISTS

Apostles claimed that he was the Messiah; which indeed is the fundamental article of the true faith. Now it is evident, to begin with, that the prophecies bearing upon the advent and nature of the Messiah were not literally fulfilled. Thus, the prophecies of the Virgin bearing a child are easily shown to refer "in their obvious and primary sense, to other matters than these which they are produced to prove." The method actually used by the evangelists and Apostles is "typical or allegorical." St. Matthew, for example, quotes the words, "He shall be called a Nazarene," which nowhere occur in the Old Testament; though Isaiah does say, that the Messiah shall dwell in Galilee, and Nazareth is a City of Galilee. Collins clearly means that the only way in which prophecies can plausibly be made to apply to Jesus is by such preposterous methods as were practised in rabbinical circles. The prophecy of Jesus that he would shortly come again was never fulfilled in any but a mystical sense. Collins therefore concludes, that, tested by the rules used in the schools, "the books of the Old and New Testament will be in an irreconcilable state, and the difficulties against Christianity will be incapable of being solved." Bishop Chandler in reply cited the prophecy of Malachi: "Behold, I will send you Elijah the prophet before the coming of the great and dreadful day of the Lord. And he shall turn the hearts of the fathers, lest I come and smite the earth with a curse." Here, it is argued, is a prophecy of the coming of John the Baptist and of Jesus. To which Collins replies, that the prophecy has nothing to do with John the Baptist, but announces the return of Elias in person; that John the Baptist himself expressly denied that he was Elias, probably in reference to this very prophecy; and, finally, that John's character is quite different from that announced in Malachi. One of the most remarkable contentions of

Collins is that in which he argues that the book of Daniel was written in the time of Antiochus Epiphanes, because the writer shows a clear knowledge of events down to that time and no later.

As Collins attacked the literal truth of the prophecies, so Thomas Woolston sought to show that the miracles narrated in scripture were purely allegorical. If they are to be taken in their literal sense, why should not the promise of removing mountains by faith be understood in the same way? The account of the resurrection of Lazarus and of Christ himself must be regarded as symbols of the rising of the spirit of the true religion from the grave of the letter. The idea thus suggested by Collins was followed out by Peter Annet (1768), who made a critical investigation into the narratives of the resurrection in the Gospels and the Acts, and denied the possibility of miracles. In support of the latter contention he not only adopted the view of Spinoza, that the laws of nature, as determinations of the divine will, are as unchangeable as God himself, but he suggested the argument, afterwards employed by Hume with telling effect, that it is impossible to prove with certainty that any alleged miracle actually took place, because there is a much greater likelihood that the narrative of the miracle is mixed up with error, self-deception or intentional deceit, than that the miracle actually occurred.

In Conyers Middleton the power of the historical method begins clearly to assert itself. The *Letter from Rome* proceeds to show in detail that the ceremonies and practices of the Romish Church are mainly derived from paganism. In his next work, he agrees with Tindal in tracing many of the Jewish practices, and especially circumcision, to the Egyptians. What dictated his method was a perception of the continuity of history, leading him to deny the literal inspiration of scripture, which virtually placed the Bible beyond the reach of criticism. Middleton sought by closer study to show that the narratives of scripture must be subjected to the same method of criticism as the records of other nations. Applying this method to the gospels, he argued that by it the trifling discrepancies between the various accounts can easily be explained. " The case is the same in theological as in natural enquiries : it is experience alone, and the observation of facts, which can illustrate the truth of principles. Facts are stubborn things, deriving their existence from nature, and though frequently misrepresented and disguised by art and false colours, yet cannot possibly be totally changed or made pliable to the systems which happen to be in fashion, but sooner or later will always reduce the opinions of men to compliance and conformity with themselves." The true source of miracles Middleton assigns to the general intellectual condition of an earlier age. Jews and Gentiles, as well as Christians, believed in diabolical possession and the efficacy of exorcism. Middleton denies that his principles apply to the narratives in the Gospels, but he finally admits that he cannot surrender them whatever the consequences may be. Why should the evangelists be believed, if we refuse to accept the miraculous stories of the Fathers ? In thus challenging the breach of continuity between sacred and profane history, Middleton brings the direct controversy to a close. He was the first to see that we are not shut up to the alternative : either supernatural interference or human imposture ; there being a third alternative, namely, that there is a scientific explanation of the history of religious development. The general course of thought from Locke to Middleton thus shows that there was a growing perception of the difficulty of maintaining the old distinction between sacred and profane history. The result of the whole movement was scepticism in regard to the traditional religion, a scepticism which was carried to its logical result by Hume in the denial of everything supernatural, including the belief in God, and the immortality of the soul. Before considering his doctrine, however, it will be necessary to form some estimate of the earlier philosophy of Locke's successor, Bishop Berkeley.

LECTURE SEVENTH.

BERKELEY AND HUME.

THE question with which Berkeley mainly dealt was that of the relation between the mind and the external world. It is important, however, to distinguish various senses in which the terms "mind" and "external world" may be understood. (1) "Mind" may mean the "sensitive being" —that which is the subject of sensations and impulses. In this sense all animals, and not merely man, may be regarded as possessed of "mind," and what is contrasted with "mind" or the "sensitive being" will be non-sensitive bodies, such as stones and even plants. Starting from the common-sense view that there exist an indefinite number of beings having sensations and impulses, it may be asked under what conditions these are excited. The answer belongs properly to psychology. It may, however, be readily shown that this way of stating the problem tacitly implies certain assumptions which not only may be, but have been, questioned. Thus, it may be denied, after the manner of Descartes, that there is any valid reason for regarding sensitive beings as different from non-sensitive —any difference, that is, in kind—for sensation and impulse, it may be said, are modes of motion, to be explained as other modes of motion are explained. On this view, the only individuality that can be attributed to living beings will be the individuality of an aggregate of material atoms with their peculiar movements. Hence, strictly speaking, there is no problem of the relation of "mind" to the "external world," since the sensitive being, like the non-sensitive, belongs to the external world. On the other hand, if it is held that sensitive beings differ in kind from non-sensitive, the question will arise in what way they do differ. Thus, individuality will have the meaning of an immediate unity, and the relation of this unity to the "external world" will not be merely mechanical, but will involve a form of reaction not found in non-sensitive beings. The sensitive life will therefore be incapable of reduction to mechanism.

(2) By "mind" may be understood, not the sensitive, but the rational life, and by the "external world" the object of reason. Here, again, different views of the rational life may be held. (*a*) It may be maintained that there is no fundamental difference between the rational and the sensitive life. From this point of view reason will consist in an aggregate of sensations and impulses, the only difference being that reason is *conscious* of the emergence of sensations and impulses, without having the power, however, to alter their nature. What reason will have to do, therefore, will be to observe sensations and impulses, keeping clear of all arbitrary additions of its own. For reality is revealed, it may be said, only in the sensitive life. The relation between "mind" and the "external world" will therefore be this, that reason becomes aware that sensations and impulses reveal the actual nature of things. (*b*) On the other hand, it may be denied that sensations and impulses give any revelation of the "external world" when taken by themselves, and it may be held that the external world cannot exist except for a rational being. Thus the only real world will be the intelligible world.

(3) By "mind" may be meant "reason" or "thought," but it may be held that thought cannot comprehend the

external world at all, because it works with elements that are not identical with the nature of things. This doctrine evidently assumes a fundamental discrepancy between what is thought and what exists, and, if pressed to its logical conclusion, it must result in the complete denial of knowledge.

(4) By "mind" may be understood "reason" or "thought" as it exists in each individual man, and by the "external world" the world that is not made by him but only revealed to him. Here a distinction is drawn between the individual man's knowledge of the world and the reality of that world. There is a compulsion laid upon him to apprehend the world as it is. The question, therefore, arises how this is to be effected. Obviously the process of the sensitive life must become an object of the individual's thought. But this will not be enough unless he is capable of going beyond the sensitive life and connecting it with other modes of existence. Here, therefore, we are forced to ask what right we have to maintain that the world revealed to the individual man coincides with the world as it is. If we answer that the world of the individual man is a "copy" of the real world, it would seem that as knowledge proceeds from part to part, the real world can never be known in its completeness. If again we say that the individual mind by its own independent activity constructs a world that is a counterpart of the real world, we shall have to assume a "pre-established harmony" between thought and reality; and then the difficulty will be to show that such a "pre-established harmony" exists. To prove the possibility of a knowledge of reality, we must therefore find some way of showing that knowledge and reality must coincide. And this is the crux.

Locke seems to have been entirely unconscious of the difference between these various senses of the term "mind" and "external world." Thus, by not distinguishing clearly between the two first senses of these terms, he was led to suppose that a feeling of touch revealed the existence of a solid body. Now, whatever the feeling of touch may reveal, it is itself a state of the sensitive subject, and as such it cannot be a property of an external body, which must be distinct and separate from that state. Moreover, the feeling of touch is transient, whereas solidity as a property is permanent. Hence the feeling as such has no object. To show that it arises only under condition of an impact communicated from an external object to the sensitive organism, does not in any way explain the knowledge of solidity, unless we conceive the feeling of touch to involve a knowledge of the object by which it is stimulated. If this is what is meant by a "feeling of touch," there is obviously no distinction between sensation and reason. But, if we so define sensation, we must be prepared to accept the consequences. A sensation which reveals the reality of a solid body involves unchangeable relations in the way of impact and resistance; for otherwise what would be revealed is not "solidity" as a property of things, but merely the transient existence for the subject of a state of feeling existing for a moment and then passing away. It is, therefore, only by endowing sensation with the power of thinking that any relation of the "mind" to the "external world" can be established. On this view, it is obviously absurd to ask whether the sensation "corresponds" to a property of the external object; it must "correspond," because the knowledge of that property is bound up with the existence of the sensation. Whether, therefore, we can say that sensation reveals an external object or not, depends upon the meaning we give to the term "sensation." If sensation is conceived to be the transient state of a sensitive being, involving nothing but itself, then sensation does not reveal an external object. But if sensation means the act of comprehending sensation as involving a relation to a real solid body, certainly it reveals a real world at the same time as it reveals itself. Interpreted in this second sense, Sensationalism and Idealism are identical in their fundamental principle. And it is only as so interpreted, that any valid theory of knowledge is possible at all. It is by confusing these two senses of "sensation" that Locke plausibly explains the knowledge of solidity on the basis of immediate sensation. He tacitly assumes a world of solid bodies, the knowledge of which can only be explained by ascribing to immediate sensation what exists only for a thought that refers sensation to an external world. If we once assume an external world, containing solid bodies related to one another and to the sensitive subject, we must suppose that there is repeated in the mind what exists externally to it. It must be observed, however, that this repetition can have a meaning only from the point of view of the individual man ; for, if there is no external world apart from the fixed constitution of things, we may indeed speak of the individual man as recognizing or representing that world, but only because in him reason operates in harmony with the reason expressed in nature. Hence the last sense (*d*) in which we can speak of the relation of mind and the external world is that the world as comprehended by thought is a fixed or stable world, which is in no way dependent on the activity of thought in this or that man, but to which that activity must conform if it is to comprehend the world as it really is. It is not unnatural to suppose that, as the world is independent of any man's thought, it must be independent of all thought. Thus the separate existence of the world seems to be established ; whereas all that is really established is its existence as independent of the thought of the individual man. And when the independence of the real world is supposed to mean its independence of all "mind," it comes to seem the abstract opposite of "mind." Thought, it is supposed, is inextended, and all its operations must be different from those of body. To think is not to know, and all knowledge must come to us through sensations as effects of the action of body. In this way arises the doctrine that the properties of things are only known because they excite "ideas" in us which are "copies" of those properties.

The world of "matter,"—which on this theory of Locke exists independently of all "mind," whether sensitive or thinking—is by Berkeley denied to have any existence. The whole theory of its action upon the mind is therefore discarded, for that which has no existence cannot act. Hence we have to account for knowledge from the nature of the human mind itself, independently of any supposed "matter." Now, there are two main factors in the human mind : (1) feelings, and (2) the operations of thought. The knowledge of real existence must therefore be derived from one of these classes of ideas ; and as Locke has discarded all the independent products of thought as fictitious, what remains for Berkeley is to explain reality by means of ideas of sensation. How, then, without taking refuge in the untenable doctrine that ideas of real things are excited in us by the things themselves, are we to explain the distinction between "fact" and "fiction" ? The independent bodily thing being discarded, the distinction must be found in the nature of the ideas themselves. We find that some of our ideas are due to our own volition, whereas others we have no power to produce. The former are, therefore, the work of the mind itself, the latter we are forced to accept whether we will or not. "It is no more than willing," says Berkeley, "and straightway this or that idea arises in my fancy ; and by the same power it is obliterated and makes way for another." But "when in broad daylight

I open my eyes, it is not in my power to choose whether I shall see or no, or to determine what particular objects shall present themselves to my view." Moreover, "the ideas of sense are more strong, lively, and distinct than those of the imagination: they have likewise a steadiness, order, and coherence, and are not excited at random, as those which are the effects of human wills often are, but in a regular train and series" (*Princ.* 28-30). But, while these characteristics are found in our sensations, they are not real because of these characteristics, but because they are independent of our will, and, in contrast to the fictions which we are conscious of ourselves producing, are "strong, lively, and distinct," and are not "excited at random." They must therefore, Berkeley concludes, be referred to a cause other than ourselves, and this cause is God.

What at once strikes us in this account is the sudden leap which Berkeley makes from the ideas of sensation to God as their cause. These ideas, Berkeley argues, are not produced by "matter," because "matter," as a reality independent of ideas, cannot be established through ideas. Granting the force of this argument, the natural inference would seem to be, that no cause other than the ideas themselves need be supposed. Berkeley assumes the validity of the reasoning from "ideas" to a cause, but the conception of "cause" itself stands in need of proof, and cannot be assumed. As Hume afterwards pointed out, it is not an idea of sensation, and therefore it must be, on Berkeley's own showing, a "fiction." And even granting that we are entitled to assign a cause for ideas of sensation, how is it proved that that cause is God? It is not plain why an infinite cause is required to explain a finite effect. And in truth Berkeley is unable to prove that ideas of sensation can only be caused by God; the most that he can possibly prove is that "something not-ideas" produces them. Granting even that this "something" must be a "mind," why should that "mind" be infinite? This is a difficulty the force of which the followers of Berkeley never seem to appreciate. Ideas, as they exist in an individual mind, are held to require a cause to account for them, and without first establishing the existence of God, they are at once referred to him as their only possible cause. It is difficult, however, to see how, from a series of transitory states of feeling in an individual mind, we can at once pass to a mind which cannot consist of such transitory states, but is eternal and immutable. Manifestly, before we do so, we must show how we can have a knowledge (1) that such a Being exists, and (2) that he is the cause of ideas in us. To take for granted his existence and causality is obviously illegitimate.

Let us, however, see what becomes of the external world on Berkeley's theory. There is no longer any external reality independent of mind, and consequently no longer any permanent substances such as common-sense is accustomed to suppose. What remains? In place of solid and extended bodies, we have a flux of feelings in an indefinite number of individual minds, a flux in which nothing is permanent but change. When I say, "that is a swallow," I do not mean that a thing, independent and distinct from my sensations, is there in space and continues to exist when I do not see it; what I mean is that a feeling has just occurred to me which raises in me a lively expectation of certain other feelings frequently associated with it. Others may have a similar feeling and a similar expectation, and what I mean by calling the object a "swallow" is that there is a certain "steadiness, order, and coherence" in my ideas, —characteristics which, as I believe, are also found in the ideas of other men. Nevertheless, the sole reality is in the ideas which so occur in my mind and the minds of other men. That is to say, there is not a single indivisible object, the " swallow," which is the same for all men, but an indefinite number of ideas of the " swallow,"—namely, all that are present to my mind and the minds of others at any time. It is obvious that, on this doctrine, our world is split up into a number of separate minds, each of which is in perpetual flux, and that the only identity to be found in them is an identity of the names applied—not to identical but—to similar successions of ideas. The doctrine, in short, leads to Nominalism. Now, Nominalism is inconsistent with any general proposition, because it regards the only reality as that of the particular—in this case, the particular ideas in an individual mind. Hence, no science of nature is possible ; for a science involves universal propositions, and Nominalism admits of none. We cannot say, *e.g.* " the planets move in ellipses," for " the planets " and " ellipses " mean the series of ideas in an indefinite number of individual minds, a series which is perpetually coming and going.

It may be objected that the same difficulty besets all doctrines that refuse to accept the independent existence of " matter." Is it not true, it may be asked, that Idealism in any form is bound to admit that nothing is real but " mind " ? and does not this imply that as there can be no " mind " in general, any more than "man" or "animal" in general, reality has no existence except in some individual mind ? No doubt, reality need not be limited to the ideas in any human mind, but surely it must either be meaningless, or, supposing all human minds annihilated, it would still exist in the divine mind ?

In answer to this argument, it may be pointed out (1) that the denial of the independent existence of an external or material world is not the same thing as its reduction to a congeries of feelings. Berkeley's simplification of Locke consists in just such a reduction; the logical consequence of which is, not that reality must consist of individual minds, but that there is no reality except the various congeries of feelings. For, as Hume soon showed, there is no more reason on Locke's premises for affirming the existence of a "substance" of mind, than for affirming the existence of a "substance" of body. The "substance" of mind, for Berkeley, must be the congeries of feelings, and any supposition of a mind distinct from that congeries must be the result of the work of the mind, and must therefore be fictitious. (2) Speculative Idealism stands on quite a different footing. It does not deny the existence of "matter," any more than of "mind": what it denies is that "matter" has any reality independent of "mind." No doubt "matter," in the sense of an actual "substrate" capable of existing apart from its properties, it does deny; but "matter" in this sense is an abstraction, based upon a false view of the nature of thought. And Speculative Idealism equally denies the existence of a "substrate" of "mind," maintaining that it is due to the same false conception of thought as a process of abstraction from the concrete. Nor does it admit with Berkeley that reality can be reduced to a congeries of feelings; on the contrary, it asserts that a congeries of feelings is just as much an abstraction as a "substrate" of "matter" or of "mind." (3) As to the doctrine that the only reality is that which is found in individual minds, Speculative Idealism begins by asking what is meant by an "individual mind." It is perfectly true that there is no real "mind in general"; for such a supposed "mind" is simply the abstraction formed by eliminating all the differences between one mind and another, and calling the emaciated remainder "mind in general" or "universal mind." But, though there is no "universal mind" (in this sense of the term) it is just as true that there is no "individual mind," if by that is meant a mind that is complete in itself in independence of all other reality. The only "individual mind" that can possibly exist is the mind which comprehends within itself all reality; in other words, the Absolute Mind or God. No human mind, on the other hand, can be called individual in the strict sense, because no human mind is self-complete or embraces all reality within itself. (4) But, though no human mind is completely individual, every human mind is capable of determining what reality in principle is. And it is so capable, in virtue of the power of thought. For thought is no vain process of abstraction, by which what presents itself to perception is converted into a phantom of itself; it is essentially concrete. The fundamental mistake of Empiricism is to overlook the fact that, from the very beginning of knowledge, there is no such thing as purely individual feeling. What is called individual feeling is in reality a complex form of consciousness, in which we can distinguish, though we cannot separate, the particular and the universal. The very simplest apprehension—say, that "there is something here"—involves the two elements "something" and "here," and "something" is obviously a universal, since it applies to every possible "something," while "here" is particular, so far as it concentrates attention upon a determination of the universal space. And this implicit grasp of universal and particular is what is meant by thought, as distinguished from feeling. There is no need to affirm that man is never in a state of "mere feeling"—that is a question in the history of the individual which must be settled by psychology—but it is safe to say that "mere feeling" gives no *knowledge* of anything whatever. Therefore, the simplest phase of knowledge is that in which the subject has emerged from the stage of "mere feeling," and has made his feeling an object. Man as knowing, in short, is a thinking being, and only as such is there for him any object whatever. He grasps the particular as a determination of the universal, and in so doing he has knowledge of "something real." From this we can see what is the fundamental mistake of Empiricism. It confuses a "feeling" with a "thinking" being, and attributes to the former what is possible only for the latter. The objective world exists only for a thinking consciousness, not for a being who is at the stage of feeling. If it is objected, that thought deals only with the abstract, and that the abstract cannot be identical with reality, the answer is that thought as thus defined is a fiction, which exists only in the minds of those who adopt a false and misleading opposition of abstract and concrete. If I apprehend "something" as "here," it is in virtue of my thought that I do so; and to exclude thought from such apprehension is to ascribe to feeling what does not belong to it, and to take from thought what does belong to it. It is to do the former, for feeling as merely particular cannot give the consciousness of anything; it is to do the latter, because thought is not limited to the universal or abstract, but is involved in the simple apprehension. And as knowledge grows, it is always in virtue of a thinking consciousness that a stable world of objects is formed. There is a correlative process of unification and differentiation. In proportion as the elements of the real world are discriminated from one another, the unity of the world becomes more concrete. When the thinking consciousness, *e.g.* grasps the law of gravitation as involved in the constitution of the external world, it does so only because it has gone through a process of discrimination by which body is distinguished from mind, and various species of body from one another. In this case, no doubt, it is the universal law upon which attention is fixed; but that is because the particulars are already assumed to be known, not because the law is an abstraction. Every body submits to the law, because the very existence of each body involves the expression of the law *in it*. The fallacy which has formulated itself in the doctrine that conceptions are " abstract ideas," is countenanced by the partial or abstract view of the concrete world which science is forced to take in order to solve its special problem. It has to treat the external object as if it were completely exhausted in being movable, overlooking its more determinate character. Not to insist upon the fact that " matter " cannot be found existing apart from " mind," it is enough to say that it is so far an abstraction, that it fixes upon a universal characteristic to the exclusion for the time being of the more concrete characteristics inseparable from actually existing bodies. Thus thought, which has already constituted a world of objects in space and time, seems to reverse its process, and take from objects by abstraction characteristics they already have; but it does so only because the temporary isolation of the common characteristics of *all* bodies is necessary to the discovery of the law involved in *each*. If it is argued that this common characteristic is found by a simple process of abstraction, the answer is plain, that by such a process no new characteristic—such as gravitation—can possibly be discovered: there must be a process of concretion or synthesis. Thus the abstraction of " matter " is but a preliminary stage in the process by which it is determined as manifesting the law of gravitation. For that law exists, not in separation from bodies, but as an integral and inseparable characteristic of them. From what has been said we may see that the comprehension of the real world is a process of combined integration and differentiation, a process which is possible only for a thinking as distinguished from a feeling consciousness. And as for the latter there exists no single object, and therefore no world of objects, it is impossible, on the basis of a merely feeling consciousness, to advance to a knowledge of God. Hence, we may be sure that Berkeley, so far as he is true to the basis of his philosophy, cannot possibly construct a theology. To remove the foundation from the external world does not lay down a foundation for a spiritual world. If what is left after the denial of external " substance " is merely a number of discrete feelings, containing no universal in them, there is no world whatever before us, and therefore no possibility of advancing from the world to its cause.

Berkeley, however, confusing particular feelings with the qualities of things, goes on to ask what is meant by general knowledge and how it is obtained. " It is, I know," he says, " a point much insisted on, that all knowledge and demonstration are about universal notions, to which I fully agree ; but then it does not appear to me that those notions are formed by abstraction—universality, so far as I can comprehend, not consisting in the absolute positive nature or conception of anything, but in the relation it bears to the particulars signified or represented by it ; by virtue whereof it is that things, names, or notions, being in their own nature particular, are rendered universal. Thus, when I demonstrate any proposition concerning triangles, it is to be supposed that I have in view the universal idea of a triangle ; which is not to be understood as if I could frame an idea of a triangle which was neither equilateral nor scalene nor equicrural ; but only that the particular triangle I considered, whether of this or that sort it matters not, doth equally stand for and represent all rectilinear triangles whatsoever, and is in that sense universal." Thus it is that " a man may consider a figure merely as triangular without attending to the particular qualities of the angles, or relations of the sides."[1]

Now (1) in rejecting the ordinary doctrine of abstraction on the ground that it eliminates all the differences of particular things—in the instance given, the differences between various particular triangles—Berkeley has undoubtedly entered upon the right track. But, though he is so far right in maintaining that there is no " abstract idea " of triangle, he wrongly takes this denial as equivalent to the affirmation that there is nothing but particular sensible triangles. For, if anything is certain at all, it is that a sensible triangle has no existence anywhere. Certainly it is not with sensible triangles that the mathematician deals. If it were, the triangle would exist only so long as it was present to the individual, and with the disappearance of the image, the triangle itself would vanish. Not only therefore could we not make any affirmation about triangles in general, but we could make no affirmation about any triangle whatever. If I say, " This figure A.B.C., now before me, is a triangle," I must grasp its universal nature, for, unless I do so, it might not be a triangle. Thus, in the particular figure, A.B.C., there is involved the universal triangle. No doubt my attention is concentrated on the determinate character of this triangle, and my judgment may, in the first instance, only be that " This equilateral figure is a triangle " ; but, though I do not in this case obtain the full extension of the subject, the predicate is a universal. Now, if in the particular figure I already virtually comprehend the universal, it is obvious that I do not first observe a particular sensible figure, and then, comparing it with others, pronounce it to be a triangle. But this is Berkeley's view. He confuses the supposed sensible particularity of a given triangle with

[1] *Principles*, 15, 16.

the individuality involved in the comprehension by thought of a figure enclosed by three straight lines. It is because the triangle is the conception of a particular determination of space—a determination based upon the unchangeable nature of space—that it has permanence or universality. Kant calls such a determinate conception a "schema," holding that it is a determination of the form of space and as such of a fixed or unchangeable character. Setting aside the untenable doctrine that space is merely a form of human perception, we may accept Kant's doctrine in this sense, that in a given triangle we have a union of universal and particular elements, which cannot be severed without fatal consequences. Eliminate the universal element, and we have nothing before us but an indeterminate image; remove the particular, and we are reduced to an impossible abstraction. And this is a universal law. No reality can anywhere be found that does not involve the inseparable union of universal and particular.

The same principle applies to the physical determination of the world. Berkeley, discarding any reality but feelings, is logically bound to hold that all physical truths are particular. When it is said that the earth moves, for example, we must interpret this to mean merely that there is a succession of ideas in this or that man. But Berkeley does not consistently maintain this view. "The question whether the earth moves or not," he says, " amounts in reality to no more than this, to wit, whether we have reason to conclude from what hath been observed by astronomers, that if we were placed in such and such circumstances, and such or such a position and distance both from the earth and the sun, we should perceive the former to move among the choir of the planets, and appearing in all respects like one of them ; and this by the established rules of nature, which we have no reason to mistrust,

THE PHILOSOPHY OF BERKELEY 249

is reasonably collected from the phenomena" (*Princ.* 58). Here, it will be observed, Berkeley assumes an " established law of nature " which may be " collected from the phenomena," according to which the motion of the earth is now going on. Obviously, therefore, it is presupposed that the feelings excited in any individual occur in accordance with an organized system of nature, a system that we are capable of recognizing. On the other hand, Berkeley's express doctrine is that there is no " necessary connection " between ideas as they arise in us, but, when one idea occurs, it is for us the sign that another idea will immediately follow.

And this brings us to Berkeley's conception of God. Having discarded as a fiction Locke's " substratum " of matter, and reduced external reality to particular ideas of sense, Berkeley has to explain how these ideas, which are not subject to our will and therefore are not produced by us, come to present themselves in our consciousness. They arise in our consciousness, he answers, because they are directly produced by God, who is their efficient cause. The soul or self, again, is a " thinking substance," and this " thinking substance " as necessarily inextended and indiscerptible he holds to be " naturally immortal."

It is obvious that Berkeley's premises cannot bear the weight of his conclusion. Granting that the soul is " inextended," it does not follow that it is " immortal," since, as Kant afterwards pointed it, it may gradually become less in degree until it disappears. Nor can it be held that the soul is " immortal " because there is an endless succession of ideas, since such a succession is not identical with immortality unless there is at the same time self-conscious identity. Now, self-conscious identity is not possible on the basis of a mere succession of ideas; it is only as the correlation of a permanent world that there can be any consciousness of a permanent self, and Berkeley, in discarding the former, has made the latter impossible. Knowledge of self is essentially correlative to knowledge of the world, and any attempt to maintain the independent reality of the one after the elimination of the other must be abortive. Thus Berkeley prepared the way for Hume's denial of " thinking substance " altogether.

God is regarded by Berkeley as the efficient cause only of ideas of sense. " There must be an active power to produce our ideas, which is not to be found in ideas themselves, for we are conscious that they are inert, nor in matter, since that is but a name for a bundle of ideas ; which must therefore be in spirit, since of that we are conscious as active ; yet not in the spirit of which we are conscious, since then there would be no difference between real and imaginary ideas ; therefore in a Divine Spirit, to whom, however, may forthwith be ascribed the attributes of the spirit of which we are conscious." Now, the assumptions here lie on the surface. It is assumed that there must be a " power " to produce certain of our ideas. But, on Berkeley's own principles, no " power " was required to produce ideas in us by " matter " ; all that appears in our consciousness are the ideas themselves, and therefore the " matter " supposed to be independent of our ideas must be discarded, and with it any " power " it was supposed to possess. Why, then, should we assume that the self-explaining ideas require any " power " to produce them ? All that we know directly are the ideas themselves, and an unknown " substrate " of mind is just as much a fiction as an unknown substrate of matter. But, with the elimination of the " thinking substance " no possibility remains of making any transition from ideas to an efficient cause. If it is said that we must explain the origin of those ideas that are independent of our will, the answer is that on Berkeley's

THE PHILOSOPHY OF HUME

premises, there is no " will," if by that is meant a " power " of originating ideas, and therefore there is no valid distinction between ideas of sense as real and ideas of imagination as fiction; whatever distinction subsists between them must be explained from the ideas themselves. Moreover, even supposing it admitted that we are conscious of originating certain ideas, how can we pass from this to a kind of " power " of which we are not conscious ?

Starting from Berkeley's simplification of Locke's doctrine by the elimination of material " substance," Hume reduces the contents of consciousness to " impressions " and " ideas," the latter being a copy of the former. Berkeley had assumed that we are entitled to explain the origin of impressions and ideas by referring the former to God as their cause, and the latter to the mind of the individual, which he conceived as thinking substance. He also virtually assumed that the self is identical with itself. Now, these three conceptions, namely, cause and effect, substance and attribute, and self-identity, must either be derived from impressions, or they must be regarded as mere " words " to which no reality corresponds. Hume distinguishes between " natural" and " philosophical " relations, the latter being fictions resulting from or rather following on the former. The " natural relations " are declared to be given in impressions. When, *e.g.*, we have the impressions of " red " and " yellow," we have at the same time a consciousness of their likeness and unlikeness. By thus assuming that " resemblance " is already implied in the impressions, Hume is relieved from the burden of seeking to derive it from impressions. Thus he is able plausibly to show that there are not even " general " ideas, such as Berkeley seemed to find in the relation of ideas to one another. All ideas being particular, all propositions must be singular. Even when a proposition is stated in a universal form, the judgment is not truly universal, but is merely a number of singular propositions, associated by the influence of " custom." We apply the same name to ideas that resemble one another, and this is the only sense in which we can speak of generality at all. The " philosophical " relations of substance, causality and identity, again, are by Hume explained away as due to the mind's " propensity to feign." What then becomes of the ideas of the soul and of God ? If the soul, as Berkeley said, is a " thinking substance," Hume asks what is " the impression that produces it " (p. 517). As there is no such impression, he infers that it is a pure fiction. And as the soul is a fiction, we cannot infer from it the existence of a spiritual cause to account for it.

Thus the presuppositions upon which Deism was based —belief in the existence of a personal God, and belief in the immortality of the soul—are expressly denied by Hume, while its doctrine of religion as natural to man, and therefore as known to him from the earliest time, is also assailed. The first is attacked in the *Dialogues concerning Natural Religion* (1778), the second in *The Natural History of Religion* (1757). In these theological writings Hume assumes the validity of our belief in the invariable order of the universe, a belief which in his metaphysical writings he denies ; in other words, his theological writings contain merely an *argumentum ad hominem*, addressed mainly to those who believed it possible to demonstrate the existence of God, the immortality of the soul, and the reality of miracles.

(1) Hume makes very short work of the *a priori* or " ontological " argument for the being of God.[1] What is the connotation of the term " God " ? It is admitted by

[1] The terms " ontological," " cosmological," and " physico-theological " are of course Kant's, not Hume's.

Malebranche and other divines that we have no positive idea of God ; when he is called a spirit, all that is meant is that he is not matter ; and no one ventures to say that his nature in any way resembles ours ; for, though we attribute to him thought, design and knowledge, these predicates do not mean what they mean when spoken of ourselves. *Our* " acts, sentiments and ideas " are distinct and successive, whereas *the mind of God*, as absolutely simple and immutable, and therefore as devoid of all distinctions of thought, will, sentiment, love or hatred, is a pure blank. Nor can a God as thus defined be proved. It is impossible to demonstrate that anything exists by *a priori* arguments. " Nothing is demonstrable, unless the contrary implies a contradiction. Nothing that is distinctly conceivable implies a contradiction. Whatever we conceive as existent, we can also conceive as non-existent. There is no being, therefore, whose non-existence implies a contradiction. Consequently, there is no being whose existence is demonstrable " (ii. 432). It may be answered, that God is a necessarily existent Being, and that if we knew his whole essence or nature, we should perceive it to be as impossible for him not to exist as for twice two not to be four. But, so long as our faculties remain the same as at present, we can always conceive the non-existence of what we formerly conceived to exist ; and therefore the combination of necessity and existence is a contradiction in terms. Moreover, if there be any necessarily existent Being, why should it not be the material universe ? The answer of Dr. Clarke is that both the matter and the form of the world are contingent, since " any particle of matter may be conceived to be annihilated ; and any form may be conceived to be altered." But, by the same argument, God may be imagined to be non-existent or his attributes to be altered. If this is denied, it must be because he possesses some unknown inconceivable qualities; and no reason can be assigned why these qualities may not belong to matter (ii. 433).

(2) The "cosmological" argument claims to be based upon experience, and therefore to be superior to the ontological. Its reasoning is, shortly: "Something exists: therefore, there is a necessary existence." The argument is based upon the necessity of assuming a first cause. But, answers Hume, it is illegitimate to apply the idea of cause in this way; for that which exists from eternity cannot have a cause, since every cause implies "priority in time and a beginning of existence." We can properly speak only of the cause of any member in a succession of events, not of a cause of the whole. If we know "the particular causes of each individual in a collection of twenty," it is very unreasonable afterwards to ask for "the cause of the whole twenty. This is sufficiently explained in explaining the cause of the parts" (ii. 433).

(3) To a consideration of the physico-theological argument Hume mainly devotes his attention. As originally stated, the argument is that the world is "nothing but one great machine, subdivided into an infinite number of lesser machines, which again admit of subdivision, to a degree beyond what human senses can trace and explain. All these various machines, and even their most minute parts, are adjusted to each other with an accuracy, which ravishes into admiration all men, who have ever contemplated them. The curious adapting of means to ends, throughout all nature, resembles exactly, though it much exceeds, the productions of human contrivance; of human designs, thought, wisdom and intelligence. Since, therefore, the effects resemble each other, we are led to infer by all the rules of analogy, that the causes also resemble; and that the Author of Nature is somewhat similar to the mind of man; though

possessed of much larger faculties, proportioned to the grandeur of the work, which he has executed" (ii. 392). The argument, objects the sceptic, is based upon analogy, and becomes weaker the less the objects compared resemble each other. The analogy between a house and the universe is so faint, that at the most we can only guess or conjecture that the causes are similar. "Thought, design, intelligence, such as we discover in men and other animals, is no more than one of the springs and principles of the universe.... But can a conclusion, with any propriety, be transferred from parts to the whole?" And if it can, "why select so minute, so weak, so bounded a principle as the reason and design of animals is found to be upon this planet? What peculiar privilege has this little agitation of the brain which we call thought, that we must make it the model of the whole universe?" (ii. 396). "In this little corner of the world alone there are four principles, reason, instinct, generation, vegetation, which are similar to each other, and are the causes of similar effects" (ii. 472). By any one of these we may form a theory of the "original" of the world, "and it is a palpable and egregious partiality, to confine our view entirely to that principle, by which our own minds operate" (ii. 423). "The world resembles a machine, therefore it is a machine, therefore it arose from design." Why not say, "The world resembles an animal, therefore it is an animal, therefore it arose from generation?" No doubt the steps are wide, but not wider in the latter than the former, and there is this superiority, that the analogy is more striking. It may be answered that it is not necessary to identify the operations of the divine mind with reason in us, but only to hold that the ideas in the divine mind correspond to the visible universe as the architect's plan to the house. But, objects Hume, if we set up an ideal world, and argue that it must have a cause, we shall be led into an infinite progression, or, if not, into an inexplicable principle. It is, therefore, no real escape to set up an ideal world, which is equally in need of explanation with the world we know. Moreover, the argument from design can at the most only prove the existence of a being in time and space, operating on matter external to himself. And as we can only infer a cause adequate to produce the effect, we cannot conclude to the infinite perfection of the cause. Nor can we even prove a single cause. The greater the power, indeed, the less close is the analogy to human art; and hence polytheism is the most natural inference. For the universe as a whole, in fact, the growth of organisms is a more fitting analogy than that of human artifice; why, then, should we not be guided by the idea of natural development rather than go beyond Nature in search of a transcendent cause? And might not the apparent adaptation of the world be merely the result of chance? Why should we not say that in the many possible combinations of elements there have arisen organisms which survive because of their harmony with the environment? On this point Hume does not dwell, however, but goes on to ask whether it is true that the world actually shows adaptation in every part. A doubtful balance of happiness over misery is not what we should expect from a Being infinite in power, wisdom and goodness. "Why is there any misery at all in the world? Not by chance surely. From some cause then. Is it from the intention of the Deity? But he is perfectly benevolent. Is it contrary to his intention? But he is almighty. Nothing can shake the solidity of this reasoning, so short, so clear, so decisive; except we assert, that these subjects exceed all human capacity, and that our common measures of truth and falsehood are not applicable to them" (ii. 446).

The only reply that the defender of the argument can

make is to admit that it establishes only a Being of "benevolence, regulated by wisdom and limited by necessity" (ii. 444)—much the same theory, it may be said in passing, as that in which John Stuart Mill later took refuge.[1] Hume, however, refuses to admit that any one, "not antecedently convinced of a supreme intelligence, benevolent, and powerful," would come to the conclusion that the world is the product of such an intelligence (ii. 445). There are four circumstances on which depend all or the greatest parts of the ills that molest sensible creatures, none of which "appear to human reason in the least degree necessary or unavoidable": (1) the existence of pain; (2) the fact that the world is conducted by general and inflexible laws, which might be suspended temporarily in order to prevent evil; (3) the sparing distribution of natural powers; (4) the "inaccurate workmanship" of all parts of the great machine, which constantly produce evils. "The whole presents nothing but the idea of a blind Nature, impregnated by a great vivifying principle, and pouring forth from her cup, without discernment or parental care, her maimed and abortive children" (ii. 446-452). It would thus seem that "the original source of all things has no more regard to good above ill than to heat above cold, or to drought above moisture, or to light above heavy " (ii. 452).

In his essay on *A Particular Providence and a Future State* Hume gives his answer to Butler's theory, that the Christian conception of the world is in harmony with the view which is suggested by a fair interrogation of nature. It is argued that the character of the world compels us to infer an intelligent creator; from which it follows that there is an intelligent government of the world. Hume starts with the principle that a cause must be proportional to its effect. And this rule "holds whether the cause assigned be

[1] See his *Three Essays on Religion*.

brute unconscious matter, or a rational intelligent being.... The knowledge of the cause being derived solely from the effect, they must be adjusted exactly to each other."[1] Hence we cannot attribute to the cause more than can be learned from the effect. Applying this principle, it is obvious that we can tell nothing about the Deity except what can be inferred from the universe as known to us. Hence we cannot reason from this world to a totally dissimilar world. It is manifestly illegitimate to argue from the failure of retributive justice in this world to its operation in a world that is quite problematical. Besides, justice does not fail in this world; for virtue brings peace, while vice is accompanied by uneasiness and unrest. Nor can we regard the instinctive desire for infinite development as a valid reason for affirming the immortality of the soul; on the contrary, the instinctive fear of death may be taken as a distinct warning not to deceive ourselves by false hopes of a future life. Nevertheless, concludes Hume, very much to our surprise, the truth of the gospel is all the more confirmed by the fact that it has revealed to us a doctrine that could never have been discovered by pure reason.

If natural theology cannot take us beyond the inference that the cause or causes of the order of the universe probably bear some distant analogy to human intelligence, how is it that religion has had so great an influence upon men? Hume's answer is given in his *Natural History of Religion*. The primitive religion was not the abstract monotheism of the deists, but polytheism, or rather fetishism. Early man naturally transferred his own emotions to things, attributing to them passions and feelings like his own. Hence he conceived of them as gods of like nature with himself, and on occasion he treated them with disrespect.

[1] Essays, IV. 112-113.

THE PHILOSOPHY OF HUME

In course of time these imaginary beings were embellished by the poets, and heroes were added to the pantheon. Thus theism did not arise from argument, but was due to the gradual promotion of some favourite deity that was finally conceived to be infinite. In this way the God of the Hebrews was formed. The contrast between religion and morality, again, was due to a survival of superstitious beliefs in a more developed stage of morality. Hume then goes on to ask whether any evidence can prove a miracle. Is it, he asks, more incredible that men should make false statements, wilfully or otherwise, than that an event should have occurred which is contrary to the order of Nature as ascertained by experience? Surely the former alternative is the only reasonable one. Thus we seem to be left with nothing but a vague belief in something behind the veil of phenomena, which perhaps may bear a remote resemblance to the intelligence of man. Hume's conception of the relations of reason and feeling did not allow him to find in experience any rational element; hence, after exposing the self-contradictory position of the deists, and discarding the supposition of a miraculous revelation and attestation of religion, nothing remained but a belief for which no reasonable ground could be assigned. Only in a philosophy which should challenge the reduction of experience to a succession of irrational feelings did there lie any hope of the reconstruction of theology on a permanent foundation. With such a challenge the philosophy of Kant begins. The way was indeed prepared for him by Lessing, who maintained that Christianity did not depend for its truth upon the dogmas of the Church or upon the literal accuracy of the biblical narratives; but it was Kant who fairly grappled, from the point of view of pure reason, with the difficulties raised by Hume.

LECTURE EIGHTH.

THE CRITICAL PHILOSOPHY.

THE development of modern philosophy, from Descartes to Hume, while it led to no perfectly satisfactory conclusion, had made certain solutions untenable. After Hume no one who stood at the level of the highest thought could suppose that any real escape from perplexity and contradiction could be found in the idea that the world was not under the sway of inviolable law, but was subject to sudden and incalculable breaks. This is a conviction that underlies the whole of the Critical Philosophy. On the other hand, neither the assumption of the school of Leibnitz that such categories as mechanical causality and teleology are self-evident, or the sceptical denial of Hume that they are more than subjective fictions, seemed to Kant admissible. If there is to be a science of nature, the law of causation must be inviolable, and therefore Hume's resolution of it into an arbitrary succession of ideas cannot possibly be accepted; while, on the other hand, the principle of final cause, though it seems essential in any reasonable explanation of the conduct of intelligent and moral beings, can hardly be satisfactorily employed in explanation of the course of nature. But, if a science of nature demands the acceptance of inviolable law, and morality the principle of final cause, it looks as if there were an insoluble contradiction between man and nature. Moreover, it is difficult to see how we can establish the existence of God without

THE CRITICAL PHILOSOPHY 261

denying the inviolability of the system of nature as well as the independence and freedom of man. These questions pressed heavily upon the mind of Kant, until after long reflection he believed that he had found the clue to the solution of the problem as to the compatibility of the system of nature with the existence of God and with the freedom and immortality of man in his distinction between phenomena and noumena, a distinction which seemed to him to reconcile mechanism and teleology. The world, as he thought could be proved, is certainly under the sway of inviolable law, and yet it can be shown that man is free and immortal, and that God exists. Man is more than "a part of this partial world": in his inner being he is not the slave but the lord of nature. Leibnitz had sought to escape from the iron chain of necessity by reducing the world of experience to a confused consciousness, which was capable of being transcended when man came to see that all real existences are independent and self-determined, the action of each on the other being an illusion that disappears when we rise to the point of view of pure thought. Kant ultimately defends the freedom and independence of man, but he denies that the world of experience is based upon a confused consciousness, or that we can bring ourselves as free beings within the sphere of knowledge. The world is a definitely articulated system, in which the slightest change in one part involves a corresponding change in all the rest, while the independence of man on nature is a matter of rational faith, not of knowledge. Nature is not a perfectly closed sphere, and therefore, inviolable as are its changes, there is nothing to hinder us from regarding them as having their real source in that which is beyond nature. The philosophy of Kant has therefore a double aspect: on the one hand, it seeks to justify the mechanical or scientific view of the world, and, on the other hand, to fix the limits of its application and so to provide a way of escape into the region of the spiritual.

The first object of Kant is to show how, in consistency with the conditions of human knowledge, there can be a science of nature. Since the special sciences may be roughly divided into the mathematical and the physical, while the former are manifestly the necessary preparation for the latter, Kant states his problem in the form: How are *a priori* synthetic judgments possible? and he begins to solve it by asking, How are *a priori* synthetic judgments of mathematics possible? As such judgments obviously deal with sensible objects and events, and these are all in space and time, he finds it necessary to enquire into the nature of space and time. Now, granting that sensible objects and events are presented to us in our immediate experience, Kant maintains that space and time are not themselves so apprehended, but are the necessary conditions under which objects and events are apprehended. The judgments of mathematics are therefore universal and necessary just because they state certain fundamental relations without which the world of experience is impossible. These relations cannot be explained away, after the manner of Leibnitz, as due to the confused consciousness of things that have no external relations to one another. At the same time, the world as determined spatially and temporally cannot be the world as it is in its true nature, for no spatial or temporal determination of things can yield a complete whole. We must, therefore, regard space and time simply as the *a priori* forms under which our consciousness of the sensible world must necessarily operate. Belonging as they do to the constitution of our perceptive faculty, they cannot be predicated of things in themselves, and therefore, while they are "empirically real," they are "transcendentally ideal." The mathematical sciences, then, are not applicable to anything but objects of sensible experience, though Kant adds that among these objects must be included states of consciousness as in time. On the other hand, in their application to such objects, or rather to the perceptual condition under which such objects are possible, they are absolute.

The next question is, How are *a priori* synthetic judgments of physics possible? in other words, how can there be such sciences as physics, chemistry and the other sciences of nature? The manner in which Kant sought to show that space and time are *a priori* forms of perception, and therefore that mathematical judgments are universal and necessary, was to point out, that, although the particular determinations of sensible objects must be simply apprehended, the perception of them as objects is possible only as the subject relates them under its own perceptive forms. Similarly, he seeks to vindicate the universal and necessary relations under which the individual objects are constituted as objects, and connected in the system of experience, by showing that apart from such relations there can be no experience, but merely a loose assemblage of sensible impressions. If we deny that in all the changes of phenomena there are permanent objects or substances, the changing states of which are connected in the way of cause and effect and which are reciprocally influenced by one another, we can have no experience of real objects as distinguished from fictions of the imagination. The proof of the principles of substantiality, causality and community cannot be based upon any number of particular instances, for in this way we could never show that they are inviolable conditions of experience. Hume, in fact, has made it plain that in this way we cannot get beyond the mere expectation that, as it has so often been so, we may assume it will always be so ; and an unprovable hypothesis of this kind is too insecure a basis upon which to rest a science. Some other method of proof is therefore required. Now, it is perfectly true that without impressions of sense we should have no experience of sensible objects; but it by no means follows that the world of our experience can be accounted for purely from such impressions. Kant, therefore, at once agrees with, and differs from, the empirical school. Nor can he admit with Leibnitz that conception is of itself a source of real knowledge. To think is not to know; for even if we could think an object in all the fulness of its predicates, we should not be able to make the transition from our conception of the object to its actual existence. It is thus plain that the mere conception of substance, or of causality, or of reciprocal action, cannot entitle us to affirm that there are substances, which undergo changes in accordance with the law of causality, and are mutually influenced in the changes of their states. But, although thought is in itself incapable of going beyond itself, it by no means follows that it is confined to the mere analysis of its own conceptions when it is dealing with the element supplied to it by sense. For there is a synthesis of imagination to which every sensible object must conform, and this synthesis, when brought to the unity of thought, is expressed in such judgments as those of substantiality, causality and community. The primary condition of experience as a system is that the thinking subject should be capable of referring all objects to the unity of one self-consciousness; and such a unity is possible only if all objects are combined in a single self-consistent system. Thus the consciousness of one world of experience and the consciousness of one self are essentially correlative. But the single world of experience implies that thought has functions of synthesis or categories by which it constitutes and connects all objects of experience in a single system. Hence, just as space and

THE CRITICAL PHILOSOPHY 265

time have been shown to be the pure forms of perception, so the categories, as we now see, are the pure forms of thought. Both are essential to experience ; for thought cannot apply its functions of synthesis except in relation to the "matter of sense," as ordered under the forms of space and time.

Granting that it has now been shown that the system of nature is absolutely determined in all its parts, the question arises, whether man must be regarded as involved in it. This is a problem of supreme interest to us ; for, if it is answered in the affirmative, there can be no freedom, morality or immortality of man, and the belief in God as a Being higher than nature must be abandoned. It thus seemed to Kant that our spiritual interests can be defended only by showing that the world of experience is not identical with ultimate reality.

Now, it has been supposed that we may infer the independent reality of the thinking subject, on the ground that we are conscious of self as permanent in all changes of consciousness, as simple, as identical with itself, and as distinct from all external objects including our own body. To Kant, however, this inference seemed based upon a confusion of thought. It is true, and indeed this is the central idea of the Analytic, that the consciousness of a single world of experience is impossible unless there is a correlative consciousness of a single self. But it is not legitimate to infer that the self is independent because it is involved in all the consciousness of objects. The very fact that there is no consciousness of self apart from the consciousness of objects shows that there are not two distinct forms of consciousness, but only one, which may be regarded either as the consciousness of objects through the unity of the self, or the consciousness of self through the unity of objects. Hence all attempts to establish the independent existence of the self really involve the substantiation of one element of consciousness in separation from the other element without which it could not exist. This is the error of Descartes, who supposed that the consciousness of self as accompanying every mode of consciousness entitled him to regard it as a " thinking substance " ; and upon this confusion between the " I think," as accompanying every determination of the world, and a separate and independent substance corresponding to it, all proofs of the independence of the thinking subject are based. In thus rejecting the method of Rational Psychology, Kant does not mean to deny the conclusion itself, but only the process by which it is reached. That man in his true being is a free spiritual subject, who is independent of nature, is his own doctrine, but he holds that it can only be established through the moral consciousness.

There is another way in which the existence of a reality higher than nature is suggested to us. The demand for completeness in the explanation of the world leads to the supposition that it is itself a whole, and that every object in it is, in the language of Leibnitz, a " monad " or individual unity. On the other hand, all our attempts to gain a knowledge of the world or of the objects in it as self-complete or unconditioned are necessarily abortive, because of the conditions under which alone knowledge is possible for us. (*a*) Since no object can be known by us that is not presented as an extensive or intensive magnitude, it is impossible for us to have any knowledge of an object that is really individual or self-complete, for the simple reason that no magnitude can possibly be truly individual. The sensible world is for us neither absolutely limited, nor absolutely unlimited, in space or in time. A first moment of time, or a last point of space, is an impossible experience ; and equally impossible is an indivisible part of space or of

THE CRITICAL PHILOSOPHY 267

body. (*b*) Again, as in time all objects of experience must be referred to a cause, and this cause must in turn be regarded as an effect, we are either forced into an infinite series of causes and effects, or we must surrender the conception of cause altogether, and assume that there is an absolutely first cause, which is not itself an effect. Similarly, in experience we find nothing but contingent objects, *i.e.* objects that exist under the condition of the existence of something else ; and it is therefore impossible to get beyond contingent objects unless we can reach a single absolutely necessary Being, or an absolute totality of contingent objects. Now, neither of the alternatives indicated is possible, because we can neither sum up an infinite series, nor reach a first cause or an absolutely necessary being. The unconditioned can never be for us an object of knowledge ; and we must, therefore, conclude that our knowledge is only of phenomena, not of ultimate reality. The source of the contradiction into which reason is forced arises from assuming dogmatically that one of the alternatives must be true, and the other false. But, when we see that the world of our experience is phenomenal, while the opposite alternatives go on the assumption that it is identical with absolute reality, the real solution suggests itself, that neither alternative is true, or that both may be true when the one is viewed as applying to phenomena and the other to things in themselves. The first two antinomies are solved by saying that we are not bound to hold phenomena to be either infinite or finite ; and the second two by the suggestion that the law of natural causality and the denial of an absolutely necessary being may be true in application to the phenomenal world, while yet the principle of free causality and the assertion of an absolutely necessary being may be true when affirmed of the noumenal world. Whether this solution is the true one can only be determined when we pass beyond the sphere of the speculative to the practical reason. It is enough at present to say that there is no contradiction in the solution suggested.

There is a third form in which reason seeks for unity besides that of the soul and the world, namely, in the idea of a Being who contains within himself all possible reality. Such an object Rational Theology affirms to exist. The Idea of God, as dealt with by Rational Theology, implies, firstly, the conception of absolutely complete knowledge; secondly, the unity of all positive predicates; and thirdly, the idea of an absolute subject-object. Now (1) there is no doubt that the idea of the world as a whole is presupposed in the consciousness of particular objects. No object can be brought within the unity of our consciousness without being related to all the other objects of our consciousness. The world of our experience is thus continually in process of being unified. Nevertheless, it can never be completely unified. No possible extension of our knowledge can yield the knowledge of reality as a perfect whole, and therefore reality as a perfect whole must always remain for us an ideal that we can never reach. Hence we cannot convert our ideal into the positive assertion of a real being corresponding to it, as is done by Rational Theology when it affirms the existence of God as an absolutely perfect Being. (2) God is held to be a Being who unites in himself all positive predicates. As a pure conception the Idea of God must exclude all negative predicates, for the law of thought is the principle of Identity or Non-Contradiction. If, then, we are to determine the Absolute Being by pure thought, we must be able to state all the positive predicates by which it is characterized. Kant does not deny that this is the ideal of Absolute Being, but he denies that Absolute Being can be known. Nothing in the nature of our experience entitles us to affirm the existence of an object that is completely determined. The idea of the complete determination of an object is therefore a mere idea. Valuable and indispensable as is the effort after that complete specification of existence which is the goal of knowledge, it can never result in any actual knowledge of an object corresponding to the idea. Without such knowledge, however, we cannot affirm that reality is completely determined. We can see that reality in its completeness would contain only positive predicates, but as complete knowledge is for us an impossibility, the most that we can say is that God, as a Being who unites in himself all positive reality, is the only Being that is consistent with our idea of an Absolute Being. Whether this Being actually exists we cannot possibly say without going beyond the consideration of our theoretical intelligence. (3) The idea of God is that of an individual subject, which is not limited in any way by an object given to it from without, but which creates its own object; in other words, it involves the conception of a subject that is its own object. The conception of a totality of being inevitably gives rise to this idea of an absolutely individual Being. That which contains in itself no negation cannot be limited by anything else. There is no possible reality that is not contained in it, and therefore it cannot be divided into various beings, which share reality among them; for, were it so divided, each of those beings would contain only a part of reality. Nor can the Being which unites all positive reality in itself, the *ens realissimum*, be regarded as merely the sum of all finite beings; for the totality of finite beings necessarily involves negation, and in the Absolute there is no negation. Nor again can finite things be parts of the Infinite; for the Infinite can have no parts, but must be absolutely indivisible. Hence God must be conceived as complete in himself apart from the world of finite beings, and therefore not as its Substance, but as its Ground or Cause. Kant's objection to Rational Theology, then, is that, as we can have no knowledge of reality as a whole, we cannot establish the existence of a Being which contains all reality within itself. In the progress of our knowledge we never reach completeness. The reality that we know is "distributive," not "collective," being found dispersed among a number of individuals, not concentrated in one. Thus a Being within which all reality exists, and is known to exist, lies beyond the range of our knowledge. If such a Being exists, it must be as a perceptive intelligence, and a perceptive intelligence cannot be understood by beings like ourselves, whose perception and intelligence operate independently of each other. Though we are not entitled to deny the existence of such an Intelligence, it is for us merely a faultless ideal, that we can never verify by any extension of our knowledge of God, all so-called proofs of his existence must be sophistical, resting as they do (*a*) upon the confusion between the idea of completed knowledge and the actual completion of knowledge, (*b*) upon the identification of the idea of a Being which is the unity of all positive predicates with the knowledge of such a Being, and (*c*) upon the equalization of this totality of positive reality with an individual Being.

At the close of the *Critique of Pure Reason* we seem to be left with an irreconcilable antagonism between the ideal of knowledge and the limited knowledge of which only we are capable. The Ideas of the Soul, the World and God no doubt reveal the limitations of our experience, but they do not enable us to go beyond it, valuable as they are in supplying us with ideals by reference to which experience is extended, specialized and systematized. But, while Kant has closed the entrance into the supersensible to knowledge, he has left the way open for a rational faith, as based upon the peculiar character of the practical reason or moral con-

THE CRITICAL PHILOSOPHY 271

sciousness. Since the whole sphere of experience is phenomenal, no conclusion can be drawn from it hostile to the existence or nature of reality as it is in itself. And when we go on to consider the peculiar character of the practical reason, we are enabled to determine positively the existence and nature of those realities that we are compelled to postulate. For, the reason why we are compelled to affirm the limited or phenomenal character of " experience " is that the world as known to us falls immeasurably short of that perfect unity of which self-consciousness is the type. Not only is the consciousness of self presupposed in the consciousness of the world, but in the consciousness of self as active or practical the self receives a new determination. Here the ideal is no longer the mere conception of a perfect unity of knowledge ; it is the ideal of the perfect self as the end which ought to be realized. From this point of view the world is not merely something that must be accepted as a fact, but something which must be brought into conformity with the ideal originated by the self. It is by reference to this ideal order of the world that we come to the consciousness of our own self-activity. It is true that the ideal can never be found realized in the world from willing it, or making it the end and principle of our action. The self that is revealed in the moral consciousness is not one object among others, and therefore it is not subject to the laws by which all objects of " experience " are determined. The subject that is conscious is also the object of which it is conscious, and there is therefore nothing to prevent the realization of the ideal self, though this does not necessarily involve the conformity of the world to this end. That we are conscious of the self as the object which is to be realized is implied in the fact that we have the idea of that which *ought* to be. Such an idea is no fact of experience, since it takes its stand upon that which *ought* to be, entirely ignoring that which *is*. The idea of the *ought* is thus a purely ideal object, and therefore it can only be possessed by a self-conscious being, who distinguishes himself from all other objects. Only in so far as I separate myself in thought from the whole knowable world, can I have the idea of myself as a being that *ought* to be that which I am not. As I cannot bend nature to myself, I must accept it as it is; but in the realm of my own self-consciousness I am absolute master. For, all that is here necessary is that I should will the ideal of myself which I undoubtedly possess. In this willing of my ideal self consists my freedom—a freedom that is in no way dependent on my power of realizing that which I will in the actual world. It is, for example, involved in my ideal of myself that I should promote the happiness of my fellow-men; and if my conduct is determined purely from regard for this object, I am free, because I am in no way influenced by anything external to my own will; and this is true even though all my efforts may prove abortive. Morality only demands that my sole motive should be that which is prescribed by my ideal of myself, and for the failure to realize the ideal in the actual world I am not responsible. This idea of goodness, Kant contends, is implied in the ordinary moral judgments of men. A man is not called good because of his superior talents or rank in society or success in life; on the contrary, he is regarded as good though his natural gifts may be poor and his well-meant endeavours are unsuccessful. Nothing is good but a good will, and a good will is one the sole motive of which is reverence for the moral law. To regulate one's conduct by the desire for the pleasure imagined to be connected with a certain object is immoral, and that whether the object is the gratification of the senses or the attainment of knowledge, or even the furtherance of the general happiness.

To this idea of morality Kant was led by his conception of the relation of the practical to the theoretical consciousness. In becoming aware of the limitations of "experience," man obtains the idea of himself as the possible subject of a knowledge that would complete his being on the theoretical side by a comprehension of reality in its completeness. Such a knowledge, however, he can never obtain, and unity with himself in the way of knowledge is therefore impossible. But self-harmony may be reached in another way. Man has the idea of himself as he would be were he capable of bringing the world into conformity with his ideal, and though he can never actually realize that ideal, he can in every act make it his motive or end. It is because the desires are regarded by Kant as antagonistic to this ideal that morality is held to be independent of them. The man who makes any particular end his motive, such as the preservation of his life, the acquisition of wealth, or the attainment of honour, is identifying his good with the realization of the lower side of his being, and therefore his conduct is immoral.

Morality, then, consists in making the moral law the only motive of action. Man, however, is not merely a moral being, but a being who on the side of his desires is part of the world, and both of these sides of his nature demand, and are entitled to receive, satisfaction. The perfect harmony of virtue and happiness constitutes what we call the *summum bonum*, and we must therefore ask what is the relation between these two elements. We cannot admit, with hedonism, that the pursuit of happiness is morality, nor can it be maintained that the willing of the moral law must result in happiness. The former view is absolutely false, for happiness, when it is made the end of action, is incompatible with virtue; the latter is not absolutely false, for it is a demand or postulate of reason that the moral man ought to be happy. In point of fact, however, man, as a being in whom there is a conflict of desire and reason, is not perfectly moral; the highest point to which he can attain is an infinite progress towards perfection; and such a progress compels us to postulate the immortality of the soul. And, as reason further demands that happiness should be proportionate to morality,—a demand that it is beyond the power of man to secure,—we must postulate the existence of God, as distinct from and yet the Author of the world. Only by the postulate of a Being at once infinitely intelligent and infinitely good, can we explain how the highest good, which involves the harmony of the system of nature with the demands of the moral law, can be realized.

In the *Critique of Judgment* Kant goes on to explain the harmony of the sensible and the supersensible by means of the idea of purpose or final cause. In the *Critique of Pure Reason* it was maintained that there are certain fundamental principles of judgment, by the exercise of which the world of experience is determined as a system of substances, their changes being inviolably connected and reciprocally determined. The principles there employed are absolutely essential to the constitution of nature, and the operation of judgment consists simply in bringing particular facts under them. From this "determinant judgment," as Kant calls it, must be distinguished the "reflective judgment," where the principle is not necessary to constitute the universal system of nature, but is a specification of that system. The whole of the special sciences are instances of the application of this latter form of judgment. Its principle is the idea of nature as a unity, all the parts of which have been purposely arranged so as to harmonize. In all scientific investigation we proceed on the principle that nature is purposive; in other words,

THE CRITICAL PHILOSOPHY

that it is so adapted to our intelligence as to be intelligible. This principle, however, Kant denies to be constitutive; it is merely a subjective principle, serving as a practical ideal in all the extension of our knowledge. Proceeding on this principle, science is continually bringing new facts under laws, and subordinating these to higher laws.

There is one special fact in reference to which the idea of purpose is especially important. Without the idea of purpose we cannot explain the distinctive character of living beings at all. Such objects we conceive as purposive, firstly, because each individual produces another of its own kind, so that we may say it is at once its own cause and its own effect; secondly, because its growth is not mere increase in size, but consists in the assimilation of material by which it develops itself; and thirdly, because every part of it has the power of self-perpetuation. A living being is thus one in which all the parts are at once end and means. It might be supposed from these considerations that Kant would maintain that purposiveness must be attributed to living beings themselves. From this conclusion, however, he dissents, on the ground that, to entitle us to affirm that anything in nature is purposive, we should require to have a complete or unconditioned knowledge of nature. The teleological judgment, he argues, could only be constitutive if we had a knowledge of the supersensible, and from such knowledge we are for ever debarred by the conditions of our experience. While therefore we cannot explain even a simple blade of grass without thinking of it as internally purposive, we cannot affirm that it actually is internally purposive. On the other hand, when the idea of purposiveness is suggested to us by the peculiar character of living beings, we must go on to conceive of all nature as a teleological system, since the existence of other forms of being must be compatible with the existence of living beings.

And this leads us to the idea that the beauty of nature may also be treated as if it were purposely intended by nature. An object is judged to be beautiful or ugly purely because of the pleasure or pain which arises from its direct contemplation. Having no relation to personal desire, the feeling is entirely disinterested. Nor does beauty imply the definite conception of an end, as in the case of that which is useful or that which is in itself good. Aesthetic satisfaction, however, does imply purpose in this sense, that in the disinterested contemplation of the object there is a consciousness of the harmony of our imagination and intelligence. Aesthetic judgment may therefore be said to rest upon a "common sense," and because aesthetic satisfaction is capable of being experienced by every one, the judgments based upon it, as expressing the harmony of faculties common to all men, are universal and necessary.

The sublime agrees with the beautiful in being a predicate not of the object but of the subject, in excluding a definite conception of the character of the object, in involving a harmony of imagination and intelligence, and in being universally valid. But there is this important difference between them, that, while the beautiful implies the presentation of an object confined within definite limits, the sublime involves the abortive effort to present a complete whole. While the former may be regarded as tending towards a specific conception of the understanding, the latter may be viewed as an implicit exercise of the reason. The pleasure which arises in the case of the sublime is not direct but indirect; for its first effect is to check the outflow of the vital forces, though its second effect is to produce a stronger outflow of them. As rather a negative than a positive feeling, the sublime is analogous to the feeling of reverence which accompanies the consciousness of the moral law. Strictly speaking, no object in nature is sublime, however it may be fitted to produce in us the feeling of sublimity by the reaction of our minds. It is the very inadequacy of the object to realize the idea of an absolute whole that excites the feeling of sublimity. The idea of purposiveness is therefore in this case connected entirely with the subject. And this explains why a certain degree of cultivation is required to appreciate the sublime in nature. Nevertheless, the sublime is in no sense arbitrary, but has its foundation in the universal nature of man ; and we may therefore fairly demand that, just as every one ought to feel reverence for moral law, so he should experience the feeling of sublimity in presence of the unlimited magnitude or power of nature.

The idea of purpose, as applied primarily in determination of living beings, and, secondarily, of nature as a whole, and also its application in explanation of our aesthetic judgments, Kant denies to be more than a regulative principle. There is, therefore, he contends, no contradiction between the mechanical and the teleological conception of the same object, when it is recognized that, while all objects in nature must be determined by the principle of mechanical causation, there is nothing to hinder us from employing the idea of purpose as a principle by which we advance our knowledge of the specific laws and forms of nature, provided only that we do not attribute purpose to nature itself. If we could penetrate behind the veil that hides the supersensible from our vision, we might find the two principles to be reducible to one ; but, limited in knowledge as we are, we must be content to say that the idea of purpose is merely subjective or regulative, though for us it has the same validity as if it were constitutive.

When, however, we turn to the moral consciousness, we

find that the only ultimate end in the world is that of rational beings as living under absolute moral laws. The moral law prescribes as an ultimate end its own complete realization, and therefore we are entitled to assume that it is capable of being realized. Only on the ground of the moral consciousness can we maintain any ultimate end of creation. Moral teleology, however, implies theology, for the possibility of the realization of morality in the world demands that we should postulate the existence of a Being who is not only independent of nature, but who is at once intelligent and moral. We must not, however, conceive of God as a Being in whom there is any separation between the idea of that which is to be realized and its actual realization; and therefore it is only analogically that we can speak of him as adapting nature to the realization of morality. It is only by analogy that we can conceive the attributes of God at all, and therefore we cannot predicate intelligence and morality of him in the same sense as that in which we affirm them of ourselves. Nevertheless, the final result of our survey of reason in all its forms is to show that God, freedom and immortality rest upon the basis of a rational faith, just because they are presupposed in our experience, limited as it necessarily is.

Morality, as we have seen, is for Kant a law prescribed by reason unconditionally. The moral law is the only object to be willed, and reverence for it the only motive. To obey the law from any consequences believed to follow from such obedience, even if these are the favour of God or eternal happiness, is to destroy the morality of our action; and therefore morality is entirely independent of religion. Though the sole motive of moral action is thus regard for the moral law, yet our acts must have certain consequences, and to these we cannot remain indifferent. Nothing short of the perfect harmony of virtue and happiness can give satisfaction to reason, and therefore morality, when considered in its relation to happiness, compels us to postulate the existence of God, in order to account for the possibility of that harmony. Thus morality, though it is not based upon religion, inevitably leads to religion.

One of the fundamental problems which fall within the sphere of religion is the problem of evil. In the oldest documents dealing with this question, we are told that man in his original state was good, but immediately fell into evil, and has been growing always more and more evil. In modern times it has on the contrary been maintained that the world, instead of growing worse with the lapse of time, has been constantly growing better. We cannot accept either of these views without reservation. Neither good nor evil can be regarded as a property belonging to man in his first state; for no man can be good or evil independently of his own free act. If, therefore, man is said to be evil by "nature," we must interpret this to mean that, notwithstanding his consciousness of moral obligation, he wills to realize his natural impulses. Evil does not consist in the mere fact that man possesses such impulses, but arises only when he takes them up into his will and determines himself by them. As evil is impossible without the free consent of the agent, the fact that man wills evil can only be explained by supposing that he has by his very nature a bias to evil, *i.e.* the disposition to act from natural desire. This bias is possible only in a free being, consisting as it does in the subject making a natural impulse the ground of his action. Why man has this bias we cannot tell, because it belongs to his inner or noumenal being, which cannot be made an object of knowledge. To say, then, that man is "evil by nature" means that it is the nature of man to violate the law which his reason prescribes, *i.e.* to subordinate the moral law to his natural inclinations; and this is the natural bias to evil. Kant refuses to admit that evil is inherited from our first parents; for evil can never exist except as the free choice of the agent. Every evil act must be viewed as absolutely originated, and we may speak, if we please, of the Fall of man as perpetually renewed. No action for which man is responsible can be explained by the influence upon him of an external force, for nothing can influence him without the consent of his own will. Scripture, it is true, speaks of evil as originating at a certain definite time; but this must be understood to mean that an evil act proceeds from the free choice of the agent, which may indeed be called the first cause of the evil act in the sense that it is not an effect of anything else. The sin of Adam is a figure of the free act of choice by which every man makes himself evil. Why man should pervert the true relation of reason and desire, subordinating the former to the latter, we cannot tell, for we cannot make the inner or noumenal self an object of knowledge. Scripture expresses this fact metaphorically, when it represents the fall of man as occasioned by an evil spirit, without attempting to explain the origin of evil itself. And when it declares that God created man upright, we must interpret this to mean that though man wills evil, his true or ideal nature is to be good. No doubt we cannot explain how man should overcome his bias to evil and become good, any more than we can explain why he exhibits this bias; all that we can say is that the possibility of willing the good is implied in the unconditional demand of reason, though, as Kant somewhat grudgingly admits, some supernatural aid may be required. There must be a revival of the primitive purity of the will and its liberation from all lower motives, and this purity implies a complete change of heart, and is therefore represented in scripture as a "new birth." But, though it is in principle an absolute change, it can only be realized in a process. To the eye of omniscience the willing of the new principle is seen as if it had accomplished its perfect work, and man is therefore regarded as already good, though for us he appears, in terms of time, as only gradually freed from the bias to evil.

In a similar way, just as Adam represents the natural man with his bias to evil, so Christ is conceived by Kant to represent man as he is in idea or after the realization of all that he is capable of becoming. As we have seen, the world gets its higher meaning from the fact that it makes possible the realization of the divine purpose, which admits of the free development of man from his original state to his ideal state of moral perfection, and as a consequence the production of complete happiness. In scripture we are told that the Word " was in the beginning with God " ; that Christ is " the only begotten Son " of God ; that it is the Word " whereby all things are made, and without which was not anything made that is made " ; that Christ is the " brightness of the Father's Glory " ; that " in him God loved the world " ; and that only by acceptance of his mind can we hope to become " children of God." All these expressions are by Kant applied to man as he is in idea. They are thus interpreted to mean that the final cause of the world is man in his moral perfection. He is the only creature that can properly be called the Son of God ; for him all other created things exist, and he is a manifestation of the divine perfection. Man is therefore the end of creation, and only in so far as individual men realize the ideal of humanity can they be called the " children of God." To this ideal of moral perfection it is the duty of every man to raise himself, and the fact that man possesses this ideal in virtue of his rational nature implies that he is capable of this self-elevation. And as this ideal is not created by us, but arises in us in an inexplicable way, we may figure it to ourselves as the Incarnation of the Son of God, who has humbled himself, and undergone suffering for the purpose of securing our moral perfection; while man, who is never free from guilt, even after he has accepted the ideal as his standard, looks upon himself as deserving whatever suffering he experiences. This ideal we must conceive in the form of a Person, who is ready to discharge all the duties of man, and to advance the course of goodness both by teaching and by example, but who resists all the seductions to evil and freely gives himself up to an ignominious death for the sake of his fellow-men, not excluding even his enemies. By " faith in the Son of God " Kant understands the condition of those who believe that they should under all temptations adhere to this ideal of humanity.

The reality of this ideal cannot be established by a proof that it has actually been realized, any more than the moral law itself can be based upon an appeal to experience; nevertheless it is implied in the ideal archetypes of our reason. To demand that the prototype of humanity should be embodied in a Person, who proves his claim to be the Son of God by miracles performed by him or upon him, is to betray want of faith in the absolute obligation of the moral law, and to substitute for it faith in a historical fact. Nor will it help in the least to suppose that the ideal of humanity has been realized in a Being preternaturally begotten, who is above the weakness of human nature; on the contrary, such a Being is unfitted to serve as the type of ordinary humanity, and therefore cannot be any guarantee to us that the ideal of humanity is practicable and attainable. On the other hand, it is natural and proper that a teacher, who though perfectly human is yet like God in nature, should speak of himself as if the ideal dwelt bodily in him, and was fully expressed in his life and teaching.

KANT'S PHILOSOPHY OF RELIGION

There are certain difficulties in regard to the possibility of realizing this ideal which must be considered. (1) The ideal demands perfect morality or holiness, and between this goal and the evil from which man starts there is an infinite distance, and an infinite distance cannot be passed over in any given time. The solution of this difficulty is that, though morality is an endless process, God regards the process as complete, when man has undergone a change of heart and is actuated in his conduct by the universal maxim of obedience to the law. (2) What guarantee is there of constancy in the pursuit of the ideal? Kant's reply is that, if a man has persevered in the higher life for a considerable period, we may reasonably conclude that he will continue in the same path. Certain knowledge on such a point seems not only unattainable but morally undesirable. (3) Though a man may undergo a change of heart, all men begin with evil; how then can the guilt of this evil be done away, since no one but the agent himself can take away his guilt, and this guilt is infinite? Kant answers that, after the inward transformation of a man's character, God, contemplating his intelligible character, regards him as a new man. In scripture this idea is expressed by saying that the Son of God is a vicarious substitute for sinners, that by his suffering and death he is their Redeemer, and that he is also their Advocate with God. That God should regard man as being actually what he is only potentially, is a work of grace, though it is quite in harmony with his justice that we for the sake of our faith are acquitted from all further responsibility. This doctrine of Justification by Faith has the important practical bearing, that no external expiation of guilt is needed or indeed possible. Only by a total change of heart can a man be absolved by God, and without such a transformation the absolution of guilt is impossible.

In order that the good principle may overcome the evil, reason demands that there should be formed an ethical society, or kingdom of virtue, comprehending the whole human race. The laws of this society are simply an expression of the ideal of morality, and therefore have no coercive power. The necessity of combination into an ethical commonwealth arises from the fact that, in the absence of a common central principle of good, each person is perpetually exposed to the assaults of the principle of evil, both in himself and in his fellow-men. The highest good cannot be attained by each man preserving separately his own moral perfection, but only by the union of all for a common end. The laws of this ethical commonwealth must be represented as founded on the commandments of God, though they are but the expression of the duties recognized by the reason of man himself. This ethical commonwealth containing the people of God can only be established by God, but it is the duty of man to proceed as if it depended entirely upon himself, and only under this condition is there ground for hoping that it will be realized in the Providence of God. The invisible Church is the idea of the union of all the virtues under the immediate divine moral government, and after the pattern of this idea the visible Church must be formed. The Church must be one, purely ethical, reciprocally free in its members, and unchangeable in its constitution, though admitting of modification from time to time according to place and circumstance. The basis of a Church Universal must be pure religious faith as founded upon reason. The true worship of God consists in the fulfilment of our duties. There can be but one religion, and that too a purely moral religion. The special ceremonial laws of a particular church must therefore harmonize with the purely moral doctrines of religion. The positive creed of the Church is never more than approximately true, but it may be regarded as a necessary preparation for the religion of reason ; and for the final establishment of this religion, it is the duty of all men to labour unweariedly.

LECTURE NINTH.

HEGEL'S RELATION TO KANT.

THROUGH the whole of the *Critical Philosophy*, as we have seen, there runs the distinction between the world of experience and the world in its ultimate nature, and indeed Kant believes that unless this opposition is granted no solution of the contradictions into which reason inevitably falls can possibly be given. Now Hegel, while he admits that there is a relative distinction between phenomena and noumena, refuses to admit that they can be contrasted as abstract opposites in the manner of Kant, and therefore he has to face the problem of resolving the contradictions of reason by reason itself, without having recourse to the fundamental distinction of the sensible world of experience and the supersensible or purely intelligible world. In attempting to give some idea of the philosophy of Hegel, and especially of his philosophy of religion, it will therefore be advisable to indicate his main differences from Kant, which may be said to revolve around their fundamental difference in regard to the relation of phenomena and noumena.

In his account of "experience" Kant maintains that without the combining or relating activity of thought there would be for us no system of "experience" or "nature." The thoughts, however, which constitute the system of experience on its formal side, while they are inseparable from the nature of the human intelligence, cannot be regarded as constituting the universe as it is in itself. To this conclusion, Kant argues, we are forced to come, because otherwise we should have to admit that reason comes into contradiction with itself. Accordingly, while he holds that the world of our experience is under necessary and universal laws, those laws cannot be regarded as determining the ultimate nature of reality, but only as the forms under which every human intelligence must operate. " Nature " is indeed subject to the principles of substantiality, causality and community, but " Nature " is not identical with the Universe, but only with the Universe as it presents itself to us under the forms of our intelligence. On this view therefore there are three terms—the knowing subject, things in themselves, and thoughts—which cannot be brought into complete harmony with one another. The subject can only think things through his thoughts, but as these thoughts do not really comprehend things but only phenomena, it follows that our thoughts actually prevent us from knowing things. Kant, therefore, absolutely separates the three terms indicated. This is the point where Hegel's divergence begins. (*a*) We exist for ourselves only in thinking ourselves, and therefore we have no meaning for ourselves apart from thought. It is only as we are objects for ourselves that our nature can be known at all, and to suppose that our thoughts prevent us from knowing ourselves is the same as saying that to make ourselves an object of thought is to make self-knowledge impossible. Such a perverse view Hegel cannot accept. (*b*) The other assumption of Kant—namely, that we have no knowledge of real objects—is equally untenable. There is no objective world, as Kant himself admits—no systematic or orderly world of nature—except that which involves thought. The world of nature has no existence anywhere but as an object of thought. Hence thoughts are not interposed between us and the world, preventing us from knowing it, but are an actual comprehension of the world. This is evident if we consider the Kantian doctrine itself, that we have no knowledge of things-in-themselves. For, what are these things-in-themselves? If they fall entirely outside of our thought, they are for us nothing whatever, but merely the absence of every object; and, obviously, the world as it exists for our thought cannot be condemned and shown to be merely "phenomenal" by a pure nonentity. Hence by "things-in-themselves" must be understood, not unthinkable being, but being that can be no further characterized. What is thus held to be a condemnation of the world as thought—the world of experience—is in reality the world as thought, but as thought in its most abstract form. It is affirmed that the system of nature is not real because it is determinate. Could anything be more perverse? We first reduce reality to pure being, and then condemn the concrete system of nature because it is not identical with this ghost of abstraction. To escape from this conclusion, we may take refuge in some form of apprehension which excludes thought altogether, either maintaining with the Neo-Platonists that the apprehension of reality excludes all definite thought and involves the abolition even of the distinction of subject and object, or falling back upon the indefiniteness and supposed fulness of mere feeling. Hegel adopts an entirely different solution. To go beyond thought, he contends, is to fall beneath it. We must therefore hold that what is beyond thought cannot possibly be real. We cannot legitimately contrast thought and reality as if they belonged to two mutually exclusive spheres. There can be no reality that is not capable of being thought, and no thought that is not a more or less complete grasp of reality. The opposition of thought and reality is essentially unmeaning; for a thought that does not grasp the nature of reality is the thought of nothing, and a reality not grasped by thought is itself nothing. What can be contrasted, therefore, is not thought and reality, but a more or less adequate or complete thought-reality. Thus, what Kant calls the "thing-in-itself" is just the simplest or most abstract comprehension of thought-reality, not reality separated from thought. With this perfectly abstract thought-reality we can contrast any more determinate thought-reality, but to contrast it with all more concrete forms of thought-reality, as that which is not thought-reality at all, is preposterous. It is legitimate to say that the world as known to us in experience involves a system of things all of which are reciprocally determinant, and this concrete world we can contrast with the utterly general characterization of the known world as simply that which is, but which is not further definable. But, when it is once seen that the purely indeterminate world and the concrete world defined as the system of nature belong to the same sphere, there can be no possible doubt as to which is the more perfectly thought-world. So poor is the former—the "thing-in-itself" as Kant calls it—that, taken by itself, it is "as good as nothing," *i.e.* it only *means* to be real. Yet it is this mere potentiality of reality that Kant imagines to be higher than the whole world of our experience.

The general contrast of Kant and Hegel, then, is perfectly simple. While admitting, or rather contending, that the known world is for us necessarily a world that exists only because we are thinking beings, Kant denies that this known world is in any respect identical with reality. Between the two worlds there is "a great gulf fixed," which can never be spanned, because our thought is essentially limited, and therefore can never stretch beyond itself and grasp reality. Kant, indeed, does not commit himself to the untenable doctrine afterwards put forward by Lotze, that reality cannot be comprehended by any intelligence, even one that is absolutely perfect, because intelligence involves the distinction of subject and object; but he maintains that it cannot be comprehended by our intelligence, and therefore that reality falls beyond knowledge. Hegel, on the other hand, regards the opposition of unthinkable reality and thinkable phenomena as fundamentally unmeaning, since the former is the absence of all objects, and the latter is a contradiction in terms. He, therefore, holds that the only intelligible contrast is not that of reality and thought, but that of a less or more complete thought-reality. And he would add, that in the former the latter is implicit. This does not mean that, if we concentrate attention upon the simplest form of thought-reality—that of " pure being "—we shall be able to derive all the more complex forms of thought-reality from it by a purely analytic process. Such a doctrine is of course nonsense. What Hegel means is that an examination of our experience, as it has developed in the process of history from its first simplest beginnings to the whole complex wealth of modern experience, shows that there is no knowable world at all apart from the constitutive forms of thought; and that when we examine this world, we find that the simplest of these forms is " pure being," while we can see how more complex forms are essential to the concrete wealth of experience, from a consideration of the inadequate and self-contradictory character of all the thoughts by which we determine the nature of the universe except that of self-conscious intelligence, which presupposes and comprehends all the rest. In this way, the opposition of subject and object is overcome, not by the obliteration of either, but by their synthesis. Hence, if we retain the Kantian distinction of phenomena and noumena, it can only be in this form, that by "phenomena" is meant the world as less adequately determined than that of "noumena"; or, otherwise stated, that in "noumena" we not only determine the world by thought, but we recognize that there is no world except that which is so determined. It should be observed that what Hegel maintains is, not that the thinking subject is identical with reality, but that the thinking subject has itself no reality except as grasping reality. What he insists upon is not their abstract self-sameness, but their inseparability. And this is true whether we are speaking of the thinking subject in general, as comprehending all possible intelligences, or of the thinking subject as a particular human being. In the most absolute sense, it is maintained that there is no reality that is not capable of being thought; and, therefore, if any one assumes a reality that by definition cannot be thought, he commits himself to what is essentially irrational and unmeaning. Then, as to the particular human subject, it is not maintained that for every human being, at all stages of his existence and at all times, the world must exist as a thought-reality. Hegel indeed holds that, in the life of every human being, there is a stage prior to thought or consciousness, in which there is no world whatever, but only a chaos of impressions and impulses. But the existence of a "feeling soul" has no real bearing on the question whether reality has any existence in distinction and opposition to thought-reality. The absence of any thought-reality for the "feeling soul" means the absence for it of all reality, since reality exists only for a thinking subject; but this has properly nothing to do with the question, whether reality has any meaning except for a thinking intelligence. It would be to the point if it could be shown that the existence of non-thinking beings is inconsistent with a philosophy which affirms that reality is necessarily thinkable or intelligible reality; but I am not aware that Hegel holds the doctrine of Leibnitz or Lotze or some of their recent followers—a doctrine which seems to me to contravene the plain facts of experience—that all particular beings must be minds; what he holds, as I understand him, is that all particular beings exist, and can only exist, in a universe that is in itself intelligible or rational; what he does not hold is that every particular being must be even dimly and blindly aware of this fact. The two questions are entirely distinct. Surely one may hold that the universe as it appears to a thinking being, as distinguished from the universe as it appears to a feeling being, much more as it does not appear to a non-feeling being, is the only universe, without maintaining that every being in the universe is a thinking being. If this latter line of thought is to be consistently maintained, we ought to hold, not only that every being thinks, but that every being thinks in the same adequate and comprehensive way; for, once admit that there are degrees of distinctness in thought, and the whole principle, that all reality must be of the nature of mind or thought, is virtually surrendered. What Hegel holds, then, is not that every being knows reality, but that, so far as any being knows reality, it is because reality, as an embodiment of thought, is capable of being grasped only by a thinking being.

Another misunderstanding against which we must guard is the assumption that by "thought" is meant only reflective thought. That the world is known only by reflective thought, is true only in the sense that reflection is essential to the explicit comprehension of reality. But this admission is very apt to be misinterpreted. It is grossly misinterpreted if it is understood to mean that the world is known only by the abstract thinker, to the exclusion of all whose ideas assume an imaginative or pictorial form. In this " old quarrel of philosophy and poetry " Hegel is no blind partisan of philosophy. The world is no more the exclusive property of the abstract thinker than is experience ; in point of fact it is the content and not the form which determines the truth of our knowledge. To assume that the world as presented to the mind of a Goethe, say, is less adequate than the world as viewed by a Moses Mendelssohn is obviously absurd. What Hegel held was that reflection in the form of philosophy was essential to a *science* of thought, *i.e.* to a systematic comprehension of what is involved in knowable reality. It may therefore fairly be said, that for him the science of thought-reality is higher in form than the intuitions of poetic genius, while yet in content the one must be identical with the other, and indeed the latter may be richer in content than the former. This shows how inept is the charge sometimes brought against Hegel that he attempted to construct the universe out of abstract thoughts or conceptions. As I understand him, he made no such attempt. What he attempted to do—and with fair success —was to bring to light in their systematic evolution the forms of thought by which particular experiences must be connected with one another if we are to have an intelligible world at all.

The thinking subject, Hegel maintains, is a thinking subject only as it thinks reality. What is denied is that there can be an intelligence which does not grasp the intelligible ; for the supposition that such an intelligence is not only possible, but actually exists in the form of the human intelligence, leads to the setting up of a mere abstraction as equivalent to reality ; *i.e.* to the view that the objects actually known are not real, while that which is real is not known, or at best is known as a bare reality incapable of further determination. Since, therefore, the intelligence comprehends itself only in so far as it is conscious of its own functions in determining reality, while these functions again are the necessary conditions of reality, it follows that in thinking itself it is at the same time thinking the world in its universal aspects. Grant that the universe is rational or intelligible, and that in man as an intelligence this rationality or intelligible reality is capable of being grasped, and it cannot be denied that the system of thought is at the same time the system of things. We must not think of the categories of thought as forms of *our* thought, which may be externally imposed upon an alien matter, supplied to us independently of thought. In the ordinary operations of the mind thought is already at work, though of this fact we are not usually aware; on the contrary, our attention being concentrated upon objects, we overlook the part played by thought in their constitution, not observing that they exist for us only in virtue of our intelligent comprehension of them. Hence we cannot say that the universal form involved in the knowledge of objects belongs purely to the subject; the form is the very nature or essence of the object, the removal of which destroys its objectivity. Thus, while we always live in an intelligible world, in the first instance that world seems to be revealed to us in immediate apprehension, and only when we have discovered the intelligible elements involved in such apprehension, do we explicitly grasp its intelligible character. The great value of this logical consideration of the intelligible forms of experience is that the mind clearly and consciously has before it the forms of thought which are involved in the real world, and thus is capable of learning their relative nature in the constitution of that world. In this way, Hegel contends, we learn that the world is an organic whole, and indeed a rational whole, which differentiates itself in the intelligible structure that may be set forth in a speculative system of logic. To have a world at all the mind must apply intelligible forms to it; but, so long as this process is not systematized, the relation of these forms to one another, and therefore their place in the whole organism of thought, is not grasped. Such a comprehension of the fundamental nature of intelligence brings to light the real nature of reality, so far as its universal character is concerned.

This relation of intelligence and reality is overlooked by the old syllogistic logic, which assumes that thought is a purely formal faculty, that in no way affects the content given to it, and proceeds on the abstract law of identity, $A = A$. If this were really the case, judgment would merely consist in affirming that the subject is, or is not, precisely the same as the predicate—a perfectly useless process, by which no advance could be made and nothing added to knowledge. A concrete speculative logic, on the other hand, will recognize that determinations of thought are not empty "forms," but phases in the process by which the universe is constituted and comprehended. Kant's untenable opposition of phenomena and noumena is due to the assumption that in its own nature thought must conform to the abstract principle of identity, and therefore that the process of thought must in itself always be analytical. Thought, in other words, can never take us beyond itself, and therefore cannot determine real existence. It follows that whenever an object is by definition supersensible, and therefore is not a possible object of sensible experience, it can only exist as an object of pure thought. But, if pure thought or reason, in the absence of all sensible content, is analytic, obviously nothing can be determined by it in regard to a reality that by definition is beyond thought. It is therefore vain to seek by pure thought to determine anything in regard to God, the soul or the world as a whole. These are no doubt thoughts or ideas in our minds, but they are " mere ideas," and, therefore, while we can state what we mean by them, we can by no means affirm that there is any reality corresponding to them. In dealing with these three objects, we inevitably fall into illusion. In the case of God, we confuse an analytic with a synthetic determination of the object; in dealing with the soul, we assume that what is true of the sensible reality is equally true of a supersensible reality; and in attempting by pure thought to grasp the world as a whole, we confuse the indefinite extensibility or divisibility of the world with its infinity.

Hegel refuses to endorse the contention of Kant that thought is in its own nature purely analytic, maintaining that a purely analytic judgment is a mere fiction. And if thought is never merely analytic, it must be capable of existential judgments. Why then does it fall into contradiction when it seeks to determine the world as it is in itself ? The reason, Hegel answers, does not lie in any inherent impotence in thought itself, but in the false assumption that it has before it a complete thought, when in reality it has before it only one element of a complete thought. If we attempt to think a centre without a circumference, we must inevitably fall into contradiction with ourselves—now affirming the unreality of the centre, and again of the circumference; and similarly, if we attempt to think the " finite " as exclusive of the " infinite," the " soul " in separation from the " body," or " God " apart from the " world," we must fall into contradiction —not because of any impotence in our thought, but because we are attempting to think abstract elements as if they were wholes. The thinking subject is very apt to fall into this mistake, just because it has naturally so strong a faith in its own power to grasp the essence of things. Filled with this idea, the first, but really partial determination of reality is assumed to be a complete and adequate determination of it ; and therefore, when by the progress of thought another and opposite aspect of it comes to light, it seems as if thought had fallen into contradiction with itself. In the overthrow of its simple faith in itself, the intelligence is apt to fall into doubt and even despair, concluding that the human mind is infected by an inherent impotence which shuts it out from reality altogether. What is not observed is, that were the human intelligence actually of this character, it would not even be troubled with the problem of its seeming self-contradiction. Where all is illusion, there is no consciousness of illusion. Even the consciousness of the contradiction between two ways of conceiving reality implies that the two ways actually are contradictory of each other, or at least seem to be so ; which they could not be, if thought were incapable of making any true judgment. Hegel does not deny that thought actually employs opposite and indeed contradictory principles in its endeavour to characterize reality. Kant was perfectly right when he said that in its self-confidence the human mind is led to conceive of reality in self-contradictory ways. What Hegel denies is the inference of Kant, that thought inevitably becomes "antinomical" when it attempts to determine reality by pure thought or on the basis of abstract identity ; in other words, that there is an incurable breach between the principle of thought and the true nature of things. Reality, Kant assumes, cannot be self-contradictory ; therefore it must be our thought which is self-contradictory. Such a doctrine Hegel cannot admit, because it sets up an absolute opposition between that which is and that which is thought. The true inference, he contends, is that a partial is taken to be a complete determination of existence. We must therefore in all cases where thought finds itself in presence of a contradiction, seek for a more comprehensive conception which will solve the contradiction. If the "finite" and the "infinite" are absolute opposites, there must be a conception which resolves this opposition; if "soul" and "body" are mutually exclusive, the true inference is that neither has any independent reality; if "God" and the "world" are destructive of each other, neither taken in isolation can be real.

Kant assumes that the forms of thought, untrue as they are from the point of view of ultimate reality, are valid for human thought in its relation to experience. He does not, however, raise the question whether they are ultimate forms of intelligence, but treats them as if they were ultimate, leaving them standing side by side in irreconcilable antagonism. How can the mind be satisfied with the conclusion that, by its very constitution, it is forced to employ mutually contradictory principles? Kant's answer is, that the principles are not mutually contradictory in themselves, but only in relation to objects of sensible experience. There is no contradiction in the thought of the "finite" as such, or in the thought of the "infinite" as such; the contradiction only arises when the sensible world, the world in space and time, is assumed to be absolutely real, and is therefore declared to be absolutely limited or absolutely unlimited. Hegel on the other hand denies that the contradiction is due to the character of the "matter" with which thought deals; the contradiction belongs, not indeed to thought in its real nature, but to thought in so far as it assumes that each of the contrasted terms is a whole thought. It is

HEGEL'S RELATION TO KANT

not because thought is applied to space or time, or to bodies in space and time, that these can be shown to be at once " finite " and " infinite " ; the truth is that " finite " and "infinite" *as thought* are mutually contradictory.[1] Undoubtedly thought cannot possibly rest in mutually contradictory conceptions ; and, therefore, instead of assuming the contradiction to be ultimate and insuperable, we must subject these ideas to the closest scrutiny, in order to see whether they are complete thoughts, or only the *disjecta membra* of complete thoughts. The importance of Kant's view of the " antinomical " character of thought is that he has stated a fundamental problem of philosophy ; but his solution, which consists in affirming that, notwithstanding the self-contradictory character of thought as employed in determination of reality, we must not ascribe contradiction to the universe, but only to the limitations of our intellect, is no real solution. It is vain to affirm that reality is not self-contradictory, if neither in experience nor in thought can we get rid of self-contradiction. This pusillanimous device Hegel absolutely rejects. The intelligence, he holds, is not ultimately in irreconcilable antagonism with itself, but is able to solve its own contradictions, the moment it discovers that its true principle is not that of abstract identity, but of organic unity.

The fundamental difference, then, between the philosophies of Kant and Hegel consists in this, that, while both agree in holding that apart from thought there can be no knowledge, Kant maintains that the system of objects constituted by thought in relation to the differences of sense is not a determination of the nature of things as they are in themselves ; whereas Hegel maintains that thought is capable of grasping the inner nature of things, provided

[1] *I.e.* when conceived as exclusive of each other, not when the "infinite" is seen to comprehend the "finite."

it does not assume the independence and equal value of its various determinations. The opposition of "experience" and "reality" Hegel therefore denies, maintaining that it rests upon an untenable dualism. "Reality" is identical with "experience" as properly understood, and the apparent opposition of that which is known and that which exists is due to the false assumption that determinations of thought are valid only as necessary but human modes of combining objects into a system; whereas in their organic connection they really enter into and constitute the living principles of reality. This conclusion, however, will become clearer by a more particular consideration of Hegel's criticisms of Kant.

The main stages in the development of the theoretical consciousness, as laid down by Kant, are sensibility, understanding, and reason. The impressions of sense, as well as the universal and necessary forms of perception in which they are ordered, are always a multiplicity; for every impression is presented as different from every other, and space and time, in which they always appear, are marked by a mutual exclusion of elements. This multiplicity of sensation and perception is reduced to unity by the understanding, and this faculty of thought presupposes the possibility of referring that multiplicity to the consciousness which Kant calls "pure apperception." The forms or categories of the understanding are functions of synthesis, which constitute and connect the differences of the sensibility in universal and necessary ways. These categories Kant derives from the classification of the kinds of judgment contained in formal logic, arguing that to judge is the same thing as to think of a determinate object. Thus, while the world of sense is characterized by externality—every "now" implying a "before" and "after," and every impression being exclusive of every other—the world as comprehended by thought is a unity, which exists only in relation to the one single self. As the world of our experience is constituted by the synthesis of the understanding, whatever cannot be brought under that synthesis —whatever, in other words, resists the application of the categories—is transcendent, or lies beyond the sphere of knowledge, while all that can be brought under that synthesis is said to be transcendental. Thus, while the categories are the instruments by which the mere perceptions of sense obtain objectivity, it is denied by Kant that they do more than constitute the world of human experience. In themselves they are empty forms without content, and therefore they can be applied only within the range of experience. It directly follows that the understanding cannot know things-in-themselves, for these cannot be presented in perception. In contrast to the understanding, Kant regards reason as the faculty which discovers the finite and conditioned nature of the knowledge comprised in experience, as contrasted with the infinite or unconditioned, which it postulates by its very nature. Thus, while the understanding with its categories cannot transcend phenomena, reason brings to light the limitations of experience, and indicates the possibility of a higher reality.

In maintaining that the categories belong purely to the knowing subject, Hegel regards Kant as endorsing the mistake of common sense, which regards the object and the subject as independent and essentially diverse in their nature. Obviously, if the understanding has peculiar functions of its own, by means of which it imposes order and connection on the sensibility, the product cannot be identical with things as they are in themselves. Now Hegel objects to this dualistic mode of conception, that it unwarrantably assumes the unintelligibility of the universe, and thereby makes it impossible to explain how knowledge is possible. Why should it be assumed that the object must be fundamentally different in nature from the intelligence? Such a doctrine can only be defended by showing either that our intelligence cannot comprehend reality because reality is itself incomprehensible, or that our intelligence is of so peculiar a nature that its determinations hold good only from our human and limited point of view. Hegel maintains that neither of these suppositions is defensible. The assumption of the unintelligibility of reality is self-contradictory, because only by comprehending reality could it be shown to be incomprehensible; and the idea that there is something peculiar to our intelligence makes it impossible for us to make any judgment whatever, since all the products of an absolutely limited intelligence must be infected with its limitations. Hegel, therefore, while agreeing with Kant that the work of the understanding is essential in the constitution of the world, denies that the world as so constituted is discrepant from the world as it truly exists. It is undoubtedly true, for example, that apart from the activity by which thought comprehends impressions, there could be no consciousness of the unity of an object, and no knowledge of two events as causally connected; but it by no means follows that unity and causal connection are not characteristics of the real world. Common sense is no doubt wrong in regarding these intelligible bonds by which the world is converted into a system as existing independently of thought; but it is a mistake to say with Kant that they are merely the modes in which *we* construct a cosmos for ourselves. What really follows from Kant's proof of the necessity of thought to the constitution of objects, is that the objective world is essentially rational or intelligible. We must not underrate the importance of Kant's Copernican transformation of the ordinary view that the world exists independently of our intelligence, and must therefore be apprehended just as it is ; for he is undoubtedly right in holding that there can be for us no objective world at all—no connected system of objects, as distinguished from a mere disconnected series of impressions—except in so far as the thinking subject is related to the object in certain universal and necessary ways. Though it is not true that there is a fundamental opposition between the real world and the world as known to us, it is true that the real world can only be comprehended by a thinking subject. Kant's mistake is to confuse this thinking subject, for which both subject and object are, with the subject of consciousness conceived as opposed to the object and having a peculiar nature of its own. What Hegel means may be expressed in the language of Aristotle by saying that "the intelligence must be pure and unmixed, if it is to comprehend or master things" ; in other words, the forms of thought are not peculiar to human intelligence, but are at once the forms of all intelligence and the universal and necessary determinations of the real world. There is nothing in the nature of intelligence which causes it to stand in its own light, and when it determines the object in certain universal ways, it is not fabricating an artificial universe, but penetrating to the secret of the universe that actually exists.

Nowhere does Kant come so near to a comprehension of the true character of intelligence as in his doctrine of the "transcendental unity of self-consciousness." In the ordinary way of thinking, the understanding is viewed as a power or property which belongs to the subject ; the subject being regarded simply as the substrate of this power or property, in the same way as flame is supposed to have the power to melt wax or to be itself hot. Kant, on the other hand, sees that the self is not merely a property that I happen to have, but is essentially a spontaneous or self-determining unity, and a unity that is conscious of itself as a unity. Nothing can present itself to the mind which is inconsistent with its nature as a unity, and therefore nothing that can prevent it from grasping itself as a unity. In the combination of the various elements of perception into the unity of an object or system of objects, consciousness must maintain its unity with itself; for otherwise the unity of the world would be destroyed. By "objectivity" must therefore be understood the unity or self-identity of consciousness in the synthesis of the various elements of perception, and without this unity no universal synthesis or activity of the understanding is possible. From this objective unity Kant distinguishes the subjective unity, *i.e.* the mere occurrence of elements of perception as successive or co-existent; the former implying the necessary unity of apperception, as differentiated in the categories, which are just the determinate ways in which the elements of perception are brought to the unity of self-consciousness. But, while the understanding thus introduces unity into our experience, Kant holds that the manifold of perception and imagination is entirely independent of the understanding. Now, this assumption of a "given manifold" seems to Hegel to be due to the way in which Kant elevates one element of a concrete whole into a false independence. When all the material of knowledge is regarded as given in sense, there is nothing left for thought to do but to impose upon it its own form; with the result that the world is conceived to be a "manifold" just as before. Hence the world presents itself as spread out in space without limit and as exhibiting an endless series of events. Thus, the only way in which reality could be known would be by a complete survey of the infinite detail of the world of sense. As such a survey is obviously impossible, it is held that thought, in order to find its way amidst the infinite mass and variety of particulars, lets all other particulars drop and concentrates its attention upon some particular phase of a thing. This process of abstraction, it is supposed, does not affect the reality of things, which still remain as before an incomprehensible mass. Thus it is due to the impotence of our understanding that it cannot deal with an infinity of particulars, and must therefore content itself with a mere abstraction.

Obviously, this view of reality makes all philosophy impossible. The work of the understanding cannot consist in merely ignoring differences; it must effect a transformation in our whole way of conceiving the world. We must distinguish between the order of our apprehension and the order of existence. In the history of the individual man it is no doubt true that what comes first is perception, in which real things seem to be a mere aggregate of particulars, and that understanding derives from the manifold so presented the universal or abstract. But philosophy, as the search for the true nature of things, seeks to understand what is at first presented as a mere succession in time. Now, the idea that conceptions are simply abstractions, each complete in itself and fixed in its absolute rigidity, rests upon the supposed independence and completeness of individual things and events. But a conception, properly understood, is a unity which differentiates itself, not a dead unmoving self-sameness. The principle of life, for example, is not simply that which is common to a number of living beings; it is essentially a principle which manifests itself in each living being, and yet never loses its inexhaustible energy. Kant is partially aware of the truth, that thought is not a mere process of abstraction, but involves the self-differentiation of an identity. When he speaks of "*a priori* synthetic judgments," he implies that thought must determine things by transforming the manifold of sense in universal and necessary ways. His "original synthesis of apperception" really implies that thought is a self-determining unity, which remains in identity with itself in all its differences; and if this is true, its activity cannot consist in the production of a mere abstract identity, but must determine the real as a unity in difference. But, while Kant has obtained a glimpse of the true nature of intelligence as essentially self-differentiating, he fails to grasp it clearly and to follow it out to its consequences. Even the use of the term "synthesis" suggests that thought merely combines or relates elements which in themselves have no inner connection, whereas the real work of thought is not to combine what in its own nature is not related, but to comprehend a connection which already subsists and only needs to be explicitly expressed. Moreover, Kant never gets rid of the idea that thought, being merely an operation of the mind for a special and limited purpose, has nothing to do with the real nature of things, and therefore that, while it imposes upon the "matter of sense" its own forms, it does not determine things as they really are.

The doctrine of the Transcendental Judgment is, in Hegel's view, one of the most important parts of the Critical Philosophy, for it is here that Kant seeks to get beyond the abstract opposition of perception and conception with which he starts. Transcendental imagination he regards as determining pure perception in conformity with the categories; and, as all objects of experience must harmonize with these determinations, or "schemata" as Kant calls them, in this indirect way they are brought under the categories. It is held, however, that the transcendental imagination, though it involves the activity of the understanding, yet limits that activity. For, though the understanding is in itself free from the necessary condition under which the imagination operates, namely, relation to time, yet as it can only come into play under that condition, the "schema" is really a limitation of the category. The category of substance, *e.g.*, is the conception of that which is necessarily subject and cannot be predicated of anything else, and thus it has a possible application beyond the world of sense; but this hypothetical extension is practically useless to us, since the category must be schematized as the permanent in time before it is available in actual knowledge. This method of first separating conception from perception, and then mediating between them by the schema, suggests that experience is a purely arbitrary process of combining what otherwise would be uncombined. Hegel, on the other hand, denies that the categories have any meaning except in relation to the world of our experience. Kant's notion that the categories might apply beyond experience arises from his abstract conception of the understanding as the capacity for thinking anything whatever, were it not limited by the necessity of thinking the sensible under the form of time. But thought is not an absolutely indefinite capability, but the capability of thinking that which actually is. The categories dealt with by Kant, which are nothing but an analysis of the mechanical system of nature, are limited in their operation, not because they are forms of thought peculiar to man, but because they are not adequate determinations of reality as a whole. Hence Hegel, rejecting the abstract opposition of subjective and objective, considers the categories from the point of view of their specific character, endeavouring to fix the place of each in the complete comprehension of the world. Just in so far as experience is an adequate comprehension of reality, to that extent knowledge is real. The categories are this comprehension itself, and therefore the categories are not all on the same level. Grant a shallower and a profounder comprehension of reality, or, what is the same thing, a narrower or wider science of experience, and we shall naturally have more or less adequate categories. And it must be possible to determine the degree of truth of a category by asking how far it is consistent with experience in its totality. Moreover, categories, in Hegel's view, are not a number of isolated points, but are all phases or moments in the one organism of thought. Hence every abstract category, *i.e.* every conception formed by treating one side or aspect of a concrete thought as if it were a whole, must inevitably give rise to its opposite or negative, and thus involve thought in contradiction with itself. But this contradiction must be capable of being solved by the discovery of the concrete conception, of which these opposites are but elements torn from their context. Hegel therefore imparts life and movement to the dead and immobile categories of Kant, (1) by taking seriously his suggestion that the third category in his list is always a synthesis of the other two—" totality," *e.g.*, being a combination of " unity " and " plurality," and " limitation " of " reality " and " negation "—and (2) by showing that the concrete categories may be arranged in the order of their comprehensiveness, or by their adequacy as characterizations of the cosmos. Thus, instead of a single abstract opposition of phenomena and noumena, Hegel finds that there are many grades of phenomena, or, better, many grades of reality and truth. These are related to one another, not as appearance to reality, or error to truth, but as lower and higher degrees of being, or lower and higher stages of truth. Like Plato, Hegel denies that a rational being can ever accept that which is absolutely

HEGEL'S RELATION TO KANT

false. The lower category therefore contains in it an element of truth, which it is the business of philosophy to point out and to develop. The simplest category is implicitly the most complex, and the intelligence can never be satisfied until it has reached the category that, as all comprehensive, cannot be transcended.

The world of experience as constituted by the application of the categories to the sensible under the forms of space and time cannot be regarded as a complete whole, and yet the mind cannot be satisfied with less than a complete whole. Kant, therefore, distinguishes reason from understanding. The former seeks for the unconditioned or infinite, while the latter is unable to rise above the conditioned or finite. Since in the phenomenal world no unconditioned object can be found, reason sets up the Idea of such an object in the three forms of the soul, the world, and God. These can never be objects of knowledge, for knowledge is limited to the world of experience. There is, however, an invincible desire to comprehend the unconditioned, and therefore reason, having no definite forms of its own, employs the categories of the understanding—the only definite forms available—in an attempt to determine the unconditioned, not observing that such an application of them is illegitimate, since the categories are by their nature fitted only for the determination of the conditioned.

Now, Hegel admits that in distinguishing between reason and understanding Kant has done valuable service to philosophy. It is of great importance to point out that the determination of the world as a mechanical system—and this is what Kant means by " experience "—cannot be regarded as a final or adequate way of characterizing reality. But Kant makes the mistake of supposing that reason, as distinguished from understanding, has to do with that which, as unconditioned, is the mere negation of the conditioned world, the world of our experience. For, when the unconditioned is thus regarded simply as the opposite of the conditioned, it becomes perfectly abstract; and it is, moreover, not really unconditioned, since, as beyond and exclusive of the conditioned, it is itself finite or conditioned. The true infinite can never be found by simply assuming a reality above the finite, but must involve the absorption of the finite in its own fuller nature. Similarly, Kant is right in declaring that the Idea of reason is higher than the categories of the understanding; but, when he conceives of this Idea as simply that which transcends the limited categories of the understanding, he empties it of all definite content, and makes the comprehension of reality through the Idea impossible. The true distinction between the understanding and the reason is a relative one. The understanding is that phase of thought in which opposite aspects of a single conception are isolated, as *e.g.* when the finite is separated from the infinite; while reason consists in the comprehension of a conception as a whole, as when the finite and infinite are seen to be correlative aspects of the conception of independent being. Kant makes a double mistake: (1) he assumes that the highest determinate categories are those implied in the mechanical determination of the world, and (2) he fails to see that even in these the Idea is already tacitly involved. When these two mistakes are detected, we begin to see that every concrete conception is implicitly the whole system of conceptions by which the universe is determined; and that, so far from the Idea of reason being empty and indeterminate, it is infinitely concrete or determinate. This doctrine Kant was prevented from holding by his assumption that the categories of the understanding, being applicable only to phenomena, give rise to illusion when they are employed in the determination of the non-

HEGEL'S RELATION TO KANT

phenomenal. Thus we do not, by means of the Ideas of reason, obtain any comprehension of the true nature of reality. Unlike the categories, the Ideas of reason are not synthetic : having no matter of sense to which they can be applied, their only value is to serve as ideals, by reference to which the understanding is guided in the process by which it combines the elements of perception into a system. Accordingly the Ideas are not constitutive but only regulative.

In his view of Dialectic, however, Kant has hit upon a profound truth, though he has not developed it to its consequences. On the ordinary view of formal logic, Dialectic is mere sophistry ; in Kant, on the other hand, it is inseparable from reason, in so far as reason seeks to comprehend reality. For reason naturally assumes that reality is knowable, and, having no other way of comprehending its nature but by the application of the categories of the understanding, it falls into the illusion that in determining reality by the only forms of thought at its disposal it is grasping the actual nature of things. What first awakens us to a consciousness of this illusion is that we unexpectedly find ourselves caught in the meshes of self-contradiction ; and, as self-contradiction is to reason intolerable, it is not unnatural to attempt to escape from the world altogether, and to set up the Idea of a reality which transcends the whole world of our experience. Kant, however, has not, in Hegel's view, found the true mode of escape from the self-contradiction in which reason finds itself immersed. His method is to hold that, as opposite ways of determining reality cannot both be true, we must set both aside, and seek for reality in that which is beyond all determination. The source of the contradiction lies, he thinks, in assuming that phenomena are things-in-themselves ; and when this assumption is discarded, the self-contradiction of reason disappears. Hegel, on the other hand, refuses to accept this facile way of eliminating contradiction. It is not true, he contends, that contradiction is due to our false identification of phenomena with things-in-themselves; the contradiction is in the world as grasped by our intelligence. Were there no contradiction in our determination of the world, how should the mind be forced to advance to a more adequate comprehension of it? Thought begins by assuming that the positive determination of things is the true determination of them; but, on closer inspection, it finds that the positive implies the negative, and that the negative, in destroying the positive, gives rise to a new and higher positive. Thus reason, in its attempt to comprehend reality, is led into contradiction, and it is this contradiction that forces it on to a higher conception. Contradiction in fact is the nerve of all natural and spiritual life; and if we are truly to characterize the Absolute, we must first of all exhaust all the contradictions which arise in our inadequate comprehension of reality; in other words, we must combine them in a unity, which is not devoid of negation, but includes all possible negations within itself.

The first of the unconditioned entities which Kant examines is the soul. "In my consciousness," he says, "I always find that I (1) am the determining subject, (2) am singular, or abstractedly simple, (3) am identical, or one and the same in all the variety of objects of which I am conscious, (4) distinguish myself as thinking from all the things outside me." Now, Rational Psychology substitutes for these statements of experience the corresponding categories or metaphysical terms. Thus there arise four new propositions: (i) the soul is a substance, (ii) it is a simple substance, (iii) it is numerically identical at various periods of its existence, (iv) it stands in relation to space.

Such a substitution of metaphysical for empirical attributes is utterly inadmissible, and therefore it is only by a "paralogism" that the latter propositions seem to be established. Now, Hegel regards Kant's criticism as valid so far as it shows that the soul cannot be correctly characterized as a substance or thing, which is simple, permanent, and one object among others. Kant, however, regards these predicates as inapplicable to the soul because, by employing them, reason is applying the categories of the understanding in determination of that which is not a possible object of experience. Hegel, on the other hand, objects to the application of such predicates on the very different ground, that they do not characterize the soul in its distinctive character. No doubt there is a sense in which the soul may be called simple, permanent and individual; it is not, however, the simplicity, permanence and individuality of a non-living thing, but of that which preserves its unity, identity and individuality through its own self-activity and self-determination. When to this it is added that the soul, in its higher form as intelligence, is not only self-active and self-determining but self-conscious, it becomes evident how inadequate it is to define it simply as a substance.

The second unconditioned object is the world. In the attempt which reason makes to comprehend the unconditioned nature of the world, it falls into what Kant calls "antinomies"; in other words, it maintains two opposite propositions about the same object, and in such a way that each of them has to be maintained with equal necessity. To Hegel's mind, the fundamental defect of Kant's view of dialectic is the supposition that thought does not by its own nature give rise to contradiction, but that contradiction essentially consists in applying to things-in-themselves conceptions which have a meaning only in reference to phenomena. In reality, the determinations of thought are in their own nature contradictory, and indeed if they were not so, the progressive comprehension of the world would be impossible : it is because the " positive " implies the " negative," and the " negative " in destroying the " positive " in its first form gives rise to a new and higher " positive," that reason is finally able to characterize reality as it actually is. The proof that existence is capable of being understood is to be found in the consciousness of the contradiction involved in every category of thought except the highest. It is because Kant is still under the influence of the old formal logic that he is blind to the fact that affirmation involves negation, and negation the unity of both. Hence he denies reality to be knowable. He is right in holding that reason does think of the world in contradictory ways ; but, governed by the false conviction that thought must either affirm or deny, he does not see that, when it properly understands itself, it always at once affirms and denies, identifies and distinguishes. To negate, in Kant's view, is to abolish, since all real being must be affirmative ; whereas, in truth, every real negation is implicitly a higher affirmation.

Kant was the first to insist that reason falls into contradiction, even when it cannot be convicted of violating the laws of formal logic. Starting with the natural assumption that thought is capable of comprehending reality, and applying to the world the categories of the understanding, we are led to frame two opposite conceptions of it, which cannot possibly be reconciled with each other. The only legitimate conclusion would therefore seem to be, that the categories of the understanding cannot be absolute determinations of reality. Reason, as Kant rightly contends, cannot rest in the conclusion that two opposite and contradictory ways of determining the world are both true. The

of the understanding, yet limits that activity. For, though the understanding is in itself free from the necessary condition under which the imagination operates, namely, relation to time, yet as it can only come into play under that condition, the "schema" is really a limitation of the category. The category of substance, *e.g.*, is the conception of that which is necessarily subject and cannot be predicated of anything else, and thus it has a possible application beyond the world of sense; but this hypothetical extension is practically useless to us, since the category must be schematized as the permanent in time before it is available in actual knowledge. This method of first separating conception from perception, and then mediating between them by the schema, suggests that experience is a purely arbitrary process of combining what otherwise would be uncombined. Hegel, on the other hand, denies that the categories have any meaning except in relation to the world of our experience. Kant's notion that the categories might apply beyond experience arises from his abstract conception of the understanding as the capacity for thinking anything whatever, were it not limited by the necessity of thinking the sensible under the form of time. But thought is not an absolutely indefinite capability, but the capability of thinking that which actually is. The categories dealt with by Kant, which are nothing but an analysis of the mechanical system of nature, are limited in their operation, not because they are forms of thought peculiar to man, but because they are not adequate determinations of reality as a whole. Hence Hegel, rejecting the abstract opposition of subjective and objective, considers the categories from the point of view of their specific character, endeavouring to fix the place of each in the complete comprehension of the world. Just in so far as experience is an adequate comprehension of reality, to that extent knowledge is real. The categories are this comprehension itself, and therefore the categories are not all on the same level. Grant a shallower and a profounder comprehension of reality, or, what is the same thing, a narrower or wider science of experience, and we shall naturally have more or less adequate categories. And it must be possible to determine the degree of truth of a category by asking how far it is consistent with experience in its totality. Moreover, categories, in Hegel's view, are not a number of isolated points, but are all phases or moments in the one organism of thought. Hence every abstract category, *i.e.* every conception formed by treating one side or aspect of a concrete thought as if it were a whole, must inevitably give rise to its opposite or negative, and thus involve thought in contradiction with itself. But this contradiction must be capable of being solved by the discovery of the concrete conception, of which these opposites are but elements torn from their context. Hegel therefore imparts life and movement to the dead and immobile categories of Kant, (1) by taking seriously his suggestion that the third category in his list is always a synthesis of the other two—" totality," *e.g.*, being a combination of " unity " and " plurality," and " limitation " of " reality " and " negation "—and (2) by showing that the concrete categories may be arranged in the order of their comprehensiveness, or by their adequacy as characterizations of the cosmos. Thus, instead of a single abstract opposition of phenomena and noumena, Hegel finds that there are many grades of phenomena, or, better, many grades of reality and truth. These are related to one another, not as appearance to reality, or error to truth, but as lower and higher degrees of being, or lower and higher stages of truth. Like Plato, Hegel denies that a rational being can ever accept that which is absolutely

HEGEL'S RELATION TO KANT

false. The lower category therefore contains in it an element of truth, which it is the business of philosophy to point out and to develop. The simplest category is implicitly the most complex, and the intelligence can never be satisfied until it has reached the category that, as all comprehensive, cannot be transcended.

The world of experience as constituted by the application of the categories to the sensible under the forms of space and time cannot be regarded as a complete whole, and yet the mind cannot be satisfied with less than a complete whole. Kant, therefore, distinguishes reason from understanding. The former seeks for the unconditioned or infinite, while the latter is unable to rise above the conditioned or finite. Since in the phenomenal world no unconditioned object can be found, reason sets up the Idea of such an object in the three forms of the soul, the world, and God. These can never be objects of knowledge, for knowledge is limited to the world of experience. There is, however, an invincible desire to comprehend the unconditioned, and therefore reason, having no definite forms of its own, employs the categories of the understanding—the only definite forms available—in an attempt to determine the unconditioned, not observing that such an application of them is illegitimate, since the categories are by their nature fitted only for the determination of the conditioned.

Now, Hegel admits that in distinguishing between reason and understanding Kant has done valuable service to philosophy. It is of great importance to point out that the determination of the world as a mechanical system—and this is what Kant means by " experience "—cannot be regarded as a final or adequate way of characterizing reality. But Kant makes the mistake of supposing that reason, as distinguished from understanding, has to do with that which, as unconditioned, is the mere negation of the conditioned world, the world of our experience. For, when the unconditioned is thus regarded simply as the opposite of the conditioned, it becomes perfectly abstract; and it is, moreover, not really unconditioned, since, as beyond and exclusive of the conditioned, it is itself finite or conditioned. The true infinite can never be found by simply assuming a reality above the finite, but must involve the absorption of the finite in its own fuller nature. Similarly, Kant is right in declaring that the Idea of reason is higher than the categories of the understanding; but, when he conceives of this Idea as simply that which transcends the limited categories of the understanding, he empties it of all definite content, and makes the comprehension of reality through the Idea impossible. The true distinction between the understanding and the reason is a relative one. The understanding is that phase of thought in which opposite aspects of a single conception are isolated, as *e.g.* when the finite is separated from the infinite; while reason consists in the comprehension of a conception as a whole, as when the finite and infinite are seen to be correlative aspects of the conception of independent being. Kant makes a double mistake: (1) he assumes that the highest determinate categories are those implied in the mechanical determination of the world, and (2) he fails to see that even in these the Idea is already tacitly involved. When these two mistakes are detected, we begin to see that every concrete conception is implicitly the whole system of conceptions by which the universe is determined; and that, so far from the Idea of reason being empty and indeterminate, it is infinitely concrete or determinate. This doctrine Kant was prevented from holding by his assumption that the categories of the understanding, being applicable only to phenomena, give rise to illusion when they are employed in the determination of the non-phenomenal. Thus we do not, by means of the Ideas of reason, obtain any comprehension of the true nature of reality. Unlike the categories, the Ideas of reason are not synthetic: having no matter of sense to which they can be applied, their only value is to serve as ideals, by reference to which the understanding is guided in the process by which it combines the elements of perception into a system. Accordingly the Ideas are not constitutive but only regulative.

In his view of Dialectic, however, Kant has hit upon a profound truth, though he has not developed it to its consequences. On the ordinary view of formal logic, Dialectic is mere sophistry; in Kant, on the other hand, it is inseparable from reason, in so far as reason seeks to comprehend reality. For reason naturally assumes that reality is knowable, and, having no other way of comprehending its nature but by the application of the categories of the understanding, it falls into the illusion that in determining reality by the only forms of thought at its disposal it is grasping the actual nature of things. What first awakens us to a consciousness of this illusion is that we unexpectedly find ourselves caught in the meshes of self-contradiction; and, as self-contradiction is to reason intolerable, it is not unnatural to attempt to escape from the world altogether, and to set up the Idea of a reality which transcends the whole world of our experience. Kant, however, has not, in Hegel's view, found the true mode of escape from the self-contradiction in which reason finds itself immersed. His method is to hold that, as opposite ways of determining reality cannot both be true, we must set both aside, and seek for reality in that which is beyond all determination. The source of the contradiction lies, he thinks, in assuming that phenomena are things-in-themselves; and when this assumption is discarded, the self-contradiction of reason disappears. Hegel, on the other hand, refuses to accept this facile way of eliminating contradiction. It is not true, he contends, that contradiction is due to our false identification of phenomena with things-in-themselves; the contradiction is in the world as grasped by our intelligence. Were there no contradiction in our determination of the world, how should the mind be forced to advance to a more adequate comprehension of it? Thought begins by assuming that the positive determination of things is the true determination of them; but, on closer inspection, it finds that the positive implies the negative, and that the negative, in destroying the positive, gives rise to a new and higher positive. Thus reason, in its attempt to comprehend reality, is led into contradiction, and it is this contradiction that forces it on to a higher conception. Contradiction in fact is the nerve of all natural and spiritual life; and if we are truly to characterize the Absolute, we must first of all exhaust all the contradictions which arise in our inadequate comprehension of reality; in other words, we must combine them in a unity, which is not devoid of negation, but includes all possible negations within itself.

The first of the unconditioned entities which Kant examines is the soul. "In my consciousness," he says, "I always find that I (1) am the determining subject, (2) am singular, or abstractedly simple, (3) am identical, or one and the same in all the variety of objects of which I am conscious, (4) distinguish myself as thinking from all the things outside me." Now, Rational Psychology substitutes for these statements of experience the corresponding categories or metaphysical terms. Thus there arise four new propositions: (i) the soul is a substance, (ii) it is a simple substance, (iii) it is numerically identical at various periods of its existence, (iv) it stands in relation to space.

Such a substitution of metaphysical for empirical attributes is utterly inadmissible, and therefore it is only by a "paralogism" that the latter propositions seem to be established. Now, Hegel regards Kant's criticism as valid so far as it shows that the soul cannot be correctly characterized as a substance or thing, which is simple, permanent, and one object among others. Kant, however, regards these predicates as inapplicable to the soul because, by employing them, reason is applying the categories of the understanding in determination of that which is not a possible object of experience. Hegel, on the other hand, objects to the application of such predicates on the very different ground, that they do not characterize the soul in its distinctive character. No doubt there is a sense in which the soul may be called simple, permanent and individual; it is not, however, the simplicity, permanence and individuality of a non-living thing, but of that which preserves its unity, identity and individuality through its own self-activity and self-determination. When to this it is added that the soul, in its higher form as intelligence, is not only self-active and self-determining but self-conscious, it becomes evident how inadequate it is to define it simply as a substance.

The second unconditioned object is the world. In the attempt which reason makes to comprehend the unconditioned nature of the world, it falls into what Kant calls "antinomies"; in other words, it maintains two opposite propositions about the same object, and in such a way that each of them has to be maintained with equal necessity. To Hegel's mind, the fundamental defect of Kant's view of dialectic is the supposition that thought does not by its own nature give rise to contradiction, but that contradiction essentially consists in applying to things-in-themselves conceptions which have a meaning only in reference to phenomena. In reality, the determinations of thought are in their own nature contradictory, and indeed if they were not so, the progressive comprehension of the world would be impossible: it is because the "positive" implies the "negative," and the "negative" in destroying the "positive" in its first form gives rise to a new and higher "positive," that reason is finally able to characterize reality as it actually is. The proof that existence is capable of being understood is to be found in the consciousness of the contradiction involved in every category of thought except the highest. It is because Kant is still under the influence of the old formal logic that he is blind to the fact that affirmation involves negation, and negation the unity of both. Hence he denies reality to be knowable. He is right in holding that reason does think of the world in contradictory ways; but, governed by the false conviction that thought must either affirm or deny, he does not see that, when it properly understands itself, it always at once affirms and denies, identifies and distinguishes. To negate, in Kant's view, is to abolish, since all real being must be affirmative; whereas, in truth, every real negation is implicitly a higher affirmation.

Kant was the first to insist that reason falls into contradiction, even when it cannot be convicted of violating the laws of formal logic. Starting with the natural assumption that thought is capable of comprehending reality, and applying to the world the categories of the understanding, we are led to frame two opposite conceptions of it, which cannot possibly be reconciled with each other. The only legitimate conclusion would therefore seem to be, that the categories of the understanding cannot be absolute determinations of reality. Reason, as Kant rightly contends, cannot rest in the conclusion that two opposite and contradictory ways of determining the world are both true. The escape from this intolerable position, according to him, is to hold that neither is true, being but the inadequate, and indeed false, modes of characterizing the world that alone are possible for us under the necessary conditions of our knowledge. Thus we are able to see that our knowledge is only of phenomena, while our idea of reality is merely negative, and therefore does not enable us to characterize it as it actually is. By the application of the categories we are led into contradictory ways of conceiving reality ; by the Ideas of reason, we only learn what reality is not ; and, thus suspended for ever between these opposite limitations, we are unable to penetrate to the real nature of the universe. This doctrine Hegel is unable to accept, though he finds in it the important truth that what Kant calls the categories of the understanding—the categories by which we characterize the world of nature—are not an ultimate determination of reality. Hegel therefore maintains that it is possible for intelligence to discern wherein their inadequacy consists, and to advance to higher categories which will determine reality. The principle of this advance is that two elements of a single conception, when they are isolated, inevitably give rise to each other ; so that the mind can find no rest until it has discovered that they have no independent reality. What really gives the antinomies their force is not the peculiar nature of the objects to which they are applied, but the character of the conceptions themselves, which in their isolation are mutually exclusive or contradictory. They affirm that reality is at once finite and infinite ; and as these terms are by definition contradictory of each other, reality, since it is thus held to be both finite and infinite, is of a self-contradictory character. Kant, it is true, does not state the problem in this logical way, but limits himself to the world, *i.e.* to the external reality, as characterized by extension in space and succession in time. Discarding this unnecessary limitation, the antinomy then runs: quantity by its very nature is finite, quantity by its very nature is infinite; or, better, quantity by its very nature is discrete, quantity by its very nature is continuous. But these opposite elements of "discreteness" and "continuity" are not really separate thoughts, since neither has any meaning apart from the other. It is impossible to think of a unit *per se*, for every unit gets its character from the whole to which it belongs; and, on the other hand, there is no whole apart from the units into which it is differentiated. When therefore we really think quantity, we combine the elements of discreteness and continuity in a single conception.

The two first antinomies of Kant are based upon the character of quantity as involving the opposite aspects of continuity and discreteness. They are therefore rightly called by Kant "mathematical" antinomies. The third and fourth antinomies, on the other hand, he designates the "dynamical" antinomies. The former of these is concerned with the opposition between mechanical causation and free or self-determined causation. Kant's proofs of the thesis and antithesis, Hegel contends, add nothing to the immediate assumption of each; for what the thesis declares is that, if we suppose free causality we contradict mechanical causality, while the antithesis declares that, if we assume mechanical causality we contradict free causality. Obviously, therefore, it is in the one case assumed that mechanical causality is absolute, and in the other case that free causality is absolute. The third supposition—which is the only tenable one—that mechanism and freedom necessarily imply each other, is not referred to. In other words, Kant here as usual assumes that thought proceeds on the principle of abstract identity; whereas, as has been already shown, the true principle of

HEGEL'S RELATION TO KANT

thought is the unification of opposites. It is true that Kant seeks to escape from the contradiction of this antinomy by his distinction of phenomena and noumena; but this desperate resort is due to his untenable doctrine that thought and reality are in irreconcilable conflict.

In the fourth antinomy the conflict is between the assumption of a self-determined Being as the source or cause of all the changes in the world and the apparent necessity of an infinite series of causes. Hegel's solution is that a self-determined being can only be self-determined in a world that is under inviolable law; while, on the other hand, a world under inviolable law necessarily presupposes a self-determined being. There is therefore no need to take refuge in Kant's opposition of phenomena and noumena; in truth the phenomenal world cannot ultimately be explained except by regarding it as an artificially isolated aspect of the real or noumenal world.

The third object of the reason is God. Here again, according to Kant, the application of the categories to an object which, if it exists at all, must be supersensible, cannot possibly be legitimate. The Idea of God is that of a Being who is the absolute totality of all reality; but, inasmuch as the objects of experience must be limited and therefore wanting in reality, by the removal of these limits we reach the conception of a Being who cannot be positively defined but is beyond all definition. Thus the conception of God is perfectly abstract, while opposed to it is Being, which is equally abstract. The union of these two abstracts is the Ideal of reason. In the attempt to effect their union, we may either begin with Being and proceed to show that it involves the conception of God, or we may start from the conception of God and seek to show that it involves Being. Now (1) Being is presented to us as a world that is infinitely various in its content. This world may be viewed either (*a*) as an assemblage of innumerable unconnected facts, or (*b*) as a body of innumerable facts all reciprocally dependent and exhibiting traces of design or purpose. The former is the aspect fastened upon in the cosmological proof; the latter is the basis of the physico-theological proof. It is argued in the one that unconnected or contingent facts imply the existence of an absolutely necessary Being as their cause, and in the other that the purpose displayed in the adaptation of innumerable facts to one another compels us to suppose the existence of a Being who by his intelligence has ordered them in this purposive way; while both arguments maintain that this Being corresponds to the conception of God. Kant's general criticism of both proofs is that the attempt to employ the laws of thought in explanation of real existence is illegitimate. Thought by its very nature can of itself determine nothing in regard to the ultimate nature of reality, and it is therefore impossible to go beyond the world of experience by any valid process of thought. When it is argued, in the cosmological argument, that the existence of contingent facts in the world of experience implies the existence of a cause beyond the world, it is not seen that every cause that we can possibly know is itself an effect, and therefore that the argument from causality cannot establish the existence of a cause that is absolutely original or primary. Such a use of the category of causation rests on a confusion of phenomena with things-in-themselves. Similarly, the argument from design cannot possibly establish the existence of God, because it is not only open to the same objection as the cosmological argument, but it illegitimately employs the idea of purposiveness, which even in relation to the world of experience is only regulative, as if it were constitutive of non-phenomenal reality. There is, therefore, no way of passing from the world to God.

To this criticism Hegel objects that it sets up an opposition between thought and being, which makes not only the knowledge of God but all knowledge impossible. These two arguments really express two stages in the ascent from the data of sense to the true comprehension of the world. The first view of the world as an assemblage of unconnected parts is found to be unsatisfactory, as Kant himself admits, and we are therefore forced to regard the world as a system in which each fact is what it is in virtue of its relation to all the rest. But it is impossible to stop here, since even the conception of a system of facts presupposes a real unity of which these are determinations. The finite necessarily presupposes the infinite. This is the truth which the cosmological argument attempts to formulate; and if it expresses the character of the infinite in terms of the limited category of cause, that does not affect the essence of the argument, which is, that finite and contingent being implies an original Being, which expresses itself in and through the finite and contingent. Similarly, what gives force to the physico-theological argument is the organic unity which characterizes the world, though this is imperfectly apprehended when it is figured as the external adaptation of a pre-existent matter to a finite end. When we see that the system of the world must involve the harmony of all its parts, it becomes evident that the physico-theological argument, as compared with the cosmological, expresses a further step in the determination of reality. The weakness of Kant's criticism of both arguments is that he does not allow for the transformation effected by the advance from a relatively superficial to a deeper conception. It is true that if the conception of the world as an aggregate of contingent facts or of final causes were absolute, the argument to the existence of God would be invalid. The real process of thought, however, does not consist in building upon absolute presuppositions, but in developing the necessary implications involved in certain presuppositions which, in their literal form, are not ultimate. It is only from the point of view of formal logic, with its assumption of abstract identity as the basis of all reasoning, that the transition from contingency or design to a higher reality is invalid; while a concrete logic is based on the principle that thought in its progress is always transforming the data from which it starts by pointing out the contradictions that they involve, and bringing to light the higher conception by which they are resolved. Thought is therefore at once negative and positive: it shows the inadequacy of the first view of things, and substitutes for it a more adequate conception. The two arguments under consideration are only defective in not accentuating the negative aspect of the process. Hence they do not make it clear that the first view of the world as contingent or externally purposive is not final and that properly understood the world is identical with God. From the ultimate point of view the finite world has no independent existence. As to Kant's objection to the employment of cause or design in the explanation of the relation of the world to God, it must be admitted that he is right in saying that these conceptions are inadequate as expressions of the true nature of the relation. At the same time they bring to light certain characteristics of reality and are essential to a full comprehension of the Idea of God. What it is important to observe, however, is that, while the determination of the world by the category of cause emphasizes the system of things, and the application of the idea of final cause brings into prominence the unity and harmony of the world, the only perfectly adequate conception of God is that of spirit or self-conscious intelligence.

HEGEL'S RELATION TO KANT

The ontological proof begins with the conception of God and reasons to his existence. Kant's objection is, that it is impossible to deduce being from thought. All that the argument shows, he argues, is that we have the conception of God, not that he actually exists. "Being" is not a property which can be predicated by any actual reality. The conception of anything is complete as a conception without the addition of " being " to it. All that " being " expresses is that a certain content is thought in a certain conception. The conception of God no doubt involves the logical attributes of " almighty," " all-wise," etc., but this conception is not amplified by saying that "God" is conceived to " be." To think that " God is " is not the same thing as saying that " God is," *i.e.* has a real or objective existence. No doubt the "content" of a conception and of a reality may be the same, but we cannot pass from the one to the other. A hundred dollars in thought and a hundred actual dollars are both a hundred, but it does not follow that to think of a hundred dollars is to possess them.

In his examination of this criticism Hegel begins by pointing out that Kant, in contending that the conception of a hundred dollars is in content the same as an actual hundred dollars, has first abstracted from the difference between them and then affirmed their identity. No doubt the conception of a hundred so understood is the same as the actual hundred, for the simple reason that, taken in this abstract way, they mean precisely the same thing. But, when Kant abolishes their distinction, and then argues that we cannot advance from conception to reality, he forgets that the conception of a hundred dollars as a mere idea and the conception of a hundred actual dollars are not identical in content, since in the latter case we are speaking of a hundred dollars in their relation to the whole of experience. It is no doubt true that when we have only before our minds certain abstract elements, we cannot say whether an actual object containing those elements is or is not; but it by no means follows that it is impossible in other ways to determine whether the object is actual or merely possible. What Kant means by the "conception" of a hundred dollars therefore is the isolated idea, as cut off from all relation to external reality and to the subject. Of course, viewed in this perfectly abstract way, the "conception" is an abstract identity, and in fact it has no reality whatever, except as an element of reality taken by the understanding as if it were a real thing. No such abstraction can possibly be real. When, however, that element is really grasped by thought, it is conceived as an element in a larger whole—in the present instance as a fact of experience relative to other facts and to the thinking subject.

Applying this principle to the Kantian criticism of the ontological proof, it is manifest that what Kant proves is merely that God, when isolated from the concrete reality of the universe, cannot be shown to have an actual existence. And this is perfectly true: a Being so conceived, as devoid of all determinations of thought, cannot be shown to exist. But the reason is not that we cannot pass from the conception of God to the existence of God, but because what is called the conception of God is no conception at all, since "pure being" is for thought indistinguishable from "pure nothing," *i.e.* is not a possible object of thought. Kant has therefore only proved that, on the assumption that the principle of thought is abstract identity, God cannot be proved to exist. But, as nothing whatever can be proved to exist if thought is assumed to work with bare abstractions, the proper conclusion is, that thought does not proceed on the principle of abstract identity, but on the principle that reality involves both "being" and "nothing," or "affirmation" and "negation." We may therefore regard the ontological proof as an imperfect formulation of the principle, that what thought in its completeness affirms to exist actually does exist; and hence that if God can be shown to be involved in the world as known to us, he must actually exist.

In the *Critique of Practical Reason* Kant goes on to consider what is involved in moral action, as distinguished from knowledge. The theoretical reason is absolutely limited by the character of what is given to it in sensible experience; for, though it discerns the limitation of the world, which arises from the application of its forms to the matter of sense, the result of this consciousness is only to suggest a reality lying beyond experience without revealing its determinate nature. Thus theoretical reason has no freedom: it can originate no reality from itself, and the objects with which it deals are merely appearances. Practical reason, on the other hand, is absolutely independent of any given element; it does not presuppose natural law or the matter of sense, but determines itself by its own nature. Its object is the moral law, and by this, and this only, it freely determines itself. Practical reason is thus a thinking will, a will which determines itself on universal principles. It is through the moral consciousness that man becomes aware of his true nature. Man as moral is conscious of his own true self, whereas in knowledge he is only conscious of himself in and through his relation to the object. Here reason supplies its own law, and this law expresses the real nature of the moral subject. True, the individual man is not immediately in harmony with his real nature, which is therefore for him an ideal, but he is conscious of this ideal as that which expresses what he truly is. Kant distinguishes between will which takes the form of natural impulse or inclination and will as such, the latter consisting in identification with a universal end. The former he absolutely condemns, on the ground that a will which seeks its good in the pleasure expected to result from its attainment is not free. This leaves as the only moral course of action that which is independent of pleasure and therefore is followed purely for itself. Morality, he therefore contends, consists in action which is conceived to be of universal application, and is done purely from reverence for the law itself, irrespective of the pleasure of pain that may accrue from it. The moral law cannot be learned from experience, for it commands absolutely or categorically even if it never has been obeyed, and hence it proceeds entirely from within. Freedom consists solely in willing this law, and any action in which the will surrenders its autonomy, and determines itself by natural inclination, is heteronomous. Man's real nature therefore consists in determining himself by the law of reason, though as a matter of fact no one is in all cases so determined.

Hegel finds in this doctrine of Kant the supremely important principle that the ultimate end of all action is the realization of freedom, so that no external authority can impose upon man anything that is inconsistent with that end. He objects, however, to Kant's conception of freedom that, just as he makes the highest idea of theoretical reason an abstract identity, so practical reason is declared to consist simply in a self-identity which has in it no definite content. The test of the universality of a moral law is for Kant the absence of self-contradiction, and no specific law can be established in that way. Here, as in the theoretical sphere, Kant falls back upon a formal identity, which is merely the principle of the abstract understanding. We are to defend our country and to promote the happiness of others purely because it is our duty to do so, and not at all because these specific ends are essential to the realization of our freedom. An abstract identity, however, affords no criterion of morality, because any content whatever may be thrown into this form. It is no doubt true that the command, " Respect all rights of property," is inconsistent with theft, but it is a universal law only because rights of property are assumed ; deny these, and there is no contradiction in the command, " Do not respect any rights of property." Thus, the law of morality is not, as Kant assumes, merely formal, but must be determined by the principle, that only that is moral which is essential to the realization of freedom. The defect in Kant's view of morality is further seen when we consider the relation of the will of the individual to the universal will. The individual man, it is said, in order to be moral, must determine his conduct purely by the moral law ; but, as there is in his nature a conflict of the higher and lower will, morality is an ideal : it is that which a man ought to be, but which he never actually is. This cleft between the actual and the ideal is due to the same abstract opposition as plays so decided a part in Kant's theoretical philosophy. Just as theoretical reason can never comprehend reality because the sensible world is irrational, so practical reason is absolutely thwarted and opposed by the natural desires and inclinations. Obviously, on this view the conflict must be eternal ; and therefore Kant postulates the immortality of the soul, in order to allow time for the harmonization of reason and desire, not seeing that even infinite time cannot harmonize two absolute opposites. The fundamental mistake of Kant is in not recognizing that desire and reason are not incompatible, but that the former is implicitly the latter.

The second postulate is the existence of God, who must be held to exist, it is argued, because otherwise the union of virtue and happiness, which reason demands, would be inexplicable. By this postulate nature is proved to be compatible with freedom or the rational will. The union of virtue and happiness, however, is only that which must be possible, not that which actually is. Because in this world virtue is not always followed by happiness, and vice by unhappiness, we must postulate the existence of God, who will ultimately bring virtue and happiness into perfect harmony and annex unhappiness to virtue. Now, as this harmony is for Kant only a prophecy, which it will require infinite time to realize, Hegel objects that the harmony can never actually be realized, and therefore that evil must be eternal. Thus after all the postulate of God does not abolish the opposition between the natural and the spiritual. The same dualism is found in the practical as in the theoretical reason. Freedom is not capable of being realized in a world that is fundamentally opposed to moral law. There is no way of escape from this contradiction except by the recognition that nature is not hostile to freedom, and therefore that morality is actually capable of being realized here and now. Morality is no mere ideal that can only be realized in a world entirely different from the world in which we live. Kant's opposition of nature and morality, instead of proving the existence of God, makes his existence incredible; for it is not possible to reason from a world that is essentially irrational and anti-moral to the existence of a rational and moral principle. To establish the existence of God, it must be shown that, properly understood, the world is rational through and through, and therefore that morality is the only principle which can possibly prevail.

The *Critique of Judgment* is in some ways the most important of all Kant's works. In it an attempt is made to show that the demand for the unity of nature and freedom is in a sense actually present in the world, and is not postponed to an unrealizable future. The understanding is unable to comprehend reality, because its laws, as merely universal, do not enable us to determine the particular. In the practical sphere, again, reason has its own laws; but, though will is action in accordance with those laws, nature is opposed to the realization of freedom. Thus, while understanding prescribes the laws of the sensible world, and reason as practical the laws of the moral world, the two realms are separate and independent of each other. Nevertheless, these two realms must be conceived as not absolutely incompatible; for the moral law ought to be realized in the world of nature, and therefore nature must be conceived as admitting the possibility of such realization. The idea of the possible harmony of nature and freedom thus implies the idea of final cause or purpose, an idea which is the principle of reflective judgment, the faculty that mediates between understanding and reason, nature and freedom. The particular laws of nature must therefore be viewed as if they have been established by an intelligence other than ours with a view to their being comprehended by us. This idea of nature as in all its diversity purposive is, however, not to be regarded as objective, but only as a principle for the extension of our knowledge.

While he finds Kant's view of the Judgment defective in so far as it affirms that the idea of final cause is merely subjective or regulative, Hegel thinks that it points " as by a side-gesture," to use Goethe's phrase, to the principle by which the universe may be rationalized. The judgment is virtually invested with the function of a perceptive intelligence, in which particulars are seen to be informed by the universal. Such a universal is not an abstract conception under which particulars are merely externally subsumed, but a living principle which moulds the particulars after its own image. The beautiful object is not something that can exist apart from the form in which it is presented, nor is the living being explicable as a merely mechanical combination of parts that have no necessary relation to one another; but an object is beautiful, or a being lives, only because it is the realization of an idea. A universal which manifests itself in the particular is not an abstract but a concrete unity. No doubt in art as in the living individual, what is realized is not an absolutely universal principle; but in the conception of the whole world as an organic unity, in which each part exists only in relation to the other parts, Kant indicates the principle which comprehends all existence. But in denying its constitutive value he again drops back into the separative or phenomenalist point of view. Hence he will not admit that it is possible to make the ultimate principle an object of thought. In the free play of genius, indeed, he sees the expression of an immediate union with reality; but he denies that it is possible to express the intuitions of genius in the form of a definite conception. Similarly, while in Taste there is a feeling of the harmony between the free play of imagination and the uniformity of understanding, we cannot, he thinks, show theoretically that this is more than a fortunate coincidence. In his conception of the living organism as the manifestation of the informing principle of final cause, Kant shows that he has risen above the mere external adaptation of means to ends. And yet, although he has thus correctly grasped the idea of final cause as immanent in, and inseparable from, the particulars, he again falls back upon the idea that teleology is a principle peculiar to our intelligence, maintaining that, from a sufficiently comprehensive point of view, it might perhaps be discovered that mechanism is an adequate characterization of the world. Now, the limitation of knowledge to the mechanical determination of the world is obviously arbitrary, even from Kant's own

HEGEL'S RELATION TO KANT

point of view. The conception of final cause, he says, is subjective or regulative ; the categories of mechanical causation are objective or constitutive. But we must remember that the latter are only objective in the sense that they are necessary to our having any world of experience at all, while yet they are not determinations of reality. Thus, after all, they are subjective. And the same thing applies to the idea of final cause, which is admittedly essential to the determination of the world of our experience, though not to absolute existence. Hence it would have been natural for Kant to admit that the idea of inward adaptation or design is constitutive in the same sense as the mechanical categories.

Applying the idea of final cause to the process of the world, we get the idea of the Good as the absolute or final purpose of the world, and this purpose must be conceived to be the realization of the idea of God. Kant, however, will not admit that the conception of final cause can be employed in this way, because he conceives the Good as only a law peculiar to our reason in its practical use. The course of the world must admit of the realization of the moral law, but it cannot be said that " morality is the nature of things." Hence the Good as final cause and the course of the world fall apart, and therefore Kant falls back upon the idea that the Good is merely that which ought to be, but is not ; it is the object of a faith that looks to some other world for the realization of that which, as involving a progress to infinity, can never be realized here. With this insoluble contradiction the philosophy of Kant ends ; and such a consummation is in itself a striking proof of the falsity of the opposition of appearance and reality, knowledge and faith.

LECTURE TENTH.

HEGEL'S PHILOSOPHY OF RELIGION.

In my last lecture I endeavoured to give some account of the criticisms by which Hegel sought to do away with the inner contradictions of the *Critical Philosophy*. The fundamental objection which he makes to it is that by its opposition of phenomena and noumena it creates a division that virtually splits up the universe into two discrepant halves. This division he regards as due primarily to the false conception of thought as in its own nature purely analytic, whereas he contends that thought always operates by way of a method which is at once analytic and synthetic or concrete. Thought is therefore, Hegel contends, adequate to the comprehension of reality, and in fact what Kant calls the categories of thought are the more or less adequate ways in which the human intelligence grasps the fundamental principles of a universe essentially rational. No doubt a long process of historical evolution must go on before this comprehension of the universe as rational is reached; but until it is recognized that the whole life of man as a spiritual being is simply the process by which he comes to know that his own rational nature is the only key to the interpretation of existence, philosophy must be burdened with doubt and contradiction. Though Hegel considers separately the process by which a successively more adequate interpretation by thought of the universe is reached, he does not mean that the whole nature of things is reducible to categories of thought; his idea is that the human mind, in the course of the experience of the race, comes to grasp the principles of that rational organism which constitutes the universe, and to set forth its structure in abstract terms. It follows that these principles are not a mere aggregate, but, like the universe of which they are the abstract formulation, constitute an organic whole, in which no single thought stands alone, but each gets its meaning from its inseparable connection with all other thoughts. For this reason Hegel protests against the method of the understanding, which consists in isolating a thought, or rather an element of a thought, and treating it as if it were complete in itself; and to this method he attributes the contradictions with which the mind finds itself confronted. And Hegel extends this principle even beyond the whole organism of thought, maintaining that the only complete liberation from contradiction consists in following the development of the universe, first in the sphere of nature, and next in the sphere of mind, until we have reached a complete comprehension of it in the Idea of the Absolute or God, which is the crowning synthesis of the whole system.

In attempting to give some idea of Hegel's Philosophy of Religion, I shall pass over his characterization of the various forms of religion, rich as it is in suggestion, and deal only with his conception of what he calls the Absolute Religion. The historical account has made it clear that the Idea upon which religion is based—an Idea obscurely present in all its forms, but only explicitly grasped in the highest—is that of the Absolute or God, defined as spirit that is conscious of itself as spirit. Religion therefore involves on the part of man the comprehension of God as the self-conscious intelligence of which the universe is the expression. Man is capable of religion, because in him there is present the principle which in its full development constitutes the very nature of the Absolute. Conversely, the Absolute is manifested in man, and apart from such manifestation it would not be the Absolute—though of course it is not limited to man, but is present in a lower or less explicit form in all modes of being. We may therefore say, either that man comes to self-consciousness in God, or that God comes to self-consciousness in man. The true self of man is the ideal self, and the ideal self is God. When Hegel says that religion is " the self-consciousness of God," he purposely unites the two ideas of (*a*) God's consciousness of himself as expressed in man, and (*b*) man's consciousness of God as identical with his own true self. As the term " consciousness " in Hegel always involves the opposition of subject and object, in affirming that religion consists in the " self-consciousness " of God, he means to deny the abstract contrast of the world and God, and to affirm that the world when fully understood is identical with God. Hence God can only be conscious of himself in being conscious of the world. To oppose Nature to God is to make both finite ; only by recognizing that Nature is God, and God is Nature, can the infinity of God be preserved. It is the very essence of God as mind or spirit to manifest himself in the world, and without such manifestation he cannot be. " God distinguishes himself from himself," says Hegel, " and is an object for himself, but in this distinction he is purely identical with himself, or is spirit." There is no abstract separation between the world and God, but, properly understood, the world is the self-differentiation of God, and therefore God exists and is self-conscious only in this differentiation. Hegel is the consistent opponent of all forms of transcendence. A God who is beyond the world can have no reality. At the same time Hegel does not accept the immediate identification of the world with God. If the world is conceived as a mere assemblage of objects in space and time, or as a mechanical system, the parts of which are externally connected with one another, or even as an organic system which is pervaded and united by the principle of life, he would deny that the world is identical with God. Only when it is seen that the world is a spiritual organism can it be said that it is identical with God ; and this spiritual organism, as we must remember, has in it much that we are not yet able to comprehend. As the universe is God as self-manifested, the " finite consciousness," Hegel tells us, " knows God only in so far as God knows himself in it." For, if the world has no existence as a merely mechanical system, but involves the existence of the " finite consciousness " as a higher manifestation of it, the latter, as involving the consciousness of Nature, is an expression of the essence of God, and therefore it " knows God " only so far as in comprehending Nature as involving mind it grasps the essence of God. This is the basis of the religious consciousness, in which man recognizes that he only truly knows himself as he knows God. " God is spirit," says Hegel, " and indeed the spirit of his Church, *i.e.* of those who reverence him." The spirit is present in all men, and is consciously present in those who comprehend and reverence God. Hegel, of course, does not mean to distinguish spirit from God, but only to emphasize the truth that God is revealed only to rational or self-conscious beings, though he is also manifested in all forms of being. Nor by the " Church " does he mean an external organization, but the spirit which pervades and reproduces itself in every rational being, and which is only imperfectly realized in any external organization. From this point of view Hegel tells us that " God is no longer conceived as a ' beyond,' an unknown, for he has made known to men what he is, and that not merely in an external history, but in consciousness." In other words, we must not think of God, after the manner of deism, as merely an Être Suprême, whose nature is absolutely incomprehensible by the human mind. Nor is it enough that God has been declared to exist in a written document, but every man must learn to know him in and through his consciousness of himself.

The Absolute Religion may properly be called the "revealed" religion; by which Hegel does not mean that it has come to man through any supernatural or miraculous channel, but that, by the normal development of the religious consciousness, the nature of God as spirit has ultimately attained to clear and explicit consciousness. This is the principle of the Christian religion, which is therefore identical with the ultimate or absolute religion. Hegel, however, would not admit that Christianity can be identified with every dogmatic system that claims to formulate it; nor would he even identify it with the particular form in which it was expressed by Jesus and much less by his followers. Christianity, as he conceives of it, is the religion which affirms the essential identity of man, as he is in idea, with God. It is this comprehension of the ultimate nature of things which makes it the Absolute Religion, and it may well be called the Revealed Religion because it has brought to light the "open secret" of the universe. Hence Hegel emphatically rejects the doctrine that the knowledge of God consists in the apprehension of a Being standing apart from the world, and especially from man, just as we learn to know that the sun or the stars exist. God is not separable from the finite consciousness, but constitutes its very essence. Religion is no mere intellectual apprehension of a Being who is one among others: it involves the response of the whole complex nature of man to that without which it could not be. Man must not only know that God is, but must experience him in the depths of his soul. On the other hand, Hegel refuses to admit that this experience of God can only take the form of immediate feeling. The truth of this contention is that there can be no religion unless the emotions as well as the intellect and will are transformed, but this truth is utterly perverted when it is held that religion consists simply in the feeling of dependence upon a Supreme Being. For, not only does this extrude God from the inner shrine of man's rational consciousness, making him an external being, but it overlooks the fact that religious feeling is only possible for a rational or self-conscious being, and therefore that the principles underlying religion are capable of being expressed in a rational system or philosophy of religion. The idea that religion is identical with a feeling that does not admit of explicit formulation seems to be due to a perverted apprehension of what was involved in the Reformation, the principle of which was that all traditional conceptions must be set aside, and man brought into immediate communication with God. It is an utter perversion of this truth to affirm that religion is purely a matter of feeling. If all conceptions are to be eliminated from religion, it obviously cannot make any difference what the content of religion may be, so long as the feeling remains. Such a distortion of religion, which regards the content as indifferent, Hegel could not possibly accept. On this false view, even if the content is that of the Absolute Religion, it remains for the subject something externally presented to him—something which he is asked to accept in blind faith—and he can therefore never rise to the truly religious consciousness of God. Such a view can only find acceptance among reasonable men from a confusion of thought between the truth that the religious man identifies himself absolutely with God, and the falsehood that this identification excludes all thought. If it is said that man is enabled to transcend the opposition of himself and God only through the "grace" of God, Hegel answers that this mechanical and external view of " grace " is incompatible with true religion, which exists only through the response of the subject himself. A free being cannot accept anything that does not appeal to his rational nature. Thus feeling must be informed with thought, and thought must comprehend the true content of religion, or religion is impossible.

The Absolute Religion, then, is based upon the idea of God, as essentially self-manifesting or self-revealing. Hegel, therefore, re-interprets the doctrine of the Church that God has " created " the world. The idea that creation is an arbitrary act, which might or might not have taken place, he entirely rejects. God did not create the world at some moment of time in the past, but he is eternally creating it, or eternally revealing himself in it. We cannot say that the world ever began to be; but from all eternity it has existed as a manifestation of the eternal nature of God. Thus creation is really an eternal process of self-revelation, in which God's " other," the universe, is posited and transcended as " other." This indeed is the essential nature of spirit. In the Absolute Religion there is an explicit consciousness of the principle involved potentially in all religion, the principle that religion is the revelation of God in all that exists, but more especially his revelation in and to the human spirit. It is also the religion of truth and freedom, in which man rises to the consciousness that in his true nature he is one with God, and discerns that true freedom consists in overcoming that alienation from God, which is his first or immediate nature.

From what has been said, Hegel's view of the relation of the Absolute Religion to historical Christianity may be readily anticipated. It is a law of mind that what is at first presented as an external fact is only subsequently grasped in its inner nature. Hence the Absolute Religion is presented in the order of time as " positive " truth, and only then does the mind return upon itself or see itself mirrored in the object. Even moral ideas are first presented to us in an outward way, being communicated by education, training and definite instruction; but the ground of their obligation lies in their essentially rational character, not in the fact that they are the customary principles of action of the age in which we live. It is in this external way that we learn the laws of society and of the state; but nothing can justify the imposition of such laws except their rationality—they are not obligatory because they are imposed by the State, but the State imposes them, or should impose them, because it is under obligation to do so. Hence the " positive " character of law does not exclude its rationality. Nothing is merely " positive " except that which is arbitrary and contingent; and whatever is of this character will inevitably disappear under the influence of man's continual effort to embody in his life that which is intrinsically rational. Applying to religion the distinction thus suggested, Hegel separates between that in historical Christianity which is rational or eternal, and that which is temporary and evanescent. The former alone belongs to the essential nature of religion, and therefore must find expression and embodiment in the Absolute Religion. The doctrines which formulate the essence of religion have a " positive " side, in so far as they are imposed by the Church, while the members of the Church are expected to believe them. But, just as the laws of morality and of the State ultimately derive their sanction solely from their rationality, so the truths of religion can have no authority but the witness of the spirit. When it is supposed that the truths of religion may be established by an appeal to miracles, which are held to attest the divinity of the person who first revealed them, it is not seen that no interference with the laws of the visible world can possibly guarantee the truth of that which is not attested by the witness of the spirit. Truth shines by its own light. All that is noble, lofty, moral and divine finds a response in our minds and hearts. This witness of the spirit presents itself in its highest form in philosophy, which is not based upon any presupposition, but appeals only to the testimony of reason itself; for philosophy rests upon the self-development of reason, and the recognition of that self-development as necessary from the very nature of reason. Hegel does not mean that we can have no true belief in God and the truths of religion except through the medium of philosophy. It is not by a demonstration of the existence of God that we first become assured of his existence; all that such demonstration can do is to assign the ground upon which a belief in his existence is tacitly based. The witness of the spirit operates in many ways. The spiritual necessities of men vary according to their stage of culture and development. " The heart or feeling of man is not like the heart or feeling of an animal; it is the heart of a thinking or rational being, and what presents itself in the human heart as the feeling for religion, exists in the thinking medium of the heart." It is no doubt true that the principles of the Christian religion are expressed in Scripture in a positive way; but these must be witnessed to by the spirit of man, which cannot accept anything that is not in harmony with his inner nature as a rational being. And just because man is a rational being, he cannot rest even in the immediate witness of his spirit to the truth, but must go on to convert what he believes into a systematic form by mediation and reflection. Thus the essence of religion is expressed in its highest and most developed form in the philosophy of religion.

In setting forth the principles of the Absolute Religion, Hegel first considers God as he is in his eternal nature; then he goes on to speak of the self-manifestation of God in time; and lastly, he considers the return of God from this self-manifestation to the realization of the divine spirit in the hearts of believers. These three phases are called, in the language of the Church, the Kingdom of the Father, the Kingdom of the Son and the Kingdom of the Holy Spirit.

By God the Father is to be understood the eternal or unchangeable essence of the divine nature as grasped by thought. Though he thus distinguishes between the idea of God and his manifestation, Hegel does not mean that the one is actually separable from the other. He does indeed say that " God may be said to be before or independent of the creation of the world "; but this only means that he may be considered in ideal abstraction from the world, not that he actually exists in separation from it. In order to make clear to ourselves what the essential nature of God is, we begin by thinking of him as he is in his essential nature apart from the explicit modes in which he is manifested; just as, in dealing with the nature of man, it is necessary to define him as a rational and self-conscious being, though his rationality and self-consciousness are possible only in and through his consciousness of the world.

When the understanding attempts to express the essence of God, it can only employ its usual method of accumulating a number of predicates, such as almighty, omniscient, etc., each of which is conceived as exclusive of the others. The subject of the judgment is regarded as in itself perfectly indefinite, and the predicates which are externally attached to it are regarded as first giving definiteness to it. But in this way the subject is merely conceived as a substrate which is independent of its determinations, and the predicates are therefore opposed to one another as mutually contradictory. Thus the real nature of God as a self-differentiating unity is destroyed. By the same abstract method the understanding attempts to express the relation of God to the world. The world is first opposed to God as an independent reality, having a nature of its own in its isolation, and the predicates affirmed of God are supposed to express his relation to it. Hence God is said to contemplate the world in its totality or to be omnipresent or infinitely wise, and to bring the world into existence by his infinite power. It is not seen that in this external mode of conception both God and the world, as separate and distinct, are really conceived as finite. In order to abolish the opposition between them, God and the world must be grasped by reason as a single ideal unity, having two terms only logically distinguishable, the former being conceived as a self-determining reality and the latter as the product of that self-determining reality, while both are combined in the idea of a self-determining Being that is its own object.

The ontological proof of the existence of God really expresses the logical process involved in the transition from the Idea of God to his existence as manifested in the world. No doubt that proof is usually stated in terms of the understanding, the conception of God being separated from his existence; but what really constitutes the persuasive force of the argument is that God must manifest or realize himself, and therefore that his existence is involved in his Idea. Hence the world is not something adscititious to the Idea of God, but is involved in that Idea. The infinitude of God just consists in this, that he is not separated from the world, but the world is a manifestation of his being.

In this speculative idea of God all externality is abolished, whether the externality of the sensible or the externality of rigidly opposed conceptions of the understanding. The fundamental characteristic of the world of sense is its externality, every object being regarded as outside of every other in space, and every event as one of a series in time. Thus the sensible world is a world of mutual externality or " otherness." But this mode of apprehending the world is merely the first superficial conception of it, in which the unity which essentially belongs to it only betrays its presence by the infinite progression into which we inevitably fall in our endeavour to reach a whole. Nor is the fundamental defect of this mode of apprehension entirely done away even when it is recognized that an object or event has an absolutely isolated being, but that all are connected by the bond of mutual dependence; for, great as is the advance implied in this mode of thought, objects and events are still regarded as outside of one another and only related through an external necessity. It is therefore impossible in this way to reach that perfect unity without which the mind cannot be satisfied. A mechanical system is not a whole, but merely a connected aggregate. Hence we must ultimately conceive the universe from the point of view of a self-differentiating Unity. There are no absolute differences in the world, but all differences are distinctions in the one absolute Unity. The only Unity which can resolve all differences is that which by its very nature is itself a many-in-one, and such a Unity exists nowhere but in mind or spirit. Hence Hegel tells us that " in so far as God is characterized as spirit, externality is done away and absorbed." This " Idea," as he calls it, differs from a category of the understanding, because it involves the absolute unity of ideal differences. In all its operations reason combines apparently contradictory elements of thought, but its perfect work consists in combining all such elements into a single unity. This constitutes its essential distinction from the understanding, which exhibits its isolating and divisive character even when it is dealing with the infinite. On the one side it sets up the infinite, on the other side the finite, with the inevitable result that the infinite becomes finite ; and thus the mind, unable to rest satisfied with anything short of a complete whole, is lured into the fruitless quest for an infinite which is the sum of all the finite. Reason, on the other hand, recognizes that the infinite is not the sum of the finite, but the unity presupposed as the possibility of any finite. There is no finite and no infinite such as understanding assumes. The understanding is equally powerless in its attempt to comprehend the nature of life. Soul and body, it assumes, are absolutely opposed to each other, and therefore their union is inexplicable. From this point of view there can be no living unity, but only the accidental relation of two things which have no inner connection. Reason, on the other hand, sees that soul is simply the unity, as body constitutes the differences, implied in the very existence of a living being. The whole process of life consists in the transcendence of differences. No doubt the existence of wants implies the presence of a contradiction in the subject of the wants, but the process by which they are satisfied is the abolition for the subject of the contradiction. Understanding sees the contradiction, but overlooks the essential point, that life just consists in its abolition. When it comes to deal with the idea of God, the understanding again employs its divisive method. For it " God is one " in the sense that by his nature he excludes all differences. Thus the Idea of God as a spirit, present in all things and yet retaining its perfect unity, is lost. It is for this reason that the doctrine of the Trinity is supposed to be mysterious and incomprehensible. The saying that " God is love " is a true and profound thought when it is properly understood. It is the nature of love to overcome the distinction which it recognizes. Hence, when it is said that " God is love," it is implied that what is opposed to God is yet in union with him. This is the profound truth which is expressed in the doctrine of the Trinity. At first no doubt this doctrine may be accepted without any insight into its real meaning, but Hegel regards it as expressing the central idea of religion, namely, that God is not a being who is complete in himself apart from the world, but one whose very nature is to manifest himself in the world and to come to self-consciousness in such manifestation. Certainly this doctrine has often been very imperfectly apprehended. Thus it is an utterly inadequate mode of apprehension to think of the distinguishable phases of God as if these involved numerical separation, for number is one of the least adequate categories of thought.

Reason does not operate with dead abstractions. The distinction between understanding and reason may be seen in their very different ways of regarding the material world. According to the former, each predicate or atom of " matter " is conceived as a separate and independent unit, whereas by the latter a unit of matter has no existence except in its dependence in the way of gravitation on all other units. When therefore the understanding applies to God its conception of abstract oneness or dead identity, it violates the true nature of God, which is grasped by reason as a unity expressing itself in an infinity of determinations. Similarly, to speak of the three " persons " of the Trinity is apt to lead to the conversion of the living distinction of God as a subject from God as object and God as self-conscious into dead and unchanging abstractions. I am a " person " in virtue of being an abstract self. Self-consciousness implies the power of absolute abstraction from all that is not self. But the freedom thus realized is abstract, since in the idea of personality each self is regarded as self-centred and in no way as involving relations to other selves. Now, a self thus isolated is not really free; for the self cannot realize itself except by transcending its separate individuality and identifying itself with the other selves distinguished from it. Abstract personality is surrendered in friendship and love, and only so is true freedom realized. If therefore we speak of " personality " in relation to God, it must be understood in this higher sense. On the other hand, to apply the conception of abstract personality to God as Trinity leads to the division of God into three individuals. A " person " who remains in isolated independence, thus refusing to recognize what is essential to the completeness of himself, is essentially evil. We must therefore regard abstract personality as abolished in the divine unity. So the terms Father, Son and Spirit are simply metaphorical and very imperfect ways of expressing the true thought, that God is self-manifesting, conscious of himself as self-manifesting, and therefore self-unifying. To obviate the defects in its formulation of the doctrine of the Trinity the Church speaks of the Son as eternally begotten ; a mode of expression by which, through the combination of the contradictory ideas of a temporary act which yet is an eternal process, the truth that God is spirit is sought to be conveyed. The doctrine of the Trinity, so far from being a "mystery" in the sense of being unintelligible, is the most intelligible of all, expressing as it does the ultimate principle of the universe. The Jewish religion isolated the Idea of God, and thus led men to conceive of him as entirely transcending the world ; Greek philosophy affirmed the immanence of God in the world and in human life ; the Christian religion, in the doctrine of the Trinity, recognizes that God is neither beyond the world nor simply the all-pervasive soul of the world, but is essentially self-manifesting, while remaining eternally self-identical in this self-manifestation. In affirming that the universe is the eternal process in which the nature of God manifests itself, we express the central idea of the Absolute Religion, and this is the idea imperfectly expressed in the Church's doctrine of the Trinity.

What has been said in regard to the Kingdom of the Father has prepared the way for Hegel's treatment of what he calls the Kingdom of the Son, in which he goes on to ask how God manifests himself in the world. There are two aspects in which the self-manifestation of God may be viewed. In the first place it must not be supposed that God is expressed in the merely sensible world—the world viewed as an aggregate of separate things and events spread out in space and following one another in time. God cannot be apprehended by sense, but exists only for a thinking or rational subject, and indeed only explicitly even for him when he rises above the divisions of the understanding. In the second place, not only is God incapable of being known otherwise than by reason, as distinguished from what Kant calls the " understanding," but he actually manifests himself and yet maintains his unity and identity in that manifestation ; in other words, God is spirit. When we concentrate attention on the manifestation of God, as distinguished from his inner essence, we are dealing with God as the " other " of himself, or what the Church calls the " Son." Thus the divine nature is essentially self-diremptive. But, because the ultimate involution of the world and God is not at first apprehended, the world appears as in perfect alienation from God, and therefore as independent of him. And indeed the world is not merely an external product of a divine Creator, but is endowed with a free existence of its own. " In God there is no envy," as Plato and Aristotle saw, and the freedom and independence granted to the world may well be attributed to the goodness of God. Thus Hegel holds that the division from God, which is characteristic of the world in its immediateness, is essential to its perfection. This first state of division, however, is not the true or ultimate nature of the world, which, as deriving its existence entirely from God, is destined to return to its origin, and to pass from division to atonement. Until the world rises to the stage of spirit or love, it does not manifest its real nature, and therefore it must pass through a process in which the transition is made from alienation to reconciliation. This process, however, does not take place in Nature itself, which is a mere assemblage of things and events in space and time connected by necessary laws, for Nature has only an apparent independence. Hence, it is meaningless to ask whether the world, by which is meant the world of matter, is eternal or began to exist in time ; for there is no independent material world. Nor can it be said that matter is " uncreated," if by this it is meant that it has any reality in itself ; it exists only as a phase in the self-manifestation of God, and in this sense may be said to be " created " by God. There is no real distinction between the creation and the preservation of the world ; for such a distinction rests upon the idea that the world was first created as an independent being, and has afterwards been continued in existence. As the world exists only as a process in the divine being, such a distinction is obviously inept. This is the truth of the ordinary view that " conservation is a kind of creation." We may, therefore, say that the world is "eternal," in the sense that it is an eternal phase in the self-manifestation of God. By the " wisdom " of God, again, must be understood the system of nature as manifested in the totality of particular beings, including living beings as its highest realization.

It is only when we go beyond the kingdom of living beings that the process of overcoming the division of the world from God comes to clear and explicit manifestation. The world of nature is not the Kingdom of the Son, which is only realized in man, as not only a natural but a spiritual being. Man as spirit is no doubt related to nature, but he employs nature only as the means by which he realizes himself. Only man is capable of comprehending that nature is a manifestation of God, and therefore it is through the self-consciousness of man that nature comes within the sphere of religion. It is an inversion of the truth to think of nature and the natural as higher than man. The true life of man consists in lifting himself above his merely natural being, and only so can he realize what in idea he is. Evil in fact consists in perpetuating the inner division between the natural and the spiritual, and so long as this division continues, man is necessarily in contradiction with himself.

There are, therefore, two aspects in which man may be regarded : he is good by nature, and he is evil by nature. By the former, it is meant that man in his ideal or essential nature is good ; by the latter, that man in his immediate nature is evil. Man, in other words, is potentially identical in nature with God, while in his first or immediate being he is in alienation from God. Thus man is essentially different from external nature, which remains true to its own essence and character, faithfully obeys its own laws, and never departs from the circle of rigid necessity which constitutes its being. Man, on the other hand, is called upon to become actually what he is essentially ; he must place himself over against his immediate nature, and enter into the division between his essence and his actual state. In this contrast to external nature consists his freedom. To will the continuance of his immediate nature is to will evil. Thus evil arises from making the natural impulses his motive, and so substituting the immediate for the ideal or essential self. Not that those impulses act externally upon his will, but he freely wills the object to which they are directed, and thus perpetuates the division between his immediate and his true nature. Man is therefore good, not by nature, but only as the result of a process which carries him beyond his merely natural state. There can be no evil without self-consciousness; for only as he is capable of distinguishing between himself as a particular subject and himself as a universal being has he a definite single will. Evil consists in willing the good of this isolated subject, as if it were the absolute good. To be good a man must regulate his conduct in accordance with general principles and laws. To will the natural man is selfishness, as distinguished from willing the universal. Hence evil is personified as the devil—" der Geist der stets verneint," as Goethe calls it—the principle which expresses the negation of the essential self. Man, however, is always good potentially, even when he wills evil, and experiences the unrest and pain which accompanies or follows the commission of evil. If it is objected that we have no experience of men who are altogether evil, and therefore it cannot be true that all men are by nature evil, Hegel answers that men living in civilized society are not in a pure state of nature, but are already educated ethically and morally, and have therefore partially realized the idea of man. As the consciousness of evil presupposes reflection, it is apt to be supposed that reflection is the source of evil. But what reflection does is not to create evil, but to bring to light the contrast or antithesis from which evil proceeds. The stone, the plant, the animal are incapable of either evil or good; for good and evil exist only within the sphere of knowledge. Evil involves the consciousness of a self which affirms itself in contrast to other selves, but the consciousness of self is at the same time the condition of the consciousness of an object which is intrinsically universal. This division into self and not-self is the condition of evil, because it is only by separating the particular from the universal self that I am capable of evil. While self-consciousness is thus the condition of evil, it is also true that only a rational or self-conscious being is capable of good, for only such a being has the idea of that which is universal or that which ought to be. Thus, while evil originates in the disunion made possible by self-consciousness, it is likewise the condition of reconciliation or atonement. The truth underlying the popular conception of inherited evil therefore is, that evil is not something peculiar to this or that individual man, but belongs to the very nature of man as self-conscious. And as the division in the nature of man is within himself, it can only be overcome by a transformation of the inner nature. Mere external obedience is not enough, but there must be a complete change of mind. The consciousness that he is evil in his immediate nature is the condition of man's higher life.

The transition from division to reconciliation involves an experience on the part of man of the uttermost depths of evil; only so can he gain experience of all that is involved in goodness. The antithesis of good and evil assumes two forms: in the first place, the fact that the antithesis exists at all is itself evil relatively to God; and, in the second place, its existence is evil relatively to the world. (*a*) As to the former, the inward consciousness that there is contradiction in the very depths of man's being, gives rise to an infinite feeling of sorrow. This feeling has as its complement the consciousness that in his true nature he is good, without which he would not be conscious that he was actually evil. Thus there is, on the one hand, the descent into himself, which involves the consciousness of evil, and, on the other hand, the ascent to the purely spiritual unity of God. The contrast of these two correlative elements therefore implies that man is not a merely natural will-less being, and that the merely natural state of innocence is itself evil. For this reason his sorrow assumes the form of humility and contrition.

(*b*) Evil in relation to the world is misery. When man feels himself in discord with the world, which is indifferent to his desires, he is driven back upon himself; when he is aware of himself as out of harmony with the higher moral demands of his nature, which are an expression of the pure will of God, he feels inwardly condemned, humbled, broken and humiliated. In the one case he seeks satisfaction by fleeing from the world and from reality, with the result that he loses all that makes life worth living, since, in becoming abstractly free, his self is at the same time emptied of all contents ; in the other case, conscious that he is unable to fulfil the demands of an absolute moral law, he falls into a hopeless despair. These two forms of the unhappy consciousness are represented historically by the Jewish and the Roman people: the former manifesting the misery of humiliation, the latter the abstract affirmation of the self and the negation of the world. Thus the division involved in the opposition of the natural to the ideal presents itself in the one as the negation, and in the other as the affirmation of the self; while "the abstract depth of the opposition demands an infinite suffering on the part of the soul and an atonement which will be correspondingly complete."

(*c*) How is the division to be healed? The subject in its essential nature is the unity which is capable of transcending the abstract opposition, and when this unity is actually realized atonement will have been made. The very consciousness of the opposition is potentially its transcendence. But atonement cannot be accomplished by the individual subject bringing his inner life into harmony with the will of God, for so long as the subject persists in the abstract freedom of isolation the opposition must remain. The natural life as finite can never express the true universal. The presupposition of atonement is the implicit unity of the divine and the human nature, and until the subject consciously recognizes that in his isolated or natural state he can do nothing good, atonement is impossible. It must be recognized that the antithesis is in essence already removed, namely, in the being of the absolute spirit, in so far as it is living unity, atoning love. Man knows himself to be taken up and accepted in God, so far as God is to him not a strange being, his relation to whom is merely outward, but only in so far as he knows that in God his own being as freedom and subjectivity is affirmed. This essential unity of the divine with the human nature is possible only by God appearing as man and man as God. Thus the sorrow which arises from the division of the finite subject disappears when it is recognized that it is the essential nature of spirit to be conscious of the unity of the divine and the human nature.

This consciousness belongs to the very nature of man. It is not the result of special training and cultivation, and hence it is not the product of philosophical speculation, but expresses the result of the experience of the race. The Church recognizes the Idea as manifest in Christ, the "Son of God," in whom there is presented in a particular individual the union of the divine and the human nature. The doctrine of the Incarnation grew up in the Church, Hegel seems to imply, because it was recognized that man in his essential nature can find atonement only in a union with God which abolishes the element of self-seeking characteristic of the natural man. It is through "faith" in Christ as manifesting the unity of the divine and the human nature, that God ceases to be a Being beyond the world and is perceived to be manifested in it. For Christ is not merely a teacher of the truth, or a martyr to it. Before his death he was a man, who by his teaching and his life revealed to others the true basis of the religious consciousness; but it is only with the death of Christ, that the Church came to recognize that only in him as a God-man was the true nature of God revealed. The consciousness that it is the essential nature of God to be reconciled with the world only dawned upon the Church in its full significance after the death of Christ. For this reason the Church teaches that the death of Christ is the central point of the atonement, seeing in it the absolute love which even in finiteness overcomes finiteness, and negates that great negation, death.

By the Kingdom of the Spirit Hegel means the realization in the spiritual community of the unity of the divine and the human nature. In order that this community may be realized in its definiteness and completeness, the utmost freedom must be allowed to all men, and no part of human nature may be regarded as common or unclean. The Divine Idea, as all-comprehensive, is capable of spiritualizing every element in the natural life, and every member of the Christian community must be inspired with love and reverence for it. The difficulty in its realization arises from the freedom of the subject, involving his consciousness of himself as having a right to infinite satisfaction. This possibility of absolute self-assertion, however, is essential to the free surrender in love of the purely individual will. Just because man so strongly recoils from the surrender of his natural self, his final self-surrender is of absolute value. "Love," says Hegel, "harmonizes all things, even absolute opposition." Even in ordinary sexual love there is complete abstraction from all worldly things and concentration on a single individual. In religion this process of abstraction is represented as absolute, all the glory of the world being despised as worthless. This idea, however, is imperfectly comprehended when the Roman Church identifies the Son with Jesus as he appeared in time, so that the intercession of Mary and the saints has to be added in order to give greater breadth to the reconciling power of the Son, while the Spirit is conceived to be present rather in the Church as a hierarchy than in the community of believers. Hence the pictorial representation of Christ in his bodily presence on the cross, the veneration of the Holy Land where he lived and moved about, and the superstitious feeling for relics. In the true spiritual community the past is viewed *sub specie aeternitatis*, and the Second Advent, instead of being sensuously represented as an event to occur at a definite time in the future, is interpreted as the realization of the Spirit in the whole community. Unlike Stoicism, Christianity does not seek for peace in the self-centred resoluteness of the individual spirit, but, absolutely surrendering all that belongs to particularity and individuality, it places an infinite value on the love that springs out of infinite sorrow. As the individual soul has an infinite value, the immortality of the soul becomes a definite doctrine of the Christian religion. Moreover, since all distinctions of authority, power, position and even of race have no longer in themselves any value, the middle wall of partition separating men from one another is broken down, and that not merely, as in the Roman Empire, on the basis of equality in the sight of the law, but through the positive principle of love to all men as arising from the negation of infinite sorrow. Pictorially this process is presented in the sufferings, death and exaltation of Christ, but the idea conveyed by this mode of representation is that every member of the spiritual community should pass through the same process. The right relation of the individual man to the truth of the atonement is that he should himself "come to this same conscious unity, should deem it good for himself, produce it in himself, and be filled with the divine spirit.

This pure self-consciousness, which knows and wills the truth, is the divine spirit in the subject." As maintaining the actual presence of God in the souls of believers, Christianity is therefore the religion of the spirit.

(*a*) The spiritual community consists of those who live in the spirit of God. Each member of this community must experience the transition from the state of natural estrangement from God to union with him, and as a condition of this transition each must have faith that the transition has already actually taken place. Thus the atonement must be represented in the first instance as a historical fact, though its truth is not in any way dependent upon historical fact. The Church, Hegel thinks, is right in refusing to countenance investigations into the alleged appearances of Christ after his death, for such enquiries proceed on the false principle that spiritual truth can be established by external evidence. This is not always realized, and hence it is supposed that the manifestation of God in the Son involves the proof that Jesus of Nazareth, the carpenter's son, was the Son of God. In truth the self-manifestation of God is the final conclusion of modern philosophy, though it is not established by mere abstract ratiocination, but is the fruit and flower of the whole process of the religious consciousness. Faith is therefore the highest form of knowledge, resting as it does, not on any external evidence such as miracles, but on the witness of the spirit.

(*b*) Viewed in its universal aspect, the spiritual community or church exists as the institution in virtue of which its members reach the truth and appropriate it for themselves. This truth consists in the doctrine of the atonement, which is regarded as known and recognized. But in the church this doctrine is further developed and obtains a more specific form. Thus, starting from an immediate intuition of the truth, the confession of faith is an expression of the system of ideas which has been developed out of the progressive experience of the race. In baptism it is declared that the child is not born into a hostile world but into the church, in which evil is overcome in principle and God is reconciled to man. All that is required is that the individual should train himself for the church by education, practice and cultivation, and should habituate himself to the good and true which is already present in him. In this consists his regeneration. "Man must be twice born, first naturally and then spiritually. The Spirit is not immediate; it is only as it gives birth to itself out of itself; it exists only as it is born again." But this regeneration is no longer that infinite sadness in which the spiritual community originates. No doubt as a potential member of the church the individual is not spared an infinitely real sorrow, for he has still to contend against his selfish inclinations; but this is very different from the fierce battle out of which the spiritual community sprung. As the child is spirit only potentially, the truth at first appears to it in the form of authority. It is the task of the church to develop in the individual the consciousness of his need of reconciliation with God, and then to lead him to identify his will with the will of God. Here there is no mere *is-to-be*, as in the Kantian philosophy; the contradiction is already implicitly solved, when evil is known as already vanquished in the spirit in principle, and the subject has only through faith in the atonement, which is already there in its essence, to make his will good, and thus to get rid of the consciousness of evil. This action is at once the action of the subject who dies with Christ, and the action of the divine spirit in him. "Faith itself is the divine spirit, which works in the individual; but the individual is not a mere passive vessel. The Holy Spirit is equally the spirit of the subject in so far as he has faith, and in the exercise of this faith he turns against his merely natural life and discards it." This truth has been stated in three different ways. In the first place, the view of Kant is that the idea of God is merely a postulate of human reason, and that the willing of the law must also be referred entirely to the human subject. The fundamental defect in this mode of conception is that it destroys the objectivity of truth. In the second place, it is held by Pietism that the law itself, and the resolution to act in accordance with it, are produced in man solely by the divine will; a doctrine which rightly affirms the objectivity of truth, but ignores the free response of the subject. Lastly, the mystical view, especially in the form expressed by Luther, holds that there is a definite relation between God and the subjective act of will,—a view which implies, though it does not perfectly express, the philosophical idea of atonement.

In the Sacrament of the Lord's Supper the presence of God in man is given as an immediate feeling in the soul of the individual of his union with God. Here also three distinct views have been held. (1) The Roman Church affirms that the host—this outward, material, unspiritual thing—is through the act of consecration transformed into the actually present God, and thus God is experienced by man in an external act. In accordance with this external conception of the divine, truth is possessed only by the Church, so that the subject must have implicit faith in that which the Church affirms. (2) The Lutheran view is that the sensible presence is in itself nothing, nor does the consecration make the host into an object worthy of adoration, but the object exists only in faith. The only sense in which transubstantiation takes place is in the abolition of what is external; while God is only present spiritually in the faith of the subject. (3) The Reformed Church holds that

God is present only as a conception in the mind, based upon a lively remembrance of the past; and hence it is defective in not recognizing a real union of the divine and human.

(c) What in worship exists only as an inner certainty in the depths of the subject must be realized objectively. The subject, when he becomes conscious in his reconciliation with God of his freedom, asserts it in the face of the whole world. The first and lowest form in which this is done is that of a monastic renunciation of the world, meaning by the term "world" the natural desires, as manifested in the family, the civic community and the State, and in devotion to art and science. This negative attitude, however, in which violence is done to the natural emotions and impulses, cannot be the last word; for it is the very nature of spirit to comprehend and transform the whole of the interests of life. Hence arises the second form of relation, in which the world, as opposed to the divine, is slavishly subjected to the Church, which alone is held to be divine. But this is no real solution; for, in usurping the functions of the world, the Church itself sinks into an unspiritual worldliness, and becomes the victim of the very passions against which it protests. Man thus loses his freedom, and disunion enters into all the relations of life. From this unreconciled contradiction he is freed only when, in the third form of relation, the principle of freedom penetrates the world as well as the Church, and moulds it in accordance with eternal truth. Thus the divine passes into the sphere of reality in the organization of the State. In morality, which is the realization of the rational will, the atonement of religion with the world is accomplished. No longer is celibacy opposed as holy to family life, or voluntary poverty to active trade and commerce, or blind obedience to the free play of intellect and will. The atonement of religion has also to be realized in the sphere of reflective thought. At first, just as in the sphere of practice, the subject asserts himself in the abstract form of negation. He turns against the world of traditional ideas, rejecting all that is contrary to the " enlightened " understanding. Fixing upon the contradiction which he finds in every religious statement, and assuming the absoluteness of the logical law of identity, he comes at last to the conclusion that God is unknowable in his inner nature, and that religion is purely a thing of individual feeling. The subject thus falls back upon the absoluteness and infinity of his own nature, with the result that not only the objectivity of God, but the supposed objectivity of the principles of justice and morality is denied, being regarded as the product of arbitrary thought. On the other hand, reflection may insist that the subject must get rid of the illusion of independence and seek only the glory of God. This is the attitude of Mohammedanism. Man is related to the One in an absolutely universal way—not, as in the Jewish religion, to the God of a particular nation. The defect of this form of religion is its abstractness. All natural inclinations and interests are removed from the sphere of religion, and are therefore allowed free scope unchecked by reflection, while there is developed a fatalistic indifference to all practical ends. The " Enlightenment " adopts the same general attitude as Mohammedanism. Conceiving of God in a perfectly abstract way, it denies the manifestation of God in the flesh, the exaltation of Christ to the rank of the Son of God, and the transfiguration of the finitude of the world and of self-consciousness until they appear as the infinite self-determination of God. Christianity is supposed to consist in a certain number of doctrines, and Christ is regarded simply as a more distinguished teacher than Socrates or Plato. The only difference between this rationalistic Enlightenment and Mohammedanism is that the former affirms the independent reality of man, which is denied by the latter. Imperfect as this form of thought is, it has the merit of bringing to clear consciousness the principle of subjective freedom, and recognizing the rightful claims of the intellect to satisfaction.

The true form must therefore combine these opposite aspects. On the one hand, the subject must be allowed to develop the content freely; but, on the other hand, this process must not be arbitrary, nor must the content be subjective and contingent. This is the point of view of speculative philosophy, which is not governed by the abstract law of identity, but in all its thought is concrete and organic. It is not, like the Enlightenment and Pietism, indifferent to content, but recognizes that reason can realize its freedom only by a comprehension of the true nature of things. While reason must be exercised, and exercised freely, before the truth can become an object of explicit reflection, it is only in the comprehension of that which is true in and for itself that satisfaction is found. Speculative philosophy thus expresses in an organic system the fundamental principles involved in religion, and justifies the faith of Christianity in the self-manifestation of God, and in the process of atonement by which man makes the transition from the condition of alienation to union with God. In its justification of the content and the forms of truth, it learns that the negative and critical attitude of the Enlightenment is only the first step in the progress to a complete comprehension of reality. To regard this first step as final leads to the sceptical conclusion, that all forms of thought are arbitrary and subjective. Hence the purely hostile attitude of the Enlightenment, not only to the popular religion, but to the deeper truth which is imperfectly expressed in it. Speculative philosophy, on the other hand, refuses to "empty out the baby with the bath"; it recognizes the inadequacy of the forms in which the truth is expressed, but at the same time it shows the relative truth that they contain. It agrees with culture and reflection that the mode of statement of the popular religion is open to objection, while differing fundamentally from the *Aufklärung* in recognizing that the ordinary religious consciousness contains substantial truth. Thus an idealistic philosophy is not merely critical, but above all constructive. For this reason it incurs the hostility of the Enlightenment, which will not admit the element of reason in the Christian religion. " In philosophy," says Hegel, " religion receives its justification at the hands of the thinking consciousness. Simple piety feels no need of the justification, but accepts the truth on authority, and by means of the truth so received it experiences the satisfaction of reconciliation. And undoubtedly the true content is present in faith, though it has not attained to the form of thought. Truth appears in various forms prior to the true form which establishes the necessity of the true content; but only thought is the absolute judge, before which the content must verify and attest its claims." The reproach that philosophy sets itself above religion is therefore unfounded. The individual feels the truth of religion, and with this feeling philosophy does not interfere; on the contrary it reveals to feeling what its content really is. Certainly philosophy cannot accept any truth that is held in an immediate and uncritical way, but the actual result of its method is to give back to faith in a higher form the truth it contains. There are three stages in the development of the spirit; firstly, simple faith; secondly, the destructive criticism of this faith as expressed by the Enlightenment; and, thirdly, the reconstructive attitude of speculative philosophy. All three are necessary, and we must not simply condemn the Enlightenment because of the unrest and pain which it produces. In the time of the Roman Empire, when the earlier faith in the divine had given place to a chaos of conflicting forms of religion and political life was devoid of principle, man in despair abandoned the search for truth, and individual well-being was made the sole object of human endeavour. So it is now, when all faith in objective truth has been destroyed, and men are fain to content themselves with the pursuit of private ends. Nothing but a philosophical reconstruction of belief, which shall reconcile reason and religion, can lift us, in these days of unrest and unbelief, above the fatal division of the heart and the head; and even this reconciliation is only for a few. How the great body of the people is to find its way out of its present unhappy state of division can only be determined by the onward march of humanity.

INDEX.

For the convenience of the reader, the Index to the complete work has been included in both volumes.

Abelard, Theory of, I. 89.
Absolute, The, of Basilides, I. 31; of Hegel, I. 32, 312, 330-331; of Philo, I. 51; of Hamilton, I. 107; of Mansel, I. 107; of Spencer, I. 107; of Kant, I. 268; Idea of, I. 243; II. 26-33, 41-46, 124-126, 189-190, 235, 248.
Absolutism, I. 72-77; II. 235, 249-250; Theory of evil in, II. 258.
Abstraction, Clement's method of, I. 46-50; Plato's tendency to, I. 48; Aristotle's tendency to, I. 48; Gnostic method of, I. 49; Philo's method of, I. 49; Neoplatonic method of, I. 49; Berkeley's method of, I. 241; Kant's tendency to, I. 305; Hegel's objection to, I. 339; Nature of, II. 49, 62, 86-89, 93-94, 99-100, 123, 151-154, 176-177, 207-211, 266-268, 272-277, 283-284.
Aesthetics, Kant's, I. 276.
Affirmation and Negation, II. 47, 240.
Agnosticism, II. 4, 189-190, 250.
Alexandria, Jewish and Greek ideas in, I. 26, 27.
Allegory, Method of, I. 33, 36, 40, 46, 55, 57, 60, 226-230.
Altruism, II. 114.
Ambrose, Influence of, on Augustine, I. 66.
Analogy, Method of, II. 251.
Analysis, Hegel's view of, I. 330; Nature of, II. 153.

Angels, Hebrew idea of, I. 27; Origen's Theory of, I. 60; Worship of, I. 64.
Animism, I. 3, 5, 25.
Annet, Historical criticism of, I. 230.
Anselm, Theology of, I. 87-89.
Anthropomorphism, II. 257.
Antinomy. *See* Contradiction.
Appearance, II. 92, 97-99, 107, 183-185, 235, 237-240, 246-248, 258-260.
Apologists, Christian, I. 28-29, 34.
Apperception, Leibnitz' idea of, I. 191.
Aristotle, Theory of, I. 12-23; Principle of contradiction in, I. 74; Influence of, on medieval thought, I. 94; Politics of, I. 133; Theory of the intelligence in, I. 303.
Arius, Theology of, I. 63; Dante's condemnation of, I. 128.
Arnold, Matthew, on morality, II. 120.
Art, Schopenhauer's theory of, II. 262-263, 268-269; Kant's theory of, II. 269; Nietzsche's theory of, II. 271, 273; Christian, II. 305; Greek, II. 305; Idea of, II. 301, 305-307.
Asceticism, Nietzsche's antagonism to, II. 271-275; Defect of, II. 300.
Associationism. *See* Empiricism.
Athanasius, Theology of, I. 63.
Atomism, II. 145-149.

INDEX 363

Atonement, Idea of, II. 290-297. *See also* Redemption.
Augustine, Theology of, I. 64-85, 116, 120; II. 124.
Authority, Cartesian view of, I. 152-153; Spinoza's view of, I. 170-171; Kant's view of, I. 152; Hegel's view of, I. 354.
Automatism, Animal, II. 179.
Averroes, Dante's view of, I. 101.

Babylonian Myths, Relation of Hebrew religion to, I. 25.
Bain, Associationism of, II. 57; Derivation of extension in, II. 73.
Baptism, Clement's view of, I. 53; Hegel's view of, I. 355.
Basilides, Theology of, I. 31; Relation of Clement to, I. 47.
Beauty, Plato's idea of, I. 9; Kant's idea of, I. 276; Hegel's idea of, I. 327-328; Relation of truth and goodness to, II. 249; Relation of, to religion, II. 305-306.
Being, Gnostic idea of, I. 31; Clement's idea of, I. 47; Locke's idea of, I. 216; Hegel's idea of, I. 289, 322; and nothing, II. 30-31, 39.
Belief, Relation of theology to, I. 6; Distinction of, from truth, II. 68.
Bergson, his contrast of life and mechanism, II. 60; Criticism of Darwinism and Lamarckianism, II. 163-170; Denial of finality, II. 168-171; Theory of the intellect, II. 170-171; Theory of Creative evolution, II. 171.
Berkeley, Philosophy of, I. 233-251; II. 72, 85; Theology of, I. 241-246.
Bernard of Clairvaulx, Theology of, I. 89-93; Anselm's relation to, I. 92; Opposition of, to Abelard, I. 93.
Body, Aristotle's idea of, I. 13; Plato's idea of, I. 14; Descartes' idea of, I. 156-163, 190; Spinoza's idea of, I. 176; Leibnitz' idea of, I. 190-191; Hegel's idea of, I. 296-298, 342; Relation of, to Mind, II. 177-189, 260, 266.

Bonaventura, Dante's relation to, I. 101.
Bouterwek, Schopenhauer's relation to, II. 258.
Bradley, F. H., Image, conception and judgment in, II. 214-216.
Brain, Relation of consciousness to, II. 178-185.
Bunyan, Religious genius of, II. 306.
Butler, Bishop, Hume's reply to, I. 257.
Byron, Pessimism of, II. 261.

Calvin, Theology of, I. 120; Spinoza's relation to, I. 172.
Carlyle, Characterization of Dante, I. 101.
Casuistry, Hebrew, I. 26.
Categories, I. 200, 219, 265, 289, 292, 298, 301, 308-317, 319, 330, 340; II. 28-32, 38-44, 49-50, 91, 109-113, 176, 195-196, 210, 214-218, 264.
Cause, First, in Aristotle, I. 19; in Clement, I. 47, 56; in Dante, I. 111, 113; in Berkeley, I. 239-250; in Hume, I. 254, 257.
Cause, Final, Spinoza's denial of, I. 187; Leibnitz' defence of, I. 191, 201, 206; Descartes' rejection of, I. 199; Hume's denial of, I. 254, 257; Kant's theory of, I. 260, 274-278; Hegel's theory of, I. 317-320, 326-329; Bergson's denial of, II. 168-171; Idea of, II. 136-140, 172-177, 195-197, 211, 226-228, 249, 256-257.
Cause, Mechanical, Descartes' view of, I. 167; Leibnitz' view of, I. 196; Locke's view of, I. 216; Berkeley's view of, I. 239, 250; Hume's view of, I. 239, 251, 254-259; Kant's view of, I. 260, 263, 266; Hegel's view of, I. 316; Idea of, II. 38-42, 50-52, 134-136, 178-179, 192, 237-239, 258-260, 264-268.
Celsus, Origen's reply to, I. 57.
Chandler, Apology for Christianity of, I. 229.
Change, Aristotelian idea of, I. 17, 19; and permanence, II. 44.

INDEX

Christ, The Church's idea of, II. 288, 295-297.
Christianity, Origin and development of, II. 22-24; Relation of, to Neo-Platonism, I. 23; Relation of, to Judaism, I. 29, 88; II. 22; Relation of, to Paganism, I. 30; II. 22; Relation of, to Philosophy, 36, 37, 39, 41, 42, 45, 54, 56; Locke's view of, I. 221, 222; Toland's view of, I. 223, 225; Tindal's view of, I. 226; Morgan's view of, I. 228; Collins' view of, I. 228; Hegel's view of, I. 334, 336; Relation of historical criticism to, II. 4-8; Primitive, II. 4-6; Basis of, II. 8, 22-24; False idea of, II. 22, 270; Practical character of, II. 309-311.
Church, The, Gnostic idea of, I. 32; Methodius' view of, I. 62; Creeds of, I. 61, 64; II. 22-24; Augustine's view of, I. 71; Augustine's influence on, I. 72, 85; Bernard's idea of, I. 92; Thomas Aquinas' idea of, I. 94, 96; Dante's idea of, I. 100, 105, 138-147; Descartes' idea of, I. 152, 170; Spinoza's idea of, I. 170; Locke's idea of, I. 213; Toland's idea of, I. 223; Tindal's idea of, I. 226; Kant's idea of, I. 284; Hegel's idea of, I. 333, 336-338, 351-359; Dualism and asceticism of, in the Middle Ages, II. 3, 24; Visible and invisible, II. 298-313.
Cicero, Augustine's relation to, I. 64-65.
Clarke, Philosophy of, I. 227.
Clement of Alexandria, Theology of, I. 37-56.
Cogito ergo sum, the Cartesian, Meaning of, I. 155-157, 164-167.
Comparison, external, Nature of, II. 207.
Conception, Hegel's idea of, I. 306, 322; Distinction of image from, II. 49-50, 214-216; Relation of, to perception, II. 82-89; True view of, II. 110-113, 216-219; Inadequate view of, II. 192-197, 205-211, 214-218.

Conditioned and unconditioned in Kant and Hegel, I. 309.
Conscience, Nature of, II. 116-119, 140-142.
Consciousness, Reflective and unreflective, I. 4-5; Nature of, II. 110, 185-188; Relation of the body to, II. 177-189; Religious, Elements in, II. 129-132, 251-253; Subliminal, II. 232-234.
Contemplation, Aristotle's exaltation of, I. 15-19; Dante's exaltation of, I. 131.
Contingency, Aristotle's idea of, I. 12; and Necessity, Hegel's view of, I. 319.
Continuity, Principle of, II. 220-225.
Contradiction, Kant's theory of, I. 267, 298, 311; Hegel's theory of, I. 296-300, 311-317, 324-325, 330, 340-343; Idea of, II. 38, 48-50, 86-89, 92, 176-177, 214-218, 235-241, 246-248, 270.
Cope, his theory of production of organic compounds, II. 158.
Crime, Distinction of Sin from, I. 121; II. 293-297.
Creation, True idea of, II. 15, 290-293; Deistic idea of, II. 133-140; View of Personal Idealism in regard to, II. 219-231; Idea of, II. 20, 34, 109-110, 113, 195, 209, 336-340, 345-346.
Credulity, Distinction of faith from, II. 13-14.
Criticism, Historical, Locke's attitude towards, I. 221; Thomas Morgan's attitude towards, I. 228; Relation of, to Christianity, II. 2-8; Relation of, to Theology, II. 3.

Dante, Theology of, I. 99-133; Relation of, to Thomas Aquinas, I. 101, 111; Relation of, to Aristotle, I. 111; Politics of, I. 133-147.
Darwinism, II. 162-165, 167.
Deism, Character of, I. 223-232; Theology of, II. 133-143, 254-257; Hume's criticism of, I. 251-252.

INDEX 365

Dependence and self-dependence, II. 50-52.
Descartes, Philosophy of, I. 152-170; Relation of, to Luther, I. 163; Leibnitz' criticism of, I. 198-201; Kant's criticism of, I. 265-266; Conception of infinite in, II. 81; Conception of matter in, II. 91.
Design, Idea of, II. 136-140.
Desire, Relation of reason to, I. 17-19; II. 269.
Deutero-Isaiah, Prophetic religion of, I. 26.
Development. *See* Evolution.
Dialectic, Kant's theory of, I. 311; Hegel's theory of, I. 311-313.
Diognetus, Epistle to, I. 36.
Dionysius the Areopagite, Theology of, I. 90-91.
Dionysus, Mystical cult of, I. 7.
Docetism, Clement's leaning to, I. 54.
Dogma, Relation of historical criticism to, II. 2-4.
Dominic, St., Dante's relation to, I. 101.
Doubt, The Cartesian, I. 152-155.
Dualism, in Plato, I. 8-12, 14; in Aristotle, I. 15; in Clement, I. 53; Medieval, I. 99 ff.; of Dante, I. 100; Origin of, II. 92-99, 249-253.

Eckhart, Theology of, I. 148-150.
Ecstasy, Mystical, II. 249-253.
Egoism and altruism, II. 115-119.
Eimer, Theory of variation in, II. 168.
Empire, Roman, Dante's theory of the, I. 133-139, 142-147.
Empiricism, Defect of, I. 241-246; Kant's relation to, I. 263-265; Older, II. 39-42, 49, 57, 59, 213; Radical, II. 33-41, 232.
Energy, Leibnitz' idea of, I. 190-193, 205; Conservation of, II. 93, 149-154, 207; Relation of, to law, II. 95, 149-154; Degradation of, II. 150-154; Liberation of, II. 160.
Enlightenment, The, Hegel's view of, I. 357-361.

Epictetus, Clement's relation to, I. 40.
Epicureanism, Clement's rejection of, I. 40.
Epiphenomenalism, II. 177-180, 266.
Error and appearance, II. 238-240.
Eschatology, Christian, I. 36; Origen's view of, I. 61; in teaching of Jesus, II. 4-8.
Essential and unessential, II. 91.
Eternal, Aristotle's conception of, I. 18-20.
Euhemerus, Conception of the gods in, I. 30.
Evil, Plato's idea of, I. 8-12; Manichaean idea of, I. 65; Neoplatonic idea of, I. 66; Augustine's idea of, I. 66-71, 83, 85-87, 112; Anselm's idea of, I. 88; Dante's idea of, I. 116-120, 122-123; Leibnitz' theory of, I. 197; Hume's theory of, I. 256; Kant's theory of, I. 279-285; Hegel's theory of, I, 343, 346-350; True and false idea of, II. 16-18, 249, 287-288, 298, 309-313; View of, in Personal Idealism, II. 221-222; Deistic view of, II. 254-264; Naturalistic view of, II. 257; Absolutist view of, II. 258; Schopenhauer's view of, II. 264, 268-270; Mystical view of, II. 275-277; Augustinian theory of, II. 278-282; as due to finitude, II. 282-284; as impulse, II. 284-285; Will as source of, II. 285-287; not absolute, II. 287; Transition from, to good, II. 288-290, 293-297, 312-313; Relation of Invisible Church to, II. 298-303, 312-313.
Evolution, Idea of I. 33; II. 102-104, 121, 278-282, 313-316; Relation of Apocalyptic hope to, II. 4-8; of Theology and Religion, II. 22-24, 126-128; Creative, II. 121-123, 170-171, 219-222, 229-231; Relation of energy to, II. 151-154; Biological, II. 161-177; Cosmic, II. 177-180; Moral, II. 278-284.

INDEX

Experience, Kant's view of, I. 260-270, 286, 300; II. 57-58; Hegel's view of, I. 299; System of, II. 35-38, 41-46, 102-104, 193-197, 200-219, 239-240; Sensible, II. 55-58, 60-63, 102, 188, 193, 200, 206-216; Perceptive, II. 67-105; Intellectual, II. 93-95, 97-106, 187-197, 207-209, 235-241; Development of, II. 104, 207, 242, 244-248; Religious, II. 120-132.

Extensity, II. 73, 77.

Externality, Derivation of, II. 70-72, 73-78.

Ezekiel, The Prophet, Theology of, I. 26.

Fact, Berkeley's distinction of fiction from, I. 238; Relation of law to, II. 37-38, 212-214.

Faith, Augustine's conception of, I. 70; Dante's conception of, I. 102; Toland's conception of, I. 223-225; Kant's conception of, I. 261, 270, 277-278, 329; II. 86, 106-108; Hegel's conception of, I. 329, 334, 351, 354-361; Nietzsche's conception of, II. 272-275; Idealistic conception of, II. 222-231; and reality, I. 12; and knowledge, I. 42-46, 95-98, 105, 261, 270; II. 11-24, 218-219; and reason, I. 102-107, 129-131, 152; II. 15-21; Relation of, to religion and theology, II. 1-15, 306-308; Justification by, I. 120-123, 283; II. 295-297, 306-308; and belief, II. 8, 9, 13-15; and will, II. 8-13; and intuition, II. 10-12; and imagination, II. 15-21; and feeling, II. 16; Elements of II. 9-13; Degrees of, II. 13-15; Reflective and unreflective, II. 13-15; Evolution of, II. 22-24; Rational, II. 121, 125, 128, 318-319, 326-328.

Fathers, Christian, Relation of, to Early Christianity, II. 2-4.

Feeling, Hegel's view of, I. 286-292, 334-338; Nature of, II. 75-79, 188-189; and thought, II. 203-205; Religious, II. 233-234.

Fichte, Relation of Schopenhauer to, II. 258, 263.

Finite and infinite, Plato's view of, I. 8; Aristotle's view of, I. 20; Mystical view of, I. 91; Dante's view of, I. 104, 105, 111, 114; Spencer's view of, I. 111; Descartes' view of, I. 157-159, 167; Spinoza's view of, I. 175, 176, 184; Leibnitz' view of, I. 195; Locke's view of, I. 216-221; Berkeley's view of, I. 239; Hume's view of, I. 254-256; Kant's view of, I. 296-299, 309-311; Hegel's view of, I. 296-299, 309-311, 316, 319, 326, 331-334, 339, 345, 350, Relation of, II. 27-31, 50-52, 63-66, 86-89, 99-102, 125-126, 226-228, 244-248, 251-253, 275-277, 282, 289-293.

Force. *See* Energy.

Form, Aristotle's conception of, I. 12-15, 21-22; Kant's conception of, II. 57-58.

Fourth Gospel, Character of, I. 30; Relation of, to Alexandrian Philosophy, II. 3.

Francis, St., Dante's relation to, I. 101.

Freedom, Stoical idea of, I. 22-23; Origen's idea of, I. 60; Manichaean idea of, I. 65; Augustine's idea of, I. 69, 83-85; Dante's idea of, I. 110, 114-118; Leibnitz' theory of, I. 195, 209-211; Toland's theory of, I. 223; Kant's theory of, I. 260, 265, 270-274, 323, 324; Hegel's theory of, I. 316, 317, 323, 324, 334-336, 343, 346, 351, 357-361; Nature of, II. 106, 113-117, 121, 123, 138-142, 154, 175-177, 209-210, 219-222, 228-231, 246-248, 254-258, 263-266, 278-280, 284-287, 290-293, 302-303; Development of, II. 117-119.

Generalization. *See* Abstraction.

Gnostics, The Theology of, I. 31-32; Hegel's contrast to, I. 31-32; Clement's antipathy to, I. 42; Origen's reply to, I. 56.

INDEX   367

God, Idea of, I. 3-12, 17-36, 41, 46-54, 57-91, 94-96, 102-122, 157-176, 195-226, 238-259, 260-279, 295-299, 309-329, 331-352; II. 13-15, 20, 26-31, 41-42, 50-54, 86, 101-107, 125-142, 188-197, 209-211, 219-231, 241-253, 254-277, 286-297, 306-323; Being of, Thomas Aquinas' proof of the, I. 94-96; Dante's proof of the, I. 102-107; Descartes' proofs of the, I. 157-161, 167-169; Leibnitz' proof of the, I. 195-197; Locke's proof of the, I. 216-221; Hume's rejection of proofs of the, I. 252-256; Kant's criticism of proofs of the, I. 268-270; Hegel's defence of proofs of the, I. 317-323, 339-343.

Goethe, View of ethnic religions in, I. 3; on Byron, I. 100; Relation of, to Hegel, I. 292-293; *Faust* of, II. 129-130; Antipathy of, to mechanical conception of the world, II. 155.

Good, The, Aristotle's idea of, I. 17; Kant's idea of, I. 270-274, 277-279; Hegel's idea of, I. 329; Nature of, II. 282-297, 309-313. *See also* Evil.

Gospels, Synoptic, as records of Christian ideas, II. 3.

Gospel, Fourth, Relation of, to Alexandrian philosophy, II. 3.

Governor, Moral, of the world, II. 140-142.

Grace, Divine, Clement's idea of, I. 48, 53; the Church's doctrine of, I. 64; Kant's view of I. 283; Hegel's view of, I. 335; Idea of, II. 296.

Gregory the Great and the papacy, I. 85.

Gravitation, Law of, I. 343; II. 48-49, 93-94, 138, 267.

Hamilton, Sir Wm., Philosophy of, I. 107.

Happiness, Kant's view of, I. 272.

Harmony, Pre-established, Leibnitz' theory of, I. 191, 192, 206-208.

Heaven, Gnostic idea of, I. 31; Origen's idea of, I. 58; Dante's idea of, I. 117-120.

Hedonism, Kant's criticism of, I. 273-274; Defect of, II. 256-258, 267-268, 309-311.

Hegel, Relation of, to Kant, I. 286-329; Theology of, I. 330-361; Conception of "objective spirit" in, II. 222.

Hildebrand, Relation of Thomas Aquinas to, I. 94.

Holiness, Different meanings of, I. 25-28.

Humanists, I. 150.

Hume, Philosophy of, I. 251-259; II. 72.

Huxley, Epiphenomenalism of, II. 177-180; View of freedom in, II. 255.

Idealism, Speculative, I. 8-10; II. 38-39; Plato's, I. 8-10; Kant's, I. 261-329; Hegel's, I. 286-361; Berkeley's, II. 72; Personal, II. 72-82, 112, 185, 191-231.

Ideas, Innate, Descartes' conception of, I. 200; Leibnitz' conception of, I. 194; Locke's rejection of I. 211-213, 219; Simple and complex, Locke's theory of, I. 213-215; of reason, Kant's view of, II. 284; of reason, Hegel's view of, I. 340-343.

Identity, Principle of, in Leibnitz, I. 194-195; Principle of, in Locke, I. 214-215; Principle of, in Hume, I. 251-254; Principle of, in Kant, I. 268; Principle of, in Hegel, I. 295-299, 321-325, 357-359; Principle of, Nature of the, II. 35-38; 49-50, 60-61, 79, 98-100, 207-209; 226-228, 290-293; Personal, II. 260, 290-293.

Ignatian Epistles, I. 30.

Image, Contrast of conception and, II. 214-216.

Immortality, Orphic doctrine of, I. 7; Ignatius' defence of, I. 30-31; Spinoza's denial of, I. 182-184; Berkeley's defence of, I. 249; Hume's denial of, I. 257-258; Kant's proof of, I. 261, 265, 273-

INDEX

274; Hegel's theory of, I. 324-325, 352-354; True and false views of, II. 14, 16-17, 222-231, 313-317.

Impulse, Relation of reason to, II. 284-286.

Incarnation, Clement's view of, I. 52-54; Irenaeus' view of, I. 62; Mathodius' view of, I. 62; Church's doctrine of, I. 64; Dante's view of, I. 120-123; Descartes' view of, I. 152-153; Tindal's denial of, I. 226-227; Kant's view of, I. 281-283; Hegel's view of, I. 351-352; Idea of, II. 288-293.

Individuality, Principle of, I. 190-206, 266-270; II. 28-30, 47-57, 73-78, 112-119, 168-171, 174-175, 191-197, 200-205, 219-231, 241, 246-249, 262-263, 271-280, 285, 290-309.

Infinite and finite. *See* Finite and infinite.

Instinct, Relation of reason to, II. 271-273.

Intellect, Bergson's view of, II. 170, 176-177; Mystical view of, II. 250-253; Schopenhauer's view of, II. 260; Nietzsche's view of, II. 271-273.

Intelligence, Relation of, to the universe, I. 74-77; II. 38, 60-61, 102-104, 314-315; Perceptive, Kant's idea of, I. 270; Perceptive, Hegel's idea of, I. 327-329.

Intuition, Spinoza's view of, I. 179-180; Locke's view of, I. 215-216; Relation of reason to, I. 95; II. 170, 249-253, 258-260, 269, 271, 275-276; Relation of religion to, II. 1, 13-15; Relation of reflection to, II. 11-13; Relation of philosophy to, II. 17-21; Relation of poetry to, II. 17-21; Mystical, II. 275-277.

Irenaeus, Theology of, I. 62.

Jehovah, Hebrew idea of, I. 25-28.

Jeremiah, Prophetic religion of, I. 26.

Jesus, Person of, Ignatius' idea of, I. 30-31; Gnostic idea of, I. 31; Apologists' idea of, I. 34-36; Clement's idea of, I. 51-54; Origen's idea of, I. 60-61; Augustine's idea of, I. 70; Anselm's idea of, I. 87-89; Thomas Aquinas' idea of, I. 96-97; Dante's idea of, I. 120-123; Locke's idea of, I. 221-223; Morgan's idea of, I. 228; Collins' idea of, I. 228-230; Kant's idea of, I. 281-283; Hegel's idea of, I. 350-354, 357-361; Teaching of, I. 28; II. 2-9, 294; Personality of, II. 4, 6-9, 294; Relation of, to his predecessors, II. 4-6.

Jewish people, Hegel's view of the, I. 350.

Job, Book of, I. 26.

Judaism, Palestinian, I. 26; Hellenistic, I. 27; Conflict of Christianity with, I. 28-30; Hegel's view of, I. 358.

Judgment, Locke's theory of, I. 213-216; Analytic and synthetic, Kant's distinction of, I. 262-265; Critique of, Kant's, I. 274-279; Hegel's theory of, I. 296-309, 326-329; Nature of, II. 63-70, 99, 112-113, 214-216.

Justin Martyr, Theology of, I. 29-30, 34-37.

Kant, Philosophy of, I. 152, 248, 260-285; II. 57-58, 86, 94-97, 102-106, 120-123, 198-199, 213-214, 284-285; Relation of Leibnitz and Hume to, I. 260-263; Relation of Hegel to, I. 286-309.

Kelvin, Atomic theory of, II. 148.

Kepler, Idea of God, I. 170.

Kingdom, of the Father, Hegel's conception of, I. 338-345; of the Son, Hegel's conception of, I. 345-352; of the Spirit, Hegel's conception of, I. 352-361; of God, Idea of, in apocalyptic writers, II. 5; Jesus' idea of, II. 4-6.

Knowledge, Plato's theory of, I. 8-13; Aristotle's theory of, I. 12-23; Hamilton's limitation of, I. 107; Spencer's limitation of, I. 107; Spinoza's stages of, I. 177-189;

INDEX

Leibnitz' theory of, I. 193-195, 198-202; Locke's theory of, 211-221; Kant's theory of, I. 260-270, 286-323; II. 58, 105-106; Hegel's stages of, I. 305-323; Nature of, I. 12; II. 49-52; 70-75; 211-219, 222-225, 258-268; Relation of faith to, I. 39-52; II. 11-21, 130, 219-231; Higher, I. 54-56; Reflective and unreflective, II. 13-15; Progress of, II. 20-21, 216-218, 283; Stages of, II. 1-24, 75-79.

Law, The, Hebrew idea of, I. 25-28; St. Paul's idea of; I. 28-29; The Deuteronomic, I. 26; of Holiness, I. 26; Inviolable, Idea of, II. 34-39, 93-98, 102, 108-109, 112, 131-133, 150, 195-197, 200, 207, 229-231, 242.

Lamarckianism, II. 162, 166-168.

Legalism, Hebrew, I. 26-27; Jesus' opposition to, I. 28.

Leibnitz, Philosophy of, I. 190-213; II. 44; Bergson's criticism of, II. 169; Relation of Personal Idealism to, II. 219, 225; Relation of deism to, II. 256.

Lessing, Relation of Kant to, I. 259.

Life, Principle of, II. 154, 156-175, 226-228, 247, 273.

Locke, Philosophy of, I. 211-222, 235-238; II. 69, 84-86, 91, 98; Theology of, I. 221-223.

Logic, Formal, I. 295-296, 311, 330; II. 99-100; Speculative, Hegel's, I. 292, 306-320.

Logos, The, Philo's idea of, I. 27; in Fourth Gospel, I, 30; in Apologists, I. 34-36; in Clement, I. 51-56; in Philo, I. 51-54; Church's doctrine of, I. 61; in Arius, 62-64; in Athanasius, I. 62-64; in Augustine, I. 67, 78; in Dante, I. 109-110.

Lord's Supper, Idea of, I. 356.

Love of God, Origen's idea of, I. 58-59; Augustine's idea of, I. 67-68, 77-78; Dante's idea of, I. 109-111, 116, 122-123; Spinoza's idea of, I. 182-184; Leibnitz' idea of, I. 198; Hegel's idea of, I. 340-343, 350-354.

Lotze, Philosophy of, I. 290; II. 112.

Luther, Theology of, I. 151, 163, 172.

Man, Aristotle's idea of, I. 20; Philo's idea of, I. 27; Apologists' idea of, I. 34; Origen's idea of, I. 59-61; Manichaean idea of, I. 65; Dante's idea of, I. 110; Leibnitz' idea of, I. 193; Kant's idea of, I. 165; Hegel's idea of, I. 331, 339, 346-347; Relation of, to nature and God, II. 1, 133-134, 140-143, 242-246, 251-253, 260, 271, 273-277; Nature of. II. 125-127, 132, 138-142, 243, 246, 254-256, 260.

Manichaeism, Augustine's relation to, I. 65, 85.

Mansel, Philosophy of, I. 107.

Many and one, II. 42-44, 219-222, 228-231, 241.

Marcion, Theory of, I. 32-34.

Mary, Virgin, Worship of, I. 64; Dante's reverence for, I. 123-127; Hegel's view of, I. 353.

Mass, Relation of, to energy, force, space and time, II. 149-155, 178, 205-211.

Materialism, Origin of, II. 237, 259.

Mathematics, Locke's Theory of, I. 215-216; Berkeley's Theory of, I. 246-248; Kant's theory of, I. 262-263, 316.

Matter, Aristotle's idea of, I. 12-17, 21; Augustine's denial of, I. 68-69, 78-83; Sensible, Kant's view of, I. 263-265; Locke's theory of, I. 213-214, 235-239; Berkeley's theory of, I. 235-246; Hegel's theory of, I. 343-346; idea of, I. 241-246; II. 137, 187, 219, 248.

Mechanism, Leibnitz' view of, I. 192-211; Kant's view of, I. 316-320; Hegel's view of, I. 316-320; idea of, I. 233-234; II. 109-112, 144-167, 176-180, 210-211, 226-228, 258-260, 264-266.

Messiah, Belief in, I. 27-29; Collins' Theory of, I. 228-230.

Metempsychosis, Basis of, II. 157.

Method of philosophy, I. 152-155; II. 207.
Middle Ages, The, Dualism of, I. 54, 99-109.
Middleton, Historical Criticism of, I. 230-232.
Millenarianism, Origen's denial of, I. 61-62.
Mill, Philosophy of, II. 57, 73.
Mind, Aristotle's idea of, I. 15-17; Descartes' idea of, I. 155-157, 164-167; Spinoza's idea of, I. 177, 185; Leibnitz' idea of, I. 204-206; Locke's idea of, I. 216-217, 235-238; Berkeley's idea of, I. 233-246; Hegel's idea of, I. 334-336; Individual and universal, II. 70-72, 75-82, 102-104, 188-191; Relation of Body and, II. 177-189, 260; Idea of, I. 233-246.
Miracles, Tindal's denial of, I. 226; Woolston's denial of, I. 230; Annet's denial of, I. 230; Middleton's denial of, I. 230-231; Hume's denial of, I. 258-259; Kant's view of, I. 281-283; Hegel's view of, I. 334, 338, 354; Belief in, II. 131.
Morality, Stoical, I. 23-24; Christian, I. 23, 28, 34-36; Manichaean, I. 64-66; Spinoza's stages of, I. 180-182; Locke's view of, I. 216-221; Kant's view of, I. 270-274, 277-285, 323-325; II. 264-266; Hegel's view of, I. 324-325, 336-338, 346-352, 357-359; Schopenhauer's theory of, II. 263-269; Nietzsche's theory of, II. 271-275; Mystical idea of, II. 275-277; Relation of knowledge to, II. 105-107; Relation of religion to, II. 118-126, 229-231, 306-312; Nature of, II. 113-119, 140-142, 278-288, 308-315; Development of, II. 280-282, 314-315.
Mohammedanism, Hegel's view of, I. 358.
Monadism, Leibnitz' doctrine of, I. 190-211.
Monasticism, Rise of, I. 64; Hegel's view of, I. 357.

Monism and Pluralism, I. 23, 72-77.
Monotheism, I. 111-113.
Morgan, Thomas, Theology of, I. 228.
Mysteries, Religious, Dante's view of, I. 107-109; Descartes' view of, I. 152-153; Locke's view of, I. 221-223; Toland's view of, I. 223-225.
Mysticism, Relation of Aristotle to, I. 21-22; Monastic, I. 62; of Joannes Scotus, I. 86; of St. Bernard, I. 89, 91-93; of Plotinus, I. 90; of Angela of Foligno, I. 90; of Dionysius, the Areopagite, I. 90-91; Relation of Pantheism to, I. 91; Augustine's, I. 91; Thomas Aquinas', I. 97-98; Dante's, I. 101; Eckhart's, I. 149-150; Spinoza's, I. 173; of Personal Idealism, II. 222; of Absolutism, II. 249-250; Defect of, II. 125, 144, 250-253, 275-277.
Mythology, The New, II. 15-24.

Nature, Aristotle's idea of, I. 13, 19-23; Kant's idea of, I. 262-265, 286-289; Hegel's idea of, I. 286-292, 331-334, 345-347; Relation of man and God to, II. 1, 50-52, 75-82, 117-119, 127-136, 195-197, 242-246, 250-253; Relation of religion to, II. 123; System of, II. 207-209.
Naturalism, Theology of, II. 143-171, 257-258; Psychology of, II. 177-189; Criticism of, by Personal Idealism, II. 205-207.
Necessity, Plato's idea of, I. 9-12; Kant's idea of, I. 260-265, 286-289; Hegel's idea of, I. 340-343.
Negation, Principle of, I. 79-82; II. 64-66, 240; Hegel's theory of, I. 311-314.
Neo-Platonism, Philosophy of, I. 22-24, 66, 72-82; Relation of Augustine to, I. 66, 72, 82; Relation of Dante to, I. 12.
Newton, Leibnitz' criticism of, I. 192.
Nicaea, Synod of, I. 61-64.

INDEX

Nietzsche, Philosophy of, II. 271-275.
Nominalism, Berkeley's, I. 240-241.
Nothing, Hegel's idea of, I. 289, 322; Relations of Being and, II. 30.
Noumena, Kant's theory of, I. 260-275; II. 32 Hegel's theory of, I. 286.

Object, Relation of idea to, II. 59-70, 104-105; "Transsubjective," II. 195, 200-205.
Observation, Stage of, II. 109-114.
One and many, Plato's theory of, I. 8-12; Spinoza's theory of, I. 184-187; Kant's theory of, I. 303-306; Hegel's theory of, I. 303-306, 340-343; Relation of, II. 42-44, 219-222, 228-231, 241.
Opinion, Plato's idea of, II. 105.
Optimism, Augustine's, I. 71; Nietzsche's, II. 272-273.
Organic world, Kant's view of, I. 275-276; Hegel's view of, I. 326-329, 331-334; Character of, II. 109-112, 156-162, 168-171.
Origen, Theology of, I. 57-61.
Orphism, Doctrines of, I. 7.

Paley, Ethics of, II. 122.
Pan-psychism, II. 112, 191-193, 198-231.
Pantheism, Greek, I. 8, 23-24; Origen's rejection of, I. 58-59; Spinoza's I. 171-175, 197-198; Leibnitz', I. 197-198; Character of, II. 144.
Parallelism, Psycho-physical, II. 180-183, 266; Phenomenalistic, II. 183-185.
Particular and universal, II. 38-44, 49-50, 64-66, 82-84, 207-209, 211-218.
Paul, St., Theology of, I. 28-30, 33, 119-120; Augustine's relation to, I. 66-67.
Palagius, Augustine's opposition to, I. 69-70, 83-84.
Penance, Doctrine of, I. 89.
Perception, Leibnitz' theory of, I. 191-195, 205-206; Kant's theory of, I. 260-265, 300-303; Hegel's theory of, I. 301-303, 306-309; Character of, II. 39-41, 67-75, 82-89, 95-102, 203-205.
Permanence, Relation of Change to, II. 42-44.
Personality, Stoical view of, I. 23-24; Hegel's view of, I. 343-345; Idea of, I. 72-77; II. 26-32.
Pessimism, in Plato, I. 10-12; in Gnostics, I. 31-32, 62; in Origen, I. 62; Schopenhauer's, II. 258-263, 266-268.
Peter the Lombard, Theology of, I. 94.
Phenomenal and intelligible, in early Greek philosophy, I. 7-8; in Plato, I. 8-12; in Aristotle, I. 12-15; in Philo, I. 48, 51-53; in Clement, I. 52-54; in Origen, I. 59; in Augustine, I. 66; in Kant, I. 260-276, 300-314; II. 32-33, 58-59, 107-108; in Hegel, I. 286-300; 306, 312-326, 330, 340-343; Distinction of, II. 92-99, 183-190, 198-200, 214-216, 219-222, 263-266.
Phenomenalism, II. 48-49, 59, 144, 183-185, 237.
Philo, Philosophy of, I. 27, 51-52.
Philosophy, Greek, Development of, I. 7-24, 34; Clement's idea of, I. 37-46; Relations of life and, II. 12-23, 269; Relations of Art and, II. 15-21, 262, 268-269, 271, 273.
Physical Science, Berkeley's theory of, I. 248-249; Kant's theory of, I. 262-265.
Pietism, Hegel's estimate of, I. 356, 359.
Plato, Philosophy of, I. 4, 8-12, 23, 118, 345; II. 44, 314; Relation of Jewish thought to, I. 27; Relation of Clement to, I. 47, 55; Relation of Origen to, I. 60; Relation of Dante to, I. 118, 129-131.
Pleasure, Schopenhauer's view of, II. 260-262, 266-268; Relations of good and, II. 284-285, 309-312.
Plotinus, Mysticism of, I. 90.

INDEX

Pluralism, I. 22-23, 72-77; II. 1-2, 209-210, 219-231.
Plutarch, Clement's relation to, I. 40.
Poetry, Nature of, II. 17-20.
Politics, Italian, History of, I. 142-144.
Positive and negative, I. 311-316; II. 64-66, 240.
Positivism, Defect of, II. 16.
Postulates, I. 323-329; II. 195-197, 263-266.
Potentiality, Aristotle's conception of, I. 12.
Power, Relation of knowledge and, II. 209-211.
Practice, Aristotle's view of, I. 15-17.
Predestination, Augustine's doctrine of, I. 70, 84-85.
Pragmatism, Defect of, II. 11, 87, 103, 209.
Progress, Conditions of, II. 315-316.
Property, Basis of, II. 117.
Prophecy, Collins' view of, I. 228-230.
Providence, Clement's idea of, I. 50, 53-54; Augustine's idea of, I. 84-85; Thomas Aquinas' idea of, I. 95-96; Kant's idea of, I. 284-285; Idea of, II. 140-142, 254-256, 309-311.
Psalms, Hebrew, II. 26.
Psychology, Empirical, I. 178, 233, 243; Rational, Kant's criticism of, I. 265-266; Hegel's view of, I. 312-313; Parallax of, II. 208.
Punishment, Medieval theory of, I. 121-123; Schopenhauer's theory of, II. 262-263, 269-270; Kant's theory of, II. 269; Object of, II. 295-297.
Purgatory, Origen's anticipation of, I. 61.
Purpose. *See* Cause, Final.

Qualities, Primary and Secondary, II. 58, 62, 91, 147-149, 236-237.
Quality and quantity, Categories of, II. 151-154.

Radbertus, Transubstantiation in, I. 86.

Rationalism and empiricism, II. 38.
Realism, II. 55-66; and the "copying" theory, II. 68-70.
Reality and appearance, II. 50-52, 57-58, 92, 97-99, 107, 237-239, 258; Nature of, II. 30-32, 67-70, 92-98, 234-241.
Reason, Plato's conception of, I. 8-12; Aristotle's conception of, I. 12-23; Relation of Intuition to, I. 95; Clement's conception of, I. 42-46, 55-56; Thomas Aquinas' conception of, I. 94-98; Dante's conception of, I. 100-109; Truths of, Leibnitz' theory of, I. 194-195, 201-202; Sufficient, Leibnitz' principle of, I. 194; Relation of, to revelation, Locke's view of, I. 221-223; Toland's view of, I. 223-225; Tindal's view of, I. 225-228; Speculative and practical, I. 268-278, 286-292, 324-329; II. 121, 263-266; Relation of desire to, I. 273-274, 278-279; II. 270; Relation of understanding to, I. 309-311, 314-316, 330-331, 340-343; II. 108; Relation of sense and instinct to, I. 233-239; II. 271-273, 284-285; Nature of, II. 25-30, 107-113, 176-177.
Reciprocal action, Kant's view of, I. 263-265; Category of, II. 217.
Redemption, Gnostic theory of, I. 31; Clement's theory of, I. 42-46, 51-53; Origen's theory of, I. 60-61; Methodius' theory of, I. 62; Augustine's theory of, I. 69-71; Anselm's theory of, I. 87-89; Dante's theory of, I. 120-123, 131-133; Kant's theory of, I. 279-285; Hegel's theory of, I. 349-356; Idea of, II. 15, 293-297, 306-311.
Reflection, Locke's view of, I. 213-214; Hegel's phases of, I. 292-293, 347-349; Aspects of, II. 98-102.
Reformation, The, Principle of, I. 107, 150-152; II. 305; Hegel's idea of, I. 335.
Regeneration. *See* Redemption.

INDEX

Relations, Locke's view of, I. 213-214; Hume's view of, I. 251-252; Idea of, II. 47-52, 64-66, 71-72, 79-84, 90-91, 235-236.
Religion, Idea of, I. 1-12, 22-24; II. 1-13, 20-21, 120-128, 290-297, 298-302; Relations of theology and, I. 4-7, 20; II. 1, 2, 8, 131; Relation of morality to, I. 4-6, 22-24; II. 119-126, 275-277, 286-287, 306-313; Relation of ritual to, II. 303-306; Greek, Development of, I. 7-8; Hebrew, Development of, I. 25-28; Jesus' idea of, I. 28; Leibnitz' idea of, I. 198; Locke's idea of, I. 221-223; Morgan's idea of, I. 228; Hume's view of, I. 257-259; Kant's view of, I. 278-285; Hegel's view of, I. 330-361; Empirical view of, II. 232-234; Schopenhauer's view of, II. 270; Nietzsche's view of, II. 271.
Renaissance, I. 150-152.
Repentance, Hegel's view of, I. 349-352.
Resemblance, Idea of, II. 49.
Responsibility, II. 197, 209-211, 248-249.
Resurrection, Doctrine of the, I. 27, 28-31, 36, 60-62.
Revelation, Locke's view of, I. 221-223; Toland's view of, I. 223-226; Tindal's view of, I. 226-228.
Ritual, Relations of religion and, I. 5-6, 64; II. 303-308; Kant's view of, I. 284-285.

Sabellius, Dante's condemnation of, I. 128.
Saints, Worship of the, I. 64.
Sacraments, Thomas Aquinas' doctrine of the, I. 96-97.
Salvation. *See* Redemption.
Scepticism, Origin of, II. 104, 112.
Schema, Kant's doctrine of the, I. 306-307; Hegel's view of the, I. 306-309.
Schiller, Idea of God in, I. 116.
Scholasticism, Clement's tendency towards, I. 42-43; Rise of, I. 87; Character of, I. 102-105, 148.

Schopenhauer, Philosophy of, II. 258-270.
Science, Natural, Locke's view of, I. 215-216; Berkeley's view of, I. 240-246, 248-250; Kant's theory of, I. 260-263; Basis of, II. 150-156; Idea of, II. 206-209, 258-266, 298-302, 308; Christian, II. 307.
Scotus, Joannes, Theology of, I. 86.
Scripture, Holy, Gnostic view of, I. 32-33; Marcion's view of, I. 32-34; Apologists' view of, I. 34-36; Clement's view of, I. 41-42; Origen's view of, I. 57-58; Dante's view of, I. 102, 105-107; Locke's view of, I. 221; Toland's view of, I. 223-226; Tindal's view of, I. 226-227; Collins' view of, I. 228-230; Middleton's view of, I. 230-232; Kant's view of, I. 279-282; Hegel's view of, I. 336-338.
Self-activity, II. 193-194.
Self-consciousness, Cartesian theory of, I. 155-157, 163-167; Spinoza's theory of, I. 176-177; Leibnitz' theory of, I. 204-205; Locke's theory of, I. 216-221; Berkeley's theory of, I. 249-251; Kant's theory of, I. 265-266, 270-273, 300-301; Hegel's theory of, I. 286-292, 301-306, 331-354; Nature of, I. 74-77; II. 26-28, 50-53, 78-82, 95, 102-104, 118, 121-128, 217-219, 243-253, 260-268, 275-277, 290-293, 298-302.
Self-realisation, II. 285-286.
Self-projection, Theory of, II. 77.
Sensation and reality, I. 235-238; Locke's view of, I. 214-215, 235-238; Berkeley's view of, I. 238-240; Mill's view of, II. 57; Bain's view of, II. 57; Kant's view of, II. 56; New realists' view of, II. 56-63; Schopenhauer's view of, II. 266; and extensity, II. 72-73; and reality, I. 234-238; II. 68-70, 73-75; and thought, II. 79-82, 198-200, 258-260; character of, II. 39-42, 55-66, 68-70.
Sensationalism, I. 234-238; II. 213.
Sensible and Supersensible, II. 104, 133-134.

INDEX

Signs, Local, Theory of, II. 73.

Similarity, Conception of, II. 207.

Sin, Idea of, I. 64-70, 83-84, 116-123, 278-281, 346-350; II. 293-297, 306-308, 314-315; Forgiveness of, II. 293-297.

Socrates, Philosophy of, I. 8, 23.

Society, Basis of, II. 114-115; Relation of individual to, II. 113-119, 278-288, 314-317; Development of, II. 283-284; Forms of, II. 298-302.

Solipsism, II. 211.

Sophists, The, I. 8; II. 311.

Soul, Plato's conception of, I. 12-15; Aristotle's conception of, I. 12-15; in Wisdom of Solomon, I. 27; Origen's idea of, I. 59-61; Methodius' idea of, I. 62; Dante's idea of, I. 109-110, 116-117; Descartes' idea of, I. 156-159, 164-167; Spinoza's idea of, I. 176-177; Leibnitz' idea of, I. 190-193; Hume's denial of, I. 252; Kant's theory of, I. 265-268, 270-273; Hegel's theory of, I. 296-299, 312-313, 340-343; Idea of, II. 14, 156-162, 187-189; The Feeling, II. 75-79.

Space, Plato's view of, I. 8-12; Aristotle's view of, I. 20-22; Origen's view of, I. 58-59; Augustine's view of, I. 68-69, 82-83; Dante's view of, I. 107-109; Kant's theory of, I. 262-265; Nature of, II. 71-78, 211-218, 237, 245.

Spencer, Philosophy of, I. 107, 111-112; II. 73.

Spinoza, Philosophy of, I. 80, 170-189; II. 42, 54, 88.

Spirit, Holy, Apologists' view of, I. 36; Origen's view of, I. 59; Latin Church's idea of, I. 86; Augustine's idea of, I. 67-68, 72-78; Dante's idea of, I. 108-109, 120-121; Hegel's idea of, I. 352-361; Nature of, II. 248.

State, The, Dante's theory of, I. 133-147; Descartes' view of, I. 152; Spinoza's view of, I. 170, 181-182; Kant's view of, I. 323-325; Hegel's view of, I. 335-338; Schopenhauer's view of, II. 262, 269-270; Idea of, II. 298-302, 315-316.

Statius, Dante's picture of, I. 128.

Stoics, The, Philosophy of, I. 22-24, 27; Influence of, on Jewish thought, I. 27; Influence of, on Christian thought, I. 35, 39-46, 55-56; Hegel's contrast of, to Christianity, I. 353.

Subject and object, II. 55-88, 95-114, 125, 195-209, 223-225, 251-253, 263-268.

Sublime, The, Kant's idea of, I. 276-277.

Substance, Idea of, in early Greek Philosophy, I. 8, 14; in Aristotle, I. 12-18; in Descartes, I. 156-170; in Spinoza, I. 171-177; in Leibnitz, I. 190-191; in Locke, I, 213-215; in Berkeley, I. 240-246, 249; in Hume, I. 242, 251-252; in Kant, I. 263-265; 312; in Hegel, I. 312-313; Nature of, I. 241-246.

Sympathy, Schopenhauer's theory of, II. 270, 272; Nietzsche's theory of, II. 272.

Synthesis, I. 262-265, 305-309; II. 94, 121-122, 153-154, 200, 207, 211, 220,

Teleology. *See* Cause, Final.

Tennyson, Antipathy to mechanical view of, II. 155-156.

Tertullian, Clement's relation to, I. 43; Augustine's relation to, I. 64.

Theology, Relations of morality and, I. 4-7; Relation of faith to, II. 13; Rational, Kant's criticism of, I. 268-270; Relations of religion and, II. 1-8, 52, 308; Relation of historical criticism to, II. 3; Development of, II. 22-24; Principles of, II. 25, 131-133. *See also under names of authors.*

Things in themselves, Kant's view of, I. 262, 265-270; Hegel's view of, I. 286-289; Idea of, II. 95-96.

Thomas Aquinas, Theology of, I. 94-98, 120; Dante's relation to, I. 101.

INDEX 375

Thought, Aristotle's idea of, I. 15-20; Spinoza's view of, I. 178-179; Leibnitz' view of, I. 193, 204-205; Kant's view of, I. 263-265, 268-270; Hegel's view of, I. 286-323, 330-338; Relation of, to reality, I. 240-247; II. 52-56, 63-66, 71-78, 82, 88, 96, 99-100, 200, 205, 234-237; Relation of, to feeling, I. 243-246; II. 72, 202, 258; Relation of, to perception, I. 263-270; Scientific, II. 207.

Time, Plato's idea of, I. 10-12; Aristotle's idea of, I. 18-21; Origen's idea of, I. 58; Augustine's idea of, I. 68-69, 82-83; Dante's idea of, I. 107-108; Kant's theory of, I. 262-265; Idea of, II. 85, 95, 211-218, 245.

Tindal, Theology of, I. 226-228.

Toland, Theology of, I. 225-227.

Totemism, I. 25.

Transubstantiation, Doctrine of, I. 86.

Trinity, Doctrine of the, I. 64, 67-68, 72-78, 86, 93, 95, 108-114, 150, 153, 340-345.

Truth, Leibnitz' theory of, I. 193, 194: Locke's theory of, I. 213-216; Form and content of, II. 13; Degrees of, II. 28, 110-114; "Copying" theory of, II. 68-70; Nature of, II. 67-70, 249.

Unchangeable, Aristotle's conception of the, I. 19-23.

Unconditioned, in Kant and Hegel, I. 309-311; II. 263-266.

Understanding, Relations of Reason and, in Kant and Hegel, I. 309-312, 330, 339-340, 343-346; Character of, II. 93-104, 107-109.

Unessential and essential, II. 91.

Universal, Origin of the, I. 48-50; Relations of particular and, I. 50, 241-248; II. 39-41, 50, 200-203, 208-219; 286-287.

Unity, Hegel's idea of, I. 340-343.

Universe and intelligence, I. 72-77; 330-331, 340-343; II. 25-46, 52.

Utilitarianism, Nietzsche's rejection of, II. 272-275.

Value, Creation of, II. 220, 229-231.

Virgil, Dante's picture of, I. 127-128.

Virtues, Dante's classification of, I. 127-133.

Vitalism, Falsity of, II. 158.

Ward, J., on Naturalism, II. 152.

Weismann, on acquired characters, II. 167.

Will, Leibnitz' theory of, I, 195; Berkeley's theory of, I. 250-251; Kant's theory of, I. 270-273, 323-325; II. 260; Hegel's theory of, I. 323-325, 347-350; Schopenhauer's theory of, II. 258-270; Relations of faith and, II. 9-13; Relations of knowledge and, II. 264-268; Relations of feeling and, II. 266; Idea of, II. 284-287.

William of Occam, Theology of, I. 148.

Wilson, G. B., on organisms, II. 159.

Wisdom of Solomon, I. 27.

Wolff, Philosophy of, I. 211.

Woolston, on miracles, I. 230.

Wordsworth, Religion in, II. 127.

World, The, Plato's idea of, I. 8-12; Aristotle's idea of, I. 19-24; Stoical idea of, I. 23; Gnostical idea of, I. 31-32; Creation of, Apologists' theory of, I. 34-36; Plato's theory of, I. 47: Origen's theory of, I. 56-59; Augustine's theory of, I. 78-82; Mystical theory of, I. 89-91; Dante's theory of, I. 109-111; Knowledge of, Descartes' doctrine of the, I. 161-163, 169-170; Spinoza's conception of, I. 172-175, 184-189; Leibnitz' conception of, I. 195-197, 204-209; Kant's conception of, I. 266-268, 270-273; Hegel's conception of, I. 288-320, 330-346; Idea of, II. 90, 102-107, 112-114, 135-140, 243, 254-256.

Worship. *See* Ritual.

DATE DUE

GAYLORD			PRINTED IN U.S.A.